"In this book Dr. Christa McKirland has given us a text that is biblically rooted, theologically sophisticated, and attuned to vital issues that we face today concerning how we treat one another and how we relate to God. She moves easily between a rich variety of literatures as she makes a clear and compelling case for the thesis that human beings are fashioned so as to need the presence of God. This is theological anthropology of a higher order."

—**Oliver Crisp**, St. Mary's College, University of St. Andrews

"Writing in a lucid style that students, church leaders, and scholars will all enjoy, McKirland has achieved something very rare. She has written a biblical theology that takes the best from analytic philosophy, drinks deeply from the wells of Scripture and biblical scholarship, and draws countless threads together with systematic creativity. *God's Provision, Humanity's Need* offers an exciting picture of humans as creatures with a fundamental need for relationship with God. Anyone looking for a Christian answer to the question, What does it mean to be human? needs to read this book."

—**Joanna Leidenhag**, lecturer in theology and liberal arts, University of Leeds

"McKirland beautifully articulates the centrality of God's presence for the well-being of the human person. Her convincing argument that human flourishing is grounded in the humanity of the Second Person of Trinity and the case she makes for relating to God's presence through a second-personal relationship are innovative. They speak to diverse cultures and contexts since, like McKirland argues, the principal goal toward which God urges humanity is the true image, Jesus Christ, who is both the teleological prototype for all humanity and the one through whom the fundamental need of all humanity is fulfilled. McKirland has written a profoundly moving must-read for anyone interested in academic theology!"

—**Sofanit T. Abebe**, Ethiopian Graduate School of Theology

God's Provision,
Humanity's Need

God's Provision, Humanity's Need

THE GIFT *of* OUR DEPENDENCE

◇

CHRISTA L. McKIRLAND

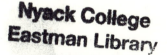

Baker Academic

a division of Baker Publishing Group
Grand Rapids, Michigan

Published by Baker Academic
a division of Baker Publishing Group
PO Box 6287, Grand Rapids, MI 49516-6287
www.bakeracademic.com

Printed in the United States of America

Library of Congress Cataloging-in-Publication Data
Names: McKirland, Christa L., 1985– author.
Title: God's provision, humanity's need : the gift of our dependence / Christa L. McKirland.
Description: Grand Rapids, Michigan : Baker Academic, a division of Baker Publishing Group,
    2022. | Includes bibliographical references and index.
Identifiers: LCCN 2021053969 | ISBN 9781540962799 (paperback) | ISBN 9781540965646
    (casebound) | ISBN 9781493436804 (pdf) | ISBN 9781493436798 (ebook)
Subjects: LCSH: Trust in God—Christianity. | Dependency (Psychology)—Religious
    aspects—Christianity.
Classification: LCC BV4637 .M386 2022 | DDC 234/.2—dc23/eng/20220107
LC record available at https://lccn.loc.gov/2021053969

Baker Publishing Group publications use paper produced from sustainable forestry practices and postconsumer waste whenever possible.

22   23   24   25   26   27   28   7   6   5   4   3   2   1

Contents

PART 4 | **Divine Presence and Needs-Based Anthropology**

Foreword

ALAN J. TORRANCE

This remarkable book represents a dynamic and constructive vision of theology and theological anthropology. Not only does it integrate resources provided by contemporary biblical exegesis, analytic philosophy, and systematic theology; it does so in a manner that is historically informed and that engages thoughtfully with the Christian tradition. The author's background in analytic theology is reflected in the lucidity, transparency, and analytic rigor with which she presents her arguments.

One might suspect that a book whose title refers to God's provision for human need is likely to be pragmatic in style and apologetically driven. Such a perception, however, could not be further from the truth. At no point do we find culturally conditioned perceptions of human need framing the interpretation of God and the Christian faith. What we have is an exercise in trinitarian and christologically focused anthropology that engages in depth and at length with biblical scholarship and key philosophical resources for the sake of the theological task.

McKirland's basic argument is that human beings have a fundamental human need for a second-personal relation to God. To describe it in these terms is to present the need as "nonderivative, noncircumstantial, and inescapable, so that the entity experiences serious harm if this need is not met." At the heart of the Christian faith, she suggests, stands the recognition that we have been created for a second-personal relationship to God. Not only is the fulfilment of this need integral to our flourishing; it is not possible to provide an account of what it is to be human that does not recognize this. We can speak of human capacities and human responsibilities, but if we have not grasped the fundamental and divinely intended feature at the heart of who we are, we have missed the defining key to what it is to be human.

Whereas attempts to outline fundamental facets of human nature can easily project individual or cultural priorities onto the interpretation of human nature, the universality of this essential human need can be affirmed, argues McKirland, without flattening out or undermining cultural diversity or human particularity. As Colin Gunton and John Zizioulas saw, second-personal relations affirm rather than dilute human particularity. What quickly becomes apparent, therefore, is that this volume upholds a fundamental feature of human nature as key to understanding our identity without succumbing to reductive or subliminally "local" assumptions as to what it is that defines us. It is pertinent to notice here that, for McKirland, a person does not have to be aware of this fundamental need—or the harm she experiences if it is unmet—for that need to be real.

All this, however, immediately raises an obvious nexus of questions: How do we recognize that this fundamental need exists, what form it takes or, indeed, that it really is a universal feature of humanity? Her answer lies unashamedly in God's self-disclosure, the witness of Scripture to the nature of humanity, and the way in which our humanity is fulfilled in communion with God. To the extent that experience serves to confirm the validity of this approach, this is only the case by way of a "backward look"—that is, looking at human nature from within the context of the reconciled experience of God's transforming presence. In short, the experience of the church testifies to the significance of the neglected but critically important insights that McKirland outlines so skillfully.

Central to McKirland's thesis is an exegetically driven theological analysis of the *imago Dei*. Her insights into what fundamental need and second-personal relations tell us about the image avoid the common trap of introspective and culturally privileged accounts of human capacity—ones that are increasingly exemplified by ill-conceived forms of dialogue with the sciences. The focus of McKirland's account is Christological—but not in a way that short-circuits the light that Israel, the theology of the temple, and, indeed, the Old Testament as a whole shed on this conceptuality. Jesus Christ is presented as the teleological prototype of humanity but also as the one in and through whom the fundamental need that defines us is fulfilled. This same concept also helps her to account not only for the commonality that the incarnate Son shares with the rest of humanity but also for key elements in his redemptive role. So why does God's engagement with humanity take this form? For McKirland, it is indicative quite simply of God's desire to dwell with humanity personally and in a way that extends and expands the divine presence. God's desire for this, moreover, is not something that God allows human sin to frustrate.

In the final chapters of the book, the theological significance of God's presence and its significance for human flourishing are explored by analyzing the metaphors of bread, water, and filial and kinship relations and by attending to the role of the tabernacle and temple in Israel's relationship to God. These discussions spell out the nature, character, and, indeed, primacy of the notion of divine presence. What becomes plain is that God did not create human beings with this fundamental need without simultaneously intending to provide the nourishment that this need requires. The whole thrust of the gospel is that human creatures are created to flourish in the context of this I-thou relationship and God's active and transformative presence in and through it. Consequently, the metaphors of bread, water, and sonship take on a whole new and profound significance in the New Testament both for Jesus and for his followers. The second-personal relation to God is fully realized through faith in Christ and through sharing in the faithfulness of Christ as the embodiment of God's second-personal presence.

To appreciate this fully, however, Logos Christology is best complemented, she argues, by a robust pneumatological focus. This constitutes the key to an integrated trinitarian account of Jesus's humanity and his divinity. Such a development provides, further, an ontological basis for the profoundly important direction in which the book seeks to take theological anthropology. The person of Jesus Christ is not only the model for human flourishing and its norm; he is also the Mediator of it—he actualizes it. This means that a person is experiencing harm if she is deprived of the relation of dependence on the personal divine presence that Jesus facilitates and mediates. What emerges here is not only a "missionary" imperative but a profound vision of the new creation as the fulfilment of human flourishing in communion with God.

There is an admirable theological modesty and, indeed, reverence in McKirland's decision not to make exaggerated claims for the theological anthropology that she develops. She refers to the "pneumachristocentric anthropology," for which she argues in her concluding chapter, as "one possible theological anthropology" that might emerge from the framework she has developed. This is in tune with her whole approach, which is intended to inspire and encourage rather than complete the theological task—a virtue, I might add, that has also characterized her unparalleled commitment to inspire and encourage women to engage in academic theology!

Usually, in writing a foreword, one tries to avoid presenting a summary of what a book contains. If I tend in that direction, it is an expression of my desire to intimate to the reader something of the range, originality, and constructive force of this volume. What one is presented with is sustained, innovative, and rigorous—an exegetically-driven, trinitarian anthropology that has profound relevance not only for academic theology but for the life and outreach of the church.

One final comment. As I have already indicated, this is not a book that attempts to shut the door on a topic—she is free of a (sometimes academic/ dogmatic) fondness for closure and control! Rather, the overarching concern of her intellectual commitment and rigorous theological scholarship is to open a cogent and compelling vista that invites the reader to develop her thesis in numerous further directions and run with it. Just one example of such an opportunity might be the significance of her trinitarian "pneumachristocentric" vision for interpreting Christ's continuing priestly role and intercessions. This would explore the significance of her concept of fundamental need and second-person relations for the theology of worship, sacramental celebration, and mediated participation in the divine life.

Acknowledgments

Every project has a story behind it, and each story involves countless influences that guide the project to its fruition. Those influences are largely personal, and this project is no different. In terms of my academic journey, Ron Pierce saw potential in me and intentionally invested in me as a person and aspiring scholar. First as my teacher, then as my mentor while I served as his teaching assistant, and eventually as my friend and colleague, he has dignified me at every step in our mentoring relationship. I did not know women could be theologians, and I did not see anyone pursuing such a vocation in my contexts, but Ron (and many others) believed in this for me. Later in my academic career, Jason McMartin helped me to "dream bigger" as I considered my next steps for my PhD. For the first time, in his class (which was my thirtieth graduate course), I read theological works by women (women who are still my heroes: Sarah Coakley and Eleonore Stump). Thanks to Jason, I was also exposed to analytic theology, a research program that immediately clicked with how my brain works and made me come alive in new ways.

Shortly after this exposure, a new institute launched at the University of St. Andrews, with fellowships funded by the Sir John Templeton Foundation. Gratefully, I received one of these fellowships, allowing me to pursue the ideas that eventually became what you will read about in this book. Through this institute, I was privileged to be supervised by Alan Torrance. He has encouraged me at every moment along the way—from before I arrived in St. Andrews to the present day. He has always treated me as a dialogue partner, even when I was his student. Due to his encouragement, I attempted to do something theologically constructive and integrative, resulting in this book. Further, he (and Andrew Torrance) recognized my passion to see more women doing theology, and together we launched Logia (now Logia International). Our tagline is "You can be what you can see," and it is an honor to be what I did not see for so much of my life.

I am also grateful for the many interactions with Andrew Torrance and the excellent conversations and ways of asking questions that he modeled. Also, Oliver Crisp, Marc Cortez, and Andrew Picard have worked through early drafts of this book and contributed to it being far better than I could have made it on my own. They too have been constant cheerleaders and encouragers that I should pursue these ideas and seek to publish them. Dave Nelson, at Baker Academic, has believed in this project from the very beginning. His tireless efforts and constant encouragement have helped shape this project into what it has become.

As one can imagine, the academic road can be quite lonely, but I am grateful to have made dear friends in the course of working out my ideas at the University of St Andrews and now at Carey Baptist College in Aotearoa New Zealand. The friendships formed and the collaborative nature of the Logos Institute have given me more food for thought than I could possibly consume. Specifically, Taylor Telford (beloved housemate!), Koert Verhagen, Kimberley Kroll, Jonathan Rutledge, Stephanie Nordby, Jeremy Rios, Justin Duff, Tamara and Ethan Knudson, Hannah Craven, Jordan Senner, Graydon Cress, Karen McClain Kiefer, Katelynn Carver, Euan Grant, Joshua Cockayne, and Joanna Leidenhag have been iron to sharpen iron on this journey. Jaimee van Gemerden has also provided multiple reads through this draft and careful attention to the tedious details of footnotes and citations, as did Grace Chamberlain during the final stages of revision (though any errors are still my own).

Further, this story would have never even begun without my family's support and belief in me since my birth (and probably, even in utero!). My brother, Josh, has shown me what bravery and perseverance look like. My mom exemplifies how having one's own thriving business as an attorney need not compromise care for one's children. My dad instilled my love for theology and always said I could do anything the Spirit led me to do. I would never have had the confidence that I now have without their consistent voices speaking into my life.

Finally, I turn to some of my most immediate influences to thank them directly. Matthew, I could not fathom a better partner. You are strong where I am weak. Yet you know my strengths and push me to be stronger. You call me out when I am defined by the voices around me, and you challenge me when I am complacent. You do not ask me to be less when cultural scripts try to demand that you should be "more." You make me laugh, encourage me to cry, and always have my back. As if this were not enough, you are an incredible father. Raya is learning from you that her value does not come from her appearance. She is learning to be brave, to ask questions, and to think critically. Johnny is learning how to be compassionate and empathic . . . as well as an antagonist. Thank you for embracing fatherhood and releasing me to embrace my expression of motherhood.

To Raya and Johnny (who, for so much of this writing project, was a child in my womb), y'all have no idea that I have been writing this with you alongside me. Thank you for grounding me. Thank you for being my constant reminder that this life is about far more than academic prestige and my number of publications. Thank you for being a living embodiment of what dependence on another can look like (especially when I was pregnant!). I am loving this adventure of a life with you.

And finally, to the One who embodies the Good News—the true image—Jesus Christ. This project has taught me more about dependence on the personal divine presence, manifested as the Spirit of Jesus, that I might become more like the author and perfecter of my faith and encourage others to do the same. Please receive this as an act of worship and continue to refine my thinking and character into your likeness.

Introduction

Theological Anthropology and Human Need

"Mom, I need a cookie," says my four-year-old.

"Sweetie, you don't need a cookie; you want a cookie,"[1] I respond. "You *need* to eat your vegetables to get strong and be healthy."

How does a four-year-old already intuitively know that the forcefulness of "need" language outweighs "want" language? I am not sure where she picked this up, but I believe her intuitions are correct. Those same intuitions drew me to this topic years ago when I first started thinking about these things. While wants are powerful, motivating, and (typically) acutely felt, they seem to be distinct from needs. Further, my daughter may not feel the need to eat vegetables, and she may not have any desire to meet that need. Yet such an absence of want does not undermine the reality of her need.

At the same time, many of our needs have continuity with the rest of creation and are not especially interesting in theological anthropology. To illustrate, a need for nutrients is shared by all known life-forms on our planet. This commonality raises questions about whether humans have one or more unique needs and if a case can be made theologically for what such a need might be. As a Christian theologian, I see specific theological questions impinging on this discussion. Does this need overlap with biblical descriptions of humans? How might the image of God relate to this need? Would this need apply to Jesus equally as the fully divine and fully human person? Would

---

1. For my non-American readers, cookies are biscuits. However, as an American Southerner by birth, I have made a committment to myself that my daughter will know what biscuits really are.

such a need imply a defect in Jesus? What about prelapsarian humanity? What about humanity in the eschaton? For a need to be fundamental, as we will see in chapter 1, it must be noncircumstantial and apply consistently to all stages of salvation history: *status integritatus, corruptionis, gratiae,* and *gloriae.*[2] Can such a need be found? These questions precipitate my research and the argument outlined in the coming pages.

I find that one's understanding of what it means to be human is inseparable from one's understanding of fundamental need,[3] because what causes harm or flourishing for a subject is bound to what kind of being it is, and fundamental needs are bound to harm and flourishing. A rose needs sunlight to flourish because it is a plant. A whale needs plankton to flourish because it is an animal. Put simply,

1. The constitution of an entity determines the fundamental needs it has.
2. An entity's possession of a thing that it needs fundamentally must causally contribute to an entity's flourishing, and the lack of that thing must causally contribute to the entity's harm.
3. Therefore, understanding what causally contributes to an entity's flourishing or harm will indicate its fundamental need(s) and constitution.

Since most theological anthropology focuses on what humans are and are moving toward, if we discover such a need, it could offer some continuity across theological anthropologies for discussing what human beings were meant for, can currently experience, and are progressing toward. Significantly, need can speak into what humans uniquely are without requiring specific views about human ontology or origin, because need is omnicompatible. I propose that a human being needs *a second-personal relation to God* to flourish, and the rest of this book will argue for this need.[4]

---

2. Kevin Timpe uses this helpful list of these epochs in human experience in *Free Will in Philosophical Theology,* 14.

3. G. Thomson, *Needs,* 31; Wiggins, *Needs, Values, Truth,* 11.

4. The nuance between having a need and getting the need met will be clarified below. In the meantime, that a rose needs sunlight is a constitutional fact about the rose. The activity of *absorbing* the sunlight is distinct from the need itself. Similarly, the human needing a second-personal relation to God is distinct from *relying* on God's second-personal presence. Finally, I should note that the second-personal presence is especially concerned with knowing a person, not simply knowing about a person. As philosopher Jill Graper Hernandez has helpfully pointed out in personal correspondence, many moral philosophers recognize that someone could be known second-personally as a "you" and still not be intimately known (such as yelling at a stranger who just clipped your car with their vehicle, "Hey you!"). While I acknowledge that this is possible, I am using a conditionalizing approach whereby second-personal knowledge is exclusively concerned with knowing a person in a relationally intimate way.

To relate second-personally is to know another person and not simply know about another person. This kind of relating involves mental states. When it comes to knowing God, to be able to relate second-personally is always a gracious act of divine accommodation. This second-personal relationship is made possible through the Spirit. In her article on autism and Christianity, Olivia Bustion helpfully captures this divine accommodation. She quotes a member of an online autistic forum saying, "The Holy Spirit is like an un-ported source code that can configure itself to any operating system, which means that the Holy Spirit can be compatible with anyone, autistic or not."[5] The extent of mental content required for this relation is debatable, but that God would accommodate Godself to various intellectual and relational capacities is presupposed throughout this book. Thus, my goal is not to say what the necessary and sufficient conditions are for a second-personal relation to "count" but to say that humans fundamentally need this kind of relation to God and that, ultimately, God provides for this need.

Filling a Gap

To date, reflection on the concept of a "fundamental need" has not occurred in biblical studies, let alone how this concept has wider theological significance. In noting this lack of reflection, I am not critiquing either discipline, since this concept has only recently received focused attention and definition. Such attention has emerged especially within analytic philosophy.[6] As we will see, when we apply fundamental need to the biblical material, the theological deliverances are rich. Given the persistent division between biblical studies and theology, this book attempts to integrate these disciplines using analytic philosophy.

For example, recent developments in temple theology, especially related to God's image and presence, have begun to gain traction in theological anthropology.[7] The biblical material is pregnant with themes and metaphors

5. Bustion, "Autism and Christianity," 675. She goes on to explain that "porting refers to the activity of adapting a computer program (or a video game) to run on different types of computers (or game platforms). A software engineer rewrites a piece of software to accommodate new hardware for which it was not originally designed. For instance, it is in virtue of porting that one can now play Super Mario Bros., a game originally designed for the Nintendo Entertainment System, on a personal computer."

6. This book focuses on the biblical and theological footing for a proposed fundamental need for humankind. Future work will turn to other sciences to further explore this proposal.

7. For instance, James Turner gives a brief defense of the need for analytic and systematic theology to take seriously the biblical scholarship regarding temple theology and holistic eschatology. J. Turner, "Temple Theology, Holistic Eschatology." For two other strong examples

that can speak into the significance of the presence of God for understanding theologically what it means to be human.[8] Further, the centrality of God's presence spans the Hebrew Bible and New Testament, offering warrant for the continuity of God's intentions and self-revelation throughout the Christian canon, which theological terms attempt to capture. This continuity provides a "unifying theme" for both a broad theological framework and a needs-based theological anthropology. Biblical scholar Samuel Terrien articulates this unifying theme in his monograph on the divine presence. He recognizes that "the presence of God" motif may enable "a unifying and yet dynamic principle which will account not only for the homogeneity of the Old Testament literature in its totality, including the sapiential books, but also for the historical and thematic continuity which unites Hebraism and large aspects of Judaism with nascent Christianity."[9] Building off of the significance of God's presence, this book integrates the particular history of God's presence with Israel and the specific predications of Jesus of Nazareth with fundamental need—extending biblical scholarship into a constructive theological proposal. On this basis, I will make claims about a universal human need that maintains the value of particularities.

Consequently, one primary outworking of this integration is to help re-ground theological anthropology in particularity.[10] While discussions of abstract human natures can yield some productive insights, we need to be wary when our theological abstractions undermine Jesus's actual humanity. He remains a male, Palestinian Jew. While fully human, he is human in this way. He also proceeded from Israel's history (even while preceding it), intentionally speaking into her present while providing Israel and humanity hope for a flourishing future.[11] Thus, our theological anthropologies can better engage how God has revealed who humans are through Israel's story.

Finally, a tendency in Western thinking is to strive for self-sufficiency and absolute autonomy. The message of this book is that such striving undermines true flourishing. We were intended to need to relate to God and others

---

of systematic theologians taking seriously the deliverances of modern biblical scholarship, see also J. Turner, "*End* of Things"; Cortez, "Idols, Images, and a Spirit-ed Anthropology."

8. For the value and appropriateness of metaphors for doing theology, see Heim, "Paths beyond Tracing Out."

9. Terrien, *Elusive Presence*, 475–76.

10. Jennings proposes a solid theological rationale for valuing particularity in *The Christian Imagination*, and a strong recent example of valuing particularity comes through in Ian McFarland's *The Word Made Flesh*.

11. This procession is the case historically, even though Christ's priesthood (as the eternal Word) is the "true and real archetypal priesthood of which all others are merely shadows (Heb. 8:5)." Greggs, *Dogmatic Ecclesiology*, 1:55.

(though the latter relation is only tacitly addressed in this work), and this is not a liability to overcome but a dignity to be embraced.

Methodology

The anthropology I propose here finds its footing in biblical texts and themes, which then are developed theologically. Recent biblical theology and New Testament theology provide the material for the broader theological claims of later chapters. An additional tool of analytic philosophy is leveraged to help clarify the language of need, including its criteria, and focus on the larger proposal. Thus, this book reads as a biblical theology that then pivots to propose a constructive theological anthropology. I accomplish this by recognizing the prevalence of God's presence in the Christian Scriptures and then connecting this to recent systematic theological anthropology via the mechanism of analytic philosophy.[12] In other words, I can imaginatively ask the biblical authors, "According to a particular analytic rubric, what do you think humans fundamentally need?" and I can abductively argue what they might say.[13] In more technical terms, I will use Nicholas Wolterstorff's category of *intended manifestational revelation*.[14] Based on that inferential reasoning, I will then be able to construct a theological anthropology.

While this method is not necessarily a robust example of analytic theology, the values of clarity and parsimony will be consistent throughout this volume. Specifically, the definition and rubric for "fundamental needs" originate from an analytic philosopher and are a load-bearing aspect of the constructive work in this book. Throughout this book, I propose a needs-based theological anthropology. My proposal is intentionally parsimonious and consonant with various theological anthropologies and various views on the origin of the human person. As we will see, structural, functional, and relational anthropologies can all work alongside a needs-based account.

12. Analytic Christian theology is typically, and most simply, "constructive, systematic, Christian theology—that uses the tools and methods of analytic philosophy." Wood, *Analytic Theology*, 3.

13. Abduction is often understood as an inference to the best explanation.

14. Nonmanifestational revelation is propositional. For an example, Wolterstorff notes that God communicated explicitly that God's reason for leading the Israelites through the Red/Reed Sea was love for Israel. This explicitly communicated reason would be nonmanifestational. However, if this act was left to the interpretation of the original community and later recipients of this event, then there is an openness of interpretation which he calls *intended manifestational revelation*. Using inference to supply a plausible reading of these themes seems to be a reasonable method to arrive at the conclusions proposed in this book. Wolterstorff, *Divine Discourse*, 27–28.

At the same time, I am conscious of the hazards of this book's integrative endeavor as I look to bring biblical studies, analytic philosophy, and systematic theology into conversation. For instance, within biblical studies there is a pronounced concern about theological prooftexting. I hope that naming and engaging "unifying" themes from biblical scholars themselves may help address what can seem to be capricious selectivity.[15] Engagement with these themes should not imply that biblical scholars agree on what these themes are or that there even are such things.[16] However, given that biblical studies scholars work closely with the biblical texts, if a theme's prevalence finds exegetical support, especially across multiple biblical scholars, its import should receive careful consideration by theologians.

On a metamethodological note, corollary reasoning in support of the claim that humans need a second-personal relation with God flows from the arguments of this book itself. If God wants to be in a second-personal relationship with humans and if this kind of relationship enables humans to become like the true image of God, Jesus Christ, it would also seem to follow that God would want us to know this.[17] Yet how is this knowledge ascertainable? We can observe our experiences and the experiences of others, but this may not reveal what is at the root of these experiences. Instead, such knowledge would seem to require some sort of communication, or divine disclosure, in human history—not only communication of the true image itself but also revelation indicating the significance of Jesus Christ.

Furthermore, since human history is dynamic, and God chose to act within this time-bound context, such disclosure would ideally be recorded so that later humans could come to know this God. A collection of those testimonies, inspired by the same God who desires to meet humankind's need for God's second-personal presence, would be a fitting way to mediate that revelation. Whether the texts are themselves revelation or a witness to the revelation does not affect the conclusions of this book, as both require that God be engaged with the created world in such a way as to be discernible by human creatures.

Since I argue that God intends that humans become like the true image, Jesus Christ, through a second-personal relationship with the divine presence (especially the Holy Spirit), the fact that this same Spirit would urge

15. The centrality of God's relational presence is the focus of Duvall and Hays, *God's Relational Presence*.

16. For an excellent example of biblical scholars who endorse both the diversity of these texts and also the possibility of unifying themes across them, see Hafemann and House, *Central Themes in Biblical Theology*.

17. I do believe this to be the case. This argument assumes that God is both all-good and all-loving and thereby wants human creatures to know their original end and provides the means for reaching this end.

humanity toward this principal goal is unsurprising. The ontology of human-ity, argued in the chapters below, reveals striking parallels to the ontology of Scripture. Humanity has a forward-moving *telos* (end, goal), needs God's second-personal presence to be what it is, and is meant to rely on the Holy Spirit. If such an understanding of humanity—of those human beings who wrote these texts in their material form—is pneumachristocentric (the an-thropology proposed in chapter 10), it seems plausible that the discourse of these texts would reflect a parallel ontology. Put another way, if God designed humanity to need God's own presence, but such a need required revelation, then a doctrine of inspiration wherein the Spirit reveals this need, while at the same time being relied on, is quite likely. While the exact role of the Spirit in the writing of these texts remains contested, I am presupposing *that* God was involved in some way. This involvement includes the authorship, redac-tion, and compilation of these texts. Such involvement makes the most sense of pervading themes and trajectories spanning the canon. This involvement also appears internally consistent with the God depicted there.

Consequently, this book works from the premise that the entire canon is a unified whole and inspired by one divine author who speaks through the voices of individuals through different genres and in other contexts. We see this within the text itself: "Even Matthew's predilection for reading prophetic texts as predictive oracles derives its theological intelligibility from his con-viction that all Scripture is a great coherent story in which the elements of Israel's past point toward a messianic consummation, in which God will at last be present with his people (cf. Matt 1:21–23, 28:20)."[18] Such a view accepts that there is some form of dual authorship of these sacred texts and that a *sensus plenior*, or "fuller sense," of the text is ascertainable through reading across books, genres, and periods.[19] Beyond the reasons already listed, this also seems reasonable given that New Testament authors use both Hebrew and Septuagint texts extensively.[20] Additionally, this method maintains the value and import of the Hebrew Scriptures even though the New Testament records Jesus inaugurating a new way of being in communion with God. Finally, this approach leaves open the possibility of a unified narrative and consequential metamessages across the canon.

---

18. R. Hays, *Echoes of Scripture in the Gospels*, 188.

19. Whether this fuller sense can be discerned apart from the illumination of the Spirit is also debated. However, minimally, the discovery of unifying themes could still occur even if their significance to the reader is not fully realized. Barker, *Imprecation as Divine Discourse*.

20. Though scholars contest the nature and extent of intertextuality, Hays makes a strong case for "reading with the evangelists" and applying their approach to reading the text today. R. Hays, *Echoes of Scripture in the Gospels*.

Finally, some readers may wonder why I begin in the Old Testament to endorse a (pneuma)Christocentric anthropology. The reasons for this are fourfold. First, the canon, as we have received it, begins with Genesis. The first uses of "image of God" occur at the beginning of Israel's Scriptures and communicate important content about understanding humanity's identity and function. To take the text on its own terms requires starting where it starts.[21] Second, and relatedly, the opening chapters of Genesis apply to all humanity, enabling universal claims for those who consider the Hebrew Scriptures to be a part of the Christian canon. Third, the connotations of the image of God as related to God's divine presence begin in Genesis and are then magnified in Christ. However, unless we first see how the authors of Genesis understood this concept, we will not understand how *imago Dei* was later applied to Christ. Tracing the continuity will help our understanding of the fundamentality of the need proposed in this book. Fourth, assuming the Christocentricity of the image of God before examining the Genesis text on its own terms can short-circuit interdisciplinary dialogue between biblical scholars and theologians. To foster more discussion between these disciplines, beginning in Genesis is important.

Scope

Given the priority of the biblical material, this book is only lightly informed by broader Christian traditions and minimally appeals to paradigmatic theological authorities. This approach thus follows a "pressure" of interpretation that moves from scriptural texts to a constructive theological proposal through the aid of an analytic rubric.[22] However, the lack of thorough engagement does not mean that "need" has not permeated Christian thinking. The idea that humans need to be in a relationship with God is something of a truism in Eastern and Western traditions. While such a need has led to various descriptions, union with God (which is one way to describe the meeting of this need) has long been the center of anthropological reflection. Supporting this pervasive theme, Vladimir Lossky summarizes the Eastern tradition:

21. Such linkage is stated explicitly by biblical scholar Claus Westermann: "The history of the people of God, which begins with the patriarchs (Gen. 12–50) and the exodus from Egypt (Exodus) and extends through the history of the Israelites to Christ and his apostles, finds in Genesis 1 a framework that links this history to the beginning of time, the world, and the human race. Everything in it is based on this beginning." Westermann, *Genesis*, 12–13.

22. I am indebted to C. Kavin Rowe for this phrase. See Rowe, "Biblical Pressure and Trinitarian Hermeneutics."

"God made Himself man, that man might become God." These powerful words, which we find for the first time in St. Irenaeus, are again found in the writings of Athanasius, St. Gregory of Nazianzus, and St. Gregory of Nyssa. The Fathers and Orthodox theologians have repeated them in every century with the same emphasis, wishing to sum up in this striking sentence the very essence of Christianity: an ineffable descent of God to the ultimate limit of our fallen human condition, even unto death—a descent of God *which opens to men a path of ascent, the unlimited vistas of the union of created beings with the Divinity.*[23]

The Latin tradition also contains this theme, as seen in Augustine, though he is not alone. He believed "that the original human was incomplete at creation because Adam foreshadowed something greater still to come. The image of God in him longed to be like God, and his humanity pointed to the means of divinization yet to come in Christ's incarnation."[24] Since *telos* has the meaning of "completion" (especially in the Sermon on the Mount) and yet does not negate the ongoing nature of the need for God's second-personal presence, incompletion is an unhelpful way to describe human persons. One can be complete and still have needs. Thus, while I will avoid the language of "incompletion," the Augustinian intuition that we have a need that only union can fulfill remains. Therefore, while historical and modern thinkers will occasionally be mentioned, this book cannot comprehensively analyze various Christian traditions. Nevertheless, the idea that humans have always required a second-personal relation to God stands on firm theological footing.

Overview

As mentioned above, I propose one fundamental need that I believe is consistent for all human beings: *a second-personal relation to God.* While there may be others, this need is necessary to be human but not sufficient to be human. If this need is not met, the lack does not undermine humanness, though it does affect flourishing. Furthermore, such a uniquely human need can apply to all humankind without flattening individual and cultural diversity. Such a need does not undermine human particularity even if the need is universal to "human" as a kind. Analogously, an orchid's need for sunlight does not negate

23. Lossky, *In the Image and Likeness of God*, 97 (emphasis added). Further, the modern-day proliferation of material discussing union with Christ and participation in Christ, which is largely concerned with the nature of this relationship with God, illustrates the centrality of this theme.

24. Beeley, "Christ and Human Flourishing," 136, referencing Augustine, *On Genesis Literally Interpreted* 3.24.

its uniqueness just because other flowers such as roses, kowhai, thyme, water lilies, and jasmine all share that same photosynthetic need.

For this argument to get off the ground, however, I must clarify what I mean by the language of need. Thus, I begin part 1 with a discussion of what I mean by "need." To do so, I draw from the work of analytic philosopher Garrett Thomson. His rigorous analysis of "fundamental need" provides criteria for determining what a need is and how basic it is for an entity's well-being.[25] He raises distinctions between need, desire, and interest, plus, importantly, he defends his understanding of harm. For Thomson, a fundamental human need is a need for something that is necessary for the well-being of the human person, even though he does not provide the specific content of well-being.[26] Ultimately, Thomson makes the case that the constitution of a creature is bound to what need(s) it has.

Once clear on our language and criteria, I turn to the abductive task in part 2. There we will look at the biblical material and ask, Does Scripture point to a fundamental human need across its diversity of texts, authors, and times?[27] However, since Scripture is not concerned with Thomson's categories, we will need to look at the terms of Scripture. Hence, an exegetical case for the minimum parameters for what it means to be human according to the Hebrew Bible will be proposed in this second chapter. We will see that this need is grounded in God's divine presence and in human flourishing as well as harm. Therefore, these themes from the Hebrew Bible and New Testament will require an examination to establish their relationship more

25. In more recent work, he is careful to distinguish between the constitution of well-being and the causes of well-being: Thomson, Gill, and Goodson, *Happiness, Flourishing and the Good Life*, 15. For the purposes of my present argument, however, we will focus on satisfaction of fundamental need as a cause of well-being. We will return to the constitution of well-being/ flourishing in chaps. 9 and 10 since there are theological reasons for understanding well-being as constituted by union with God.

26. G. Thomson, *Needs*, 88–89. "Well-being" and "flourishing" will be used interchangeably throughout this book to communicate a degreed state that can change through time. Such interchangeability is also found in Thomson, Gill, and Goodson, when they state, "What counts as greater well-being for a person as a child and for the same person as a young adult will differ in many regards from what constitutes her well-being as an older person. The same point would apply to 'flourishing.' Indeed, a full theory of well-being would be at the same time an account of some aspects of human development." See *Happiness, Flourishing and the Good Life*, 11. In fact, it is the developmental aspect of well-being and flourishing that has so much potential for future research, especially how fundamental need might comport with social and developmental psychology.

27. What I mean by "Scripture" is a "medium for divine discourse." Such language is meticulously articulated by Nicholas Wolterstorff in *Divine Discourse*, 131. Further, the interpretive methodological approach with which I most resonate and apply throughout is articulated by Kit Barker and found in his *Imprecation as Divine Discourse*.

fully.[28] Scripture makes claims implicitly and explicitly about what humans are, especially as they relate to God. Consequently, chapter 2 examines the Hebrew Bible and its uses of "image of God" language for the initial humans.

Chapter 3 will turn to the New Testament to see what it contributes to the image of God concept. These parameters will form the constraints for any Christian theological anthropology for those holding to Scripture as the norming norm for all theology. From this explanation, I will argue in support of Christ as the teleological prototype for all humans.[29] While this claim is not new, the integration of fundamental need to help connect Christ's humanity and common humanity is new. If he is the perfect expression of humanness, then Christ's need for this divine presence provides substantial evidence for all humanity needing this divine presence.[30] I will also argue that the *imago Dei* serves as the mechanism connecting the Son's humanity and universal humanity.[31]

After drawing heavily from the biblical scholarship about the image of God, in chapter 4 I will supplement chapters 2 and 3 by looking at what Israel and the surrounding cultures understood the image of God to be—specifically, how this relates to the divine presence in their contexts, including the role of temples and world building for conceiving of humanity and the cosmos. This chapter will conclude that being in the image of God supplies the identity of human persons with attendant functions. These functions do not constitute the image of God. Still, they are expressions of this identity—an identity grounded in the humanity of the second person of the Trinity, who has the same fundamental need as all other humans. This need characterizes both the identity and function of individuals and the nation of Israel and, consequently, the Christian community. Such an identity is teleological, as the divine-human

28. For this project, the recorded divine disclosure under examination is restricted to the Hebrew Bible and the New Testament.

29. The most robust formulation of a Christocentric anthropology takes shape in the work of Karl Barth. For this reason, Cortez concludes: "It would seem that more work remains for those who would like to continue affirming that Jesus reveals what it means to be truly human, either building off the work of Karl Barth and strengthening the methodological framework that he left us, or building a Christological anthropology off an as-yet-underdeveloped basis." While this book will have points of overlap with Barth, it will also attempt the latter option Cortez elucidates, by proposing a needs-based anthropology. Cortez, "Madness in our Method," 26. See also Cortez, *ReSourcing Theological Anthropology*, 22.

30. "Christ," as understood in this book, indicates the incarnate Logos.

31. By "mechanism," I mean the teleological relation that connects the prototypical image of God with those patterned after this image. This mechanism is bound to divine intention, in a way analogous to how the copies of a certain product are patterned after the original. The intention of a manufacturer is that the copies replicate the original. The *imago Dei* functions like this intention. Adam's image is one of derivation from the true image of the Second Adam. The true image is the eschatological *telos* of humanity and will be addressed more fully in later chapters.

image sets the pattern or blueprint for human beings. Humanity is meant to become like this image in a creaturely way. However, this *telos* requires relating to God's second-personal presence. Such a *telos* is not contingent on sin, the form of embodiment, or ability. It is God's intended *telos* and, as a divine intention, is sufficient to ground the identity and value of each human being. The capacity to become like the true image requires being a sort of creature who can rely on God's personal presence. Such a reliance is itself a gift of the Spirit's action in humanity, including Christ's faithful humanity. At the same time, while all humans share this need for reliance on God's presence, the incarnate Son is also in a category of his own.

Part 3 will move into geographical, metaphorical, and relational language to describe the centrality of divine presence for human flourishing. Chapter 5 maintains the importance of scriptural language that communicates the centrality of God's presence for humanity's flourishing, especially the language of bread, water, and filial (kinship) relationship and the importance of the tabernacle and temple for Israel. The sixth chapter will then address how this need finds expression in the life of Christ. While these are all experienced realities of Israel, there are also symbols of this divine presence via metaphors: bread, water, and filial language. The New Testament leverages these concepts to contextualize the coming of the "messiah-of-the-Spirit."[32] This reflection on central metaphors will naturally lead to the role of the Spirit in the life of Jesus. The sixth chapter will also discuss the *extent* to which Jesus of Nazareth is both the prototype and the goal for all humans to embody—while holding firmly to the continuity of this fundamental need even for his own humanity. The seventh chapter will conclude this section with the textual prominence of Spirit dependence for those who follow Jesus, especially related to those geographical, metaphorical, and relational terms.

We will find that both in Scripture and in Thomson's framework, the kind of need a creature has is bound to what kind of creature something is, and what kind of creature something is also determines its function. For these reasons, both identity and function flow from an understanding of fundamental need. Further, the meeting of this need causally contributes to human flourishing. So, after arguing for that fundamental need from Scripture, we will turn to a theological case for that need, first by looking at how this may enable further comprehension of Christ's humanity in chapter 8. While chapters 2 through 7 primarily build on the work of biblical scholars, the eighth chapter will return to Thomson's rubric to explore how the prior material relates to Jesus himself. Since Thomson gives general definitions of

32. M. Turner, *Power from on High*, 199.

these terms from his analytic training, this book aims to integrate these terms into a Christian perspective.[33] We will examine the four-stage anthropology (*status integritatus, corruptionis, gratiae*, and *gloriae*) to see if this need holds across each human experience. If this need applies to all stages of anthropology, then this is an inescapable and noncircumstantial need, contributing to the warrant for its fundamentality.

As mentioned above, given the methodological priority of relying on the Christian Scriptures for this book's argument, there will not be space to engage thoroughly with specific theologians. However, to strengthen the theological robustness of this argument, the ninth chapter will engage with Kathryn Tanner's understanding of weak and strong participation in the image of God, of Christocentric anthropology, and of the doctrine of God. Tanner's Christocentric anthropology fits well with the fundamental need proposed here, though she makes her case more by exegeting the Christian tradition than by exegeting the biblical texts. Within the Christian tradition, she engages especially with patristic theologians and is well versed in the later Western Church tradition, raising fruitful avenues for further historical work to be done as it relates to fundamental need. Given her engagement with the church fathers, her work provides a helpful supplement to the biblical material that will be the focus of this book.

Having argued that fundamental need is sustainable, in chapter 10 I will propose a theological anthropology that supports this disposition: a pneumachristocentric anthropology. The emergent picture is that need, as it relates to the divine presence, proves foundational to anthropology—an anthropology that recognizes the necessity of the Trinity as a whole without limiting or dismissing the Spirit. While some have noticed the tendency in theology for a Spirit-*less* anthropology, a thoroughly pneumachristocentric anthropology has only begun to receive theological attention.[34] Thus, this book will argue for a pneumachristocentric anthropology as the best way to accommodate the fundamental need for God's second-personal presence.

At root then, I propose that humans bear an intended fundamental need. As such, it is not necessarily constituted by lack or defect of any kind. This need was designed to be discovered in a context of abundance, an abundance of what (or, better, who) would continually meet this need: God's very own presence. Yet when sin entered human history, scarcity and toil took the place

---

33. By "analytic" I mean a way of approaching systematic theology that foregrounds transparency, simplicity of expression, and clarity.

34. Cortez, "Idols, Images, and a Spirit-ed Anthropology." Cortez also notes the work of Yves Congar and Colin Gunton as examples of this approach, even though their focus is not primarily exegetical.

of abundance and rest.[35] Accordingly, this need was not an imperfection but integral to what it means to be human. While having needs is often understood negatively, on this view, such need indicates, instead, the greatest creaturely dignity God could have granted humankind. Humankind is intended to experience dynamic flourishing in and through personal communion with the very triune life of God. Such communion is possible through the incarnation of the Logos, the firstborn of creation, putting on human form, depending on the Spirit, and giving the Spirit so that all humanity might flourish both now and always.

35. For a defense of the compatibility of the traditional account of the doctrine of sin— which would include a historical human pair who were uniquely related to God and whose sinful actions precipitated human death—with contemporary genetic science and paleoanthropology, see Thomas McCall's overview in the appendix of *Against God and Nature*, 576–86.

PART 1

Introducing Need

ONE

Defining Fundamental Human Need

Words matter. While we probably use the word "need" every day, we rarely mean it in a robust philosophical sense. However, to capture the theologically rich potential of this word, we need to establish what we mean by "need" as well as the content of the need. To do this clearly and simply, I utilize analytic philosopher Garrett Thomson's approach. This chapter will briefly lay out his understanding of fundamental need and associated load-bearing concepts for his framework. Such a starting point does not presume that philosophy has epistemic priority over theology or biblical studies. However, Thomson's pursuit of clarity through criteria to measure a fundamental need provides a semantic and conceptual genesis for this project. We will return to Thomson's criteria in chapters 8 through 10 after surveying the biblical material to see if anything from that material has met the analytic standard of "fundamental need" and if anything about the analytic standard can be improved.

Clarifying Terms

The fundamental human need advocated in this book is that humans need *a second-personal relation to God*. Humans are meant to relate to God as a subject, not as a list of facts.[1] In theological shorthand, this has taken the form of

---

1. For an excellent exposition of this idea, specifically through Kierkegaard's work, see Cockayne, "Contemporaneity and Communion."

expression that humans need *union* with God.[2] In biblical shorthand, though a much broader category, we might say humans are intended for and need *shalom*.[3] However, the state of union with God and *shalom* are the meeting of the need. The reason is that meeting the need involves mental acts. By contrast, a fundamental need is a passive disposition. It is meant to be intentionally engaged by human persons because its satisfaction causally contributes to human flourishing.[4] Put succinctly, it is the meeting of the need that is a mental act, rather than the need itself. My focus will be on the precondition for human flourishing in that humans are creatures of a certain sort that require a second-personal relation with God to flourish. I will also address the justification for identifying human flourishing (or at least one significant aspect of it) with relating to God second-personally. Finally, the language of second-personal relation is a more precise way of describing the fundamental need seen across the testaments than is the language of relating to God third-personally. However, even though God is doing more than relating third-personally, the language of *union* seems too robust to capture the postlapsarian epoch of human experience.[5] Instead, God's desire for humans to relate second-personally seems better to capture the continuity across all of those periods.

Given that fundamental needs are dispositional, what I mean by a "disposition" is also significant. In everyday use, we often think of a disposition as a propensity to act a certain way. When we say someone is an angry person, we typically mean they tend to become angry over a slight provocation. In that case, the disposition has been shaped by other mental states and is already formed. However, I am understanding disposition in a more innate sense. On this account, it is a property that responds to certain stimulus conditions. For example, glass has a disposition to break when struck. Thus, it is not a mental state but a property to respond in a specific way when certain stimulus conditions are met.

---

2. How this union occurs is highly contested; however, the point of my argument is *that* we need union. For this reason, Eleonore Stump's account given below (which comports with the recently defended view in Porter and Rickabaugh, "Sanctifying Work of the Holy Spirit") will be understood as the minimum for what is occurring metaphysically regarding indwelling.

3. "The Old Testament understanding of peace (in Hebrew, *shalom*) conveyed much more than the absence of conflict or disorder. Peace, rather, had a positive connotation. To live in peace was to live in right relations with God, oneself, one's neighbors and indeed the whole of creation. Righteousness, therefore, was constitutive of peace. Living within covenant communion with God provides the best image of what peace would mean; it was a state of overall well-being." Schreiter, "Peacemaking and Reconciliation," 638.

4. Other concepts communicate this same idea: dependence, surrender, trust, reliance, etc. However, the act of getting the need met is distinct from the need itself.

5. Recall that those epochs of human experience are prelapsarian, postlapsarian, redeemed, and glorified.

My argument is that humans have a disposition (as a nonmental property) to relate to God second-personally (the stimulus condition). Of course, the analogy breaks down since the glass's disposition to shatter when struck is a much more straightforward stimulus response than a human's disposition to flourish when second-personally relating to God. Relating to God is complex, since "relating to" can take many forms—both on the part of God and on the part of the human. However, the point remains that the *disposition* to relate to God does not require mental states. The complexity is that God's movement toward humanity is the initiating stimulus condition while the human response is the secondary stimulus condition. Put most simply, the disposition is intrinsic to the human person; the stimulus is external to the human person since even the response to God's movement toward humanity is a gift of faith. Therefore, the disposition is a property with a stimulus-response structure, and the chapters that follow will examine the disposition and this stimulus in more detail.[6] However, for the sake of concision, when I say that humans need a second-personal relation with God, I am always understanding this to be first initiated by God as the provision for that need, even if I am speaking in terms of human response to that provision. Humans dispositionally need a second-personal relationship with God in order to flourish. Such a disposition is constitutional in such a way that any entity of the kind "human" will have this disposition. All fundamental needs are dispositional in this way. Consequently, since all human persons have this dispositional property, personhood is not degreed; however, flourishing is degreed.[7] Because flourishing is degreed, it is also developmental and able to increase or decrease.

The degreeing of flourishing reveals another disconnect between inanimate dispositions and human dispositions. In teasing out the difference between animate and inanimate objects, Thomson clarifies that inanimate objects can need something in the sense of Jupiter's needing to have a certain momentum to stay in orbit around the sun. However, inanimate objects "can need, but cannot have needs, because they do not have aims and purposes, and because they cannot be harmed."[8] Having an aim and purpose and being able to be harmed separate animate from inanimate entities. However, such aims and purposes

---

6. I am indebted to Dr. Elanor Taylor for this succinct way of framing how dispositions are typically understood in philosophy of science. E. Taylor, "More on Dispositions?" The typical way of framing dispositions can be found in Choi and Fara, "Dispositions."

7. This degreeing of humanness is a significant problem in relational anthropologies that require a certain complexity of cognitive abilities in order to be fully human. For an excellent discussion of this problematic, see Leidenhag, "Challenge of Autism."

8. G. Thomson, *Needs*, 11. "'Need' contains the idea that A needs X to be A or to function as A, and it implies that the 'purpose' for which X is needed by A is defined by A's essential nature" (124).

are intentionally thin on Thomson's account and related more to organismic maturation and development than toward anything explicitly teleological. At the same time, a richer *telos* is compatible with Thomson's account.

While the need is itself constitutional, the meeting of this need is not. Whether or not someone is relating second-personally to God, the need remains. Even as I drink water, I need water. To have this need for water met involves mental states, which can then be described as they are acted on. Similarly, because the need for a second-personal relationship to God cannot be observed in itself, this serves as another reason that the arguments across this volume must be abductive. We will look at texts and biblical ideas that largely describe acts, not dispositions. Since relying on God's personal presence (union) is the act of responding to God's provision for a second-personal relationship with Godself, seeing the centrality of this dependence across testaments and times will strengthen the case for the dispositional need proposed herein.[9]

Further, the example of drinking water raises a distinction between survival and flourishing in that water is fundamentally needed to both survive and flourish. In contrast, one can survive without meeting the need for a second-personal relationship with God but not fully flourish. The same could be said of the fundamental need for human-to-human relationships in that one can survive without them but not flourish. This book is concerned with flourishing, not survival. I am also focusing on a distinctly *human* need.[10] In the case of a need for water, humans are not the only creatures with this need. However, at points, the parallels of food and water with the fundamental need of a second-personal relation to God will be used to illustrate that specific need's significance.

The reason for qualifying the presence as "second-personal" is that this need goes beyond a kind of existence-relation, recognized as properly basic, and consisting of the necessary dependence of all contingent beings on God for their existence, the only necessary being. Such a dependence is unintentional on the part of the creature and could be had whether God is personal or not. Instead, the fundamental need proposed here requires that a mutual relationship exist between God and human persons, even though the need is unilateral. In the theological tradition, this has typically been understood

9. Scripture is not a book on philosophy of mind, and so distinctions such as mental and nonmental states are not the concern of biblical writers and redactors. However, the fact that something is underdetermined does not mean it cannot be discussed. My main concern will be consistency and noncontradiction with what has been communicated in Scripture.

10. Arguably, angels could also relate to God second-personally. However, this relation does not seem oriented toward union, which is distinctive for this human need.

covenantally. Human persons are uniquely related to God in that God desires to have a covenantal relationship with humans, in which we respond by relating to God.[11]

Eleonore Stump's work is helpful here as she explains, "Typically, this kind of presence [second-personal] is characterized as presence *with* or presence *to* another person. I will call this kind of presence 'personal presence.'"[12] Such a second-personal presence becomes even more intimate when we introduce the divine person into the discussion. While remaining second-personal, the human-to-divine relation is even deeper than what a human-to-human second-personal presence could be. This inherent human-to-human limitation is the case because God can indwell human beings in a way that transcends human-to-human relations.[13] Thus, humans need the second-personal relation to God (a disposition), which will be met by their relying on God in a relationally intimate way (involving some sort of mental state).

We will focus on the centrality of a second-personal relation to God and whether this can fit the category of a "fundamental need." However, to clarify,

11. While recognizing that relating back to God is a gift of the Spirit's work (in light of its being redeemed in Christ's faithful human obedience to the Spirit's empowerment), we should be cautious as we seek to define what is required for this "relating back." For example, in Luke 18:17, Jesus says: "Truly I tell you, whoever does not receive the kingdom of God as a little child will never enter it." Commentator John Nolland says, "Though Jesus will be no romantic about children, somewhere among their openness, willingness to trust, freedom from hypocrisy or pretension, conscious weakness, and readiness for dependence Jesus finds those qualities that are essential for entry into the kingdom of God." *Luke 9:21–18:34*, 883. See also Leidenhag, "Does the Indwelling of the Holy Spirit Require a Neurotypical Brain?" She says, "If the relationship between God and humanity, particularly the one referred to in Christian theology as the indwelling of the Holy Spirit, is asymmetrical then we are able to say that a neurotypical brain is not a necessary requirement for relationship with God in every case, but that it may be employed in some cases. Similarly, a neurodivergent brain is also not necessary, neither an advantage nor disadvantage to the Spirit's indwelling, but may be employed in some cases, and differences in religious experience and perception may result. The Holy Spirit can accommodate to whatever neurological or other physiological conditions mark a particular human life."

12. Stump, "Omnipresence, Indwelling," 30. See also Stump, *Wandering in Darkness*, chaps. 4 and 6. For some of the instigating scholarship on this topic see Alston, "Indwelling of the Holy Spirit"; Alston, *Divine Nature and Human Language*. Most recently, Kimberley Kroll builds on and pushes against prior scholarship in "Indwelling without the Indwelling Holy Spirit."

13. Elsewhere, Stump explains: "For lack of a better term, I will use an old theological term and refer to this most intimate and powerful kind of second-personal presence between God and a human person as God's 'indwelling' a human person." "Omnipresence, Indwelling," 31, 46. For a similar framework and an argument for the merits of what might be called an "interpersonal" model of the indwelling, see Porter and Rickabaugh, "Sanctifying Work of the Holy Spirit." Finally, whether or not humans could be indwelt by God's Spirit prior to the incarnation is debatable. However, as we will see in chap. 8, the permanence of that kind of relationship becomes possible through the incarnation.

the mechanics of *how* this need is met (i.e., how human agency and divine agency interact) will not be my focus. To address those issues, a range of possibilities is available that are compatible with the theological anthropology I will propose below. The aim of this book is less comprehensive. Of course, even my proposed minimalism (that humans need a second-personal relation to God) raises questions that deserve brief attention at the outset.

Regarding God's personal presence, questions may immediately come to mind about the difference, if there is one, between God's omnipresence and localized presence. In other words, if God is already everywhere, is God then *more* present when related to second-personally? The distinction between God's omnipresence and manifest presence is a difficult question that philosophers of religion continue to debate today.[14] The debates lie beyond the scope of this book, and I offer a conditionalizing approach in which I assume the following: that omnipresence is not undermined by the different experiences of God's presence attested to throughout the Hebrew Bible and New Testament, that this presence occurs in space and time, that God's withdrawal of presence is in some way actual, and that God's presence, especially when localized, seems especially perceptible to human persons.[15] Consequently, the idea that humans are meant to second-personally relate to God *beyond* mere existence, which is made possible and is preceded by God's omnipresence, will be assumed for the sake of argument. At the same time, that anything instead of nothing exists remains a supreme gift! I do not want to undermine the gift of creaturely existence or the significance of God's omnipresence, even if this gift of existence is in some way distinct from God's localized presence. Therefore, for the sake of clarity, when I use "God's presence" or "divine presence" throughout this book, this refers to God's localized, personal presence.

That this presence is personal is also reasonable given how God's presence is described in Scripture. For instance, the most frequently used word for God's presence in the Old Testament is the Hebrew word *panim*, literally, "face." Unlike hand or eye, the face carries with it the ability to express emotions and reactions. "It also carries strong connotations of relationship."[16]

14. For a helpful overview of various positions in this debate, see Inman, "Omnipresence and the Location of the Immaterial"; Inman, "Retrieving Divine Immensity and Omnipresence."

15. These criteria are held in common with Gordon, "ReThinking Divine Spatiality," 538. He outlines the major philosophical and theological views, including their costs and benefits. For a biblical theology of God's relational presence that argues for the centrality of this concept spanning from Genesis to Revelation, see Duvall and Hays, *God's Relational Presence*.

16. Duvall and Hays, *God's Relational Presence*, 13. For this reason, when "person" is used, it means more than simply hypostasis. Instead, this is a relational personhood. I appreciate Tom McCall's definition of divine persons: "necessarily existent entities who enjoy 'I-Thou'

This is a being who creates, calls, admonishes, rescues, and loves the created order. Yahweh is consistently described using language for how persons act. Even when impersonal language is used, such as "glory," it becomes personified:

> For example, in the exodus, God's "glory" led his people. As in the Hebrew Bible (Isa 60:1–3), Judaism continued to associate an ultimate revelation of "glory" with the eschatological time. "Glory" when applied to God may invite comparison with the related Jewish concept of Shekinah, which appears especially in rabbinic literature. These texts personify the Shekinah but do not hypostatize it; it functioned essentially as a circumlocution for God, indicating his nearness. God himself could be addressed as "Glorious One" or called "the Glory of the World." God's presence could be banished by sin or invited by merit. Although these associations can vary widely, they typically involve the divine.[17]

We see in this that God's presence is personal yet distinct from omnipresence. Thus, the idea that humans are intended to relate to God's personal presence, not only God's omnipresence, is the focus of this argument.

Fundamental Need

With these terms clarified, we can turn to Thomson's work on fundamental need. To begin, Thomson distinguishes between instrumental and fundamental needs. An instrumental need is derivative in some way, while a fundamental need is not. For instance, while I need to work, a key aspect of that need is that I need to work to earn money to buy food to feed myself. Hence, when thinking about work as a means to sustenance, I see that it is (in that case) instrumental.[18] He then moves on to offer a case for each criterion that determines a need's fundamentality: the need must be nonderivative, inescapable, and noncircumstantial. Most simply, a fundamental human need is a need for that which is necessary for the well-being of a certain entity and is inseparable

---

relationship within the triune life." McCall, "Relational Trinity," 116. The basis for that assertion is how God has revealed Godself in Scripture, which McCall also briefly summarizes (117–21).

17. Keener, *Acts*, 2:1632. See also Johnson, *Hebrews*, 69: "The term 'glory' (*doxa*) is used in Scripture with reference above all to the visible presence of God among the people (see Exod 16:7, 10; 24:16; Lev 9:6; Num 14:10; Deut 5:24; Ps 18:1; Heb 9:5). The association of God's presence with *light*, furthermore, is common (Exod 10:13; Pss 4:6; 35:9; 77:14; 88:15; 118:105). It is natural, then, for 'glory' to carry the connotation of 'radiant light,' as we see elsewhere in the New Testament (John 1:4–14; 2 Cor 3:7–18)." Cf. Hansen, *Letter to the Philippians*, 136–37; and for a theological approach, see Arcadi, "God Is Where God Acts," 637.

18. Though this is not to negate the role that work may play in other aspects of flourishing. This extends beyond the scope of this book.

from the constitution of that entity.[19] Needs "are never mental acts, but are passive dispositions to suffer certain harms because of certain lacks. There is no act of needing water."[20] So, when someone does not have water and is dehydrated, this is a case of needing what one lacks. However, one could be fully hydrated and not in a state of lack, and yet still need water. In both cases, the need is not a mental act. Hence, to be fundamental, this kind of need "indicates a disposition and does not imply a lack."[21] Thomson challenges the intuition that to need something is to necessarily lack something. Instead, a need is a passive disposition, which is why it is tied to a subject's ontology.[22]

A fundamental need is a necessary condition for an entity's nature and existence. Thomson states, "To claim that X is a fundamental need for person A is to assert that X is a non-derivative, non-circumstantially specific and an inescapable necessary condition in order for the person A not to undergo serious harm."[23] So, if someone does not have the need met or have the means to have this need met, then she is necessarily harmed. To be harmed is to be deprived of intrinsic goods, which is the opposite of flourishing and is discussed below. Thomson defines the strength of fundamental needs as that of a necessary condition for understanding an entity's nature.[24] He then elaborates on this necessity, which is tied to the nature of the entity as it relates to harm: "The antecedent of a need is necessary in the sense that it is essential to A. 'Need' contains the idea that A needs X to be A or to function as A, and it implies that the 'purpose' for which X is needed by A is defined by A's essential nature. The rich sense of 'need' determines that the antecedent of a 'need'-statement must be A's life or the quality of his life, or more specifically, the avoidance of an especially serious type of harm."[25] In sum, a fundamental need is inextricably bound to an entity's nature, whereby the meeting of the need directly contributes to the entity's well-being, and not having the need met contributes directly to the entity's experience of harm. Before looking at Thomson's understanding of harm, we will turn to his criteria for determining whether a need is indeed fundamental instead of instrumental.

---

19. G. Thomson, *Needs*, 88–89. Given that this project is concerned with human persons (and not other creatures), the fundamental needs necessary for each human person's well-being are the focus here.

20. G. Thomson, *Needs*, 100.

21. G. Thomson, "Fundamental Needs," 175.

22. G. Thomson, *Needs*, 100.

23. G. Thomson, "Fundamental Needs," 175. There are many nonfundamental needs, or instrumental needs, that do not meet these criteria, but those are not the focus of this book.

24. G. Thomson, *Needs*, 124.

25. G. Thomson, *Needs*, 124. See also Brock and Miller, "Needs in Moral and Political Philosophy," on relating basic needs to the human constitution.

The criteria for fundamentality are that the need must be nonderivative, noncircumstantial, and inescapable. First, in saying that a need is nonderivative, Thomson means that this need is necessary in and of itself. It is not a need that has another need undergirding it, since any additional scaffolding would make the need instrumental instead of fundamental. So, while it would be true that a person needs money to buy a car, the money is instrumental to the purchase of the car. The acquisition of the car does not make the need for the car a non-derivative need, since having the car meets the need of driving to work, which meets the need of earning money, which is again instrumental to buying food, which is then the object of the necessity to satisfy hunger. The need for food is the nonderivative need, hunger is the indication of that need, and eating food satisfies the need even though it does not negate the disposition of the need for food. Importantly, the need for food and the food itself are two different things. So, a need can be nonderivative while still being instrumental in terms of contributing to what is good or bad for a person. What is good or bad for a person is deemed an "inescapable interest" for Thomson.[26] Schuppert elaborates on this (using the language of "fundamental interest") as "the goods and things a person necessarily requires in order to realize a shared, universally valuable and non-contingent end."[27] In the case of eating food, the universally valuable end—or, to use Thomson's language, "inescapable interest"—is survival. Like surviving, flourishing is a universally valuable end of humans and is therefore an inescapable interest. We will return to inescapable interests below.

The second criterion is that of being noncircumstantial. Thomson explains how a need is noncircumstantial: a human being "needs food because of his physical make-up. . . . The need for food can be called 'a constitutional need' and the need for bread 'a circumstantial need.' A constitutional need is, in a sense, a need whatever the circumstances."[28] In other words, the person has this need regardless of her situation.[29] Whether living on Mars, lounging on a beach, submerged in a submarine, or in any other context, this need must persist. Again, for Thomson, the constitution of the subject determines the kind of needs it has, such that "the need is innately, rather than environmentally

---

26. Thomson, *Needs*, 88.

27. Schuppert, "Distinguishing Basic Needs," 32. Schuppert's interaction with Thomson's work is especially helpful in teasing out more fully how Thomson is using the language of interests as it relates to needs. However, Schuppert ultimately proposes a "shift of focus" from fundamental needs to fundamental interests (Schuppert, 24). His critique of needs-theories, Thomson's included, does not undermine the major points of my proposal, primarily because I am seeking to maintain the importance of both fundamental/inescapable interests as well as fundamental needs.

28. G. Thomson, *Needs*, 21. "Food" is here understood as a nutritional input of some kind.

29. G. Thomson, "Fundamental Needs," 177.

and socially determined."[30] Thus, the internal structure of the entity is the final criterion that must be applied for a need to be deemed fundamental.

A need is inescapable if there is nothing a human being can do to avoid having this fundamental need. This unavoidability can be put more stringently: "The concept of a fundamental need restricts the viable courses of action down to only one."[31] Either I eat food, or I suffer and die. Either I breathe oxygen, or I suffer and die. So, whereas fundamental need is noncircumstantial regarding external contexts of the person, it is inescapable internally in that no matter what the subject does or does not do, having this need is required due to her nature.[32] In other words, the need is unsubstitutable by anything else, which means that if the subject does not have what she needs, she is harmed. We also see the language of interests coming up again, which brings us to further clarification, especially as it relates to harm.

Harm

Undergirding all these criteria is the notion of harm.[33] Thomson defines "harm" as being "deprived of engaging in non-instrumentally valuable experiences and activities as well [as] of the possibility of appreciating them."[34] To clarify what we are deprived of and to distinguish his theory of harm from desire-based theories of harm, Thomson introduces the category of an "inescapable interest."[35] An inescapable interest tells us what we are deprived

30. G. Thomson, *Needs*, 32.

31. G. Thomson, *Needs*, 27–28; cf. 126.

32. For more on the distinction between fundamental need, an addiction, and a false need, see G. Thomson, *Needs*, 28–30. David Wiggins, another analytic philosopher specializing in need, supports and even furthers this understanding of the rigorous conditions a need must meet to qualify as fundamental (though he uses the language of "absolute"), in that "any statement of the form 'y needs x [absolutely]'" presents "a challenge to imagine an alternative future in which y escapes harm or damage without having x, or an alternative where y's vital interests are better adjusted to others' vital interests than they would be if x were what he had." *Needs, Values, Truth*, 22. Wiggins also affirms Thomson's views on fundamental needs, but I will only cite him when he brings out a significant nuance.

33. In many theories of harm, desire satisfaction plays a critical role. Thomson seeks an alternative theory of harm that denies that well-being must consist of desire satisfaction or that desires are entirely inconsequential to understanding harm and well-being. See G. Thomson, *Needs*, 63. Further, Thomson articulates this by utilizing the concept of interests. They "define what types of activity we are deprived of when we are harmed" (88). These interests reveal what are of primary value to us (77–78).

34. G. Thomson, *Needs*, 178.

35. G. Thomson, "Fundamental Needs," 185. Cf. G. Thomson, *Needs*, 88–89: "The value of needed things should be explained in relation to harm and, thus, interests. Interests define what harm consists of; needs are necessary to avoid that harm."

of and what consequential desires *may* emerge from that experience. This understanding is possible because "the concept of an interest demonstrates in what sense our well-being consists in living in accordance with our nature, rather than consisting of getting what we desire."[36] So, regarding the relationship between harm, inescapable interests, and fundamental needs—an interest explains harm, and harm is necessary to understanding fundamental need.[37] Inescapable interests "provide a certain starting-point for deliberation and a certain fixedness in what is to count as good or bad for a person."[38] Put a little differently by another philosopher, "Basic [fundamental] needs are needs which possess absolute necessity for achieving a universally valuable end."[39] So, the interest tells us what we are deprived of when we are harmed. The fact that we would be harmed without satisfying the interest is what makes that satisfaction fundamentally needed. Desires may or may not map onto fundamental need and thus cannot be used to understand harm. Instead, inescapable interests indicate why we desire what we do instead of indicating the content of that desire. Thomson further explains that interests "constitute a way of characterising the content of a desire that is distinct from specifying its object. Descriptions that specify a person's interests inform us of why a person desires non-instrumentally what she does, but without telling us what she desires."[40] We can apply this theologically: (1) We have an inescapable interest to flourish. (2) We fundamentally need a second-personal relation to God to flourish. (3) When that need is not met, we are therefore harmed.

Put differently, the fundamental need for a second-personal relation to God is instrumentally valuable for the universally valuable end of flourishing. This mix of fundamental and instrumental language may seem confusing given the distinction between fundamental and instrumental needs. However, a need can still be fundamental even if it is instrumental to satisfying the interest. Returning to the glass example, three things are going on—the disposition of the glass to break when struck, being struck, and breaking. For humans, we have the disposition to flourish when second-personally relating to God;

36. G. Thomson, "Fundamental Needs," 185.
37. G. Thomson, "Fundamental Needs," 185.
38. G. Thomson, "Fundamental Needs," 185. Thomson goes into more detail in his book-length treatment of needs: "A deprivational view of harm also clarifies the relationship between need and survival. The need for food, water, and air are commonly thought to be among our basic fundamental needs. Yet people have a need for friendship even when it is clear that they won't die without it. So, survival needs can count as fundamental needs, and yet fundamental needs cover more than survival." G. Thomson, *Needs*, 38.
39. Schuppert, "Distinguishing Basic Needs," 27. I will argue, as a theological project, for what is revealed as universally valuable for humankind based on revelation.
40. Thomson, Gill, and Goodson, *Happiness, Flourishing and the Good Life*, 191.

we second-personally relate to God, and we flourish (at least via a divine-to-human relationship). Flourishing is valuable in itself and, as such, is an inescapable interest. The inescapable interest is the motivational source of desire. And yet "desires for very different things can have a similar motivational source," which is why desires may be diverse but motivated by the same end, yet that end and the means to meet it may not be apparent.[41]

For this reason, Thomson strongly critiques desire-based theories of harm. Instead of desires determining what is valuable, they function as a guide to what is valuable. He provides three primary objections to desire-based theories of harm: that desires can only mislead if based on false beliefs; that desires are value-dependent; that things are good not merely because we want them. Regarding the first objection, he asserts, "Preferences (however well-informed) can fail to track the relevant kind of intrinsic value not only because of cognitive errors but also because of affective or emotional failures, such as an obsessive hatred or being in a bad mood. For instance, when I feel vile, my desires will be obnoxious. More knowledge is not always the cure." This point seems extremely self-evident. I can know that underneath my fingernails are all kinds of germs and disgusting microbes, but this will not necessarily change my preference for biting my nails. Theologically, of course, the pervasiveness of sin's effects on cognition, emotion, and affection can also obscure what is intrinsically valuable—second-personally relating to God.[42] Thomson goes on to state that "sometimes, what one needs for improved well-being may be a transformation of desire rather than obtaining what one wants," though any suggestions for this kind of transformation go beyond Thomson's purview.[43]

I propose that humans have intentionally been given a constitution that is disposed to flourishing when its fundamental need for relating to God's presence second-personally is met. While many creatures beyond humankind likely desire the inescapable interest of flourishing, the fundamental need of a second-personal relationship with God seems to be a uniquely human need. Further, humans likely recognize their desire to flourish but may not discern the content of what would meet those desires.

To develop the second objection, Thomson asks the Socratic question: "Which way does the explanation run: from desire to being valuable or from being valuable to desire?"[44] The desire theory of harm requires that desire indicates value. However, if someone changes their preferences because of new

---

41. Thomson, Gill, and Goodson, *Happiness, Flourishing and the Good Life*, 190.
42. We will return to this in chap. 10.
43. Thomson, Gill, and Goodson, *Happiness, Flourishing and the Good Life*, 82–84; quotes are from 83.
44. Thomson, Gill, and Goodson, *Happiness, Flourishing and the Good Life*, 84.

information, it is the facts about those new options that are compelling. In Thomson's words, "The change in preference merely indicates A's sensitivity to the comparative preferability of the options; it is not constitutive of that preferability, but merely reflects it."[45] Desires are not the kinds of things that determine value; they can only indicate it.

Finally, there are times when we want what is not good for our well-being, and there are things that are good for our well-being that we do not want. Eating a whole chocolate cake is indicative of the former, just as exercise is one example of the latter. Such misalignment further supports the notion that desire is insufficient to determine what has noninstrumental value.

To summarize, a fundamental need is a passive disposition.[46] Harm consists of being deprived of what one has an inescapable interest in when one does not get what one needs. When this need is not met, the human person does not experience full flourishing, and this experience is harmful. Desires for full flourishing are motivated by this inescapable interest to pursue other means of fulfillment. Still, desires may or may not indicate the true inescapable interest at their motivational root.

To discern this motivational root, Thomson proposes two questions by which to analyze harm: What does harm deprive humans of? And why is that thing good?[47] This "good" can even be something that the human person has never experienced, such that her quality of life is affected without her knowing it. This ignorance is possible since harm is primarily about deprivation, explaining why "harm need not be felt."[48] Consequently, harm is inherently difficult to identify, as it is characterized by what it is not (flourishing) or by its effects (deprivation). Someone can be ignorant of having a specific

---

45. Thomson, Gill, and Goodson, *Happiness, Flourishing and the Good Life*, 84. Cf. G. Thomson, *Needs*, 46–49. Interestingly, Thomson makes a further clarifying remark regarding how this might work for an omniscient, perfectly rational being in that this being "would reflect perfectly the non-instrumentally valuable nature of the activities in question. They would track it perfectly. But they would not constitute it." Thomson, Gill, and Goodson, *Happiness, Flourishing and the Good Life*, 84.

46. A quick note is in order here about need being a passive disposition. While someone attuned to Aquinas's idea of obediential potential may see overlap of that concept with need, fundamental need is stronger than nonrepugnance. Further, obediential potency leaves too much room for life apart from grace. Fundamental need is also distinct from Rahner's supernatural existential for a few reasons. First, fundamental need does not necessarily orient us to God. It indicates a lack (due to sin), but because one can be entirely ignorant of any harm she is experiencing by not strongly participating in God, the orientation is more neutral than anything else. Second, fundamental need is a constituent of human nature, whereas the supernatural existential is not. For a summary of Rahner's view as it relates to the supernatural existential as developed throughout his theological project, see Coffey, "Whole Rahner on the Supernatural Existential."

47. G. Thomson, *Needs*, 44.

48. G. Thomson, *Needs*, 36–37.

fundamental need and yet not negate the actuality of the need's existence.[49] Thomson gives an example of a people on the fictitious planet of Kakapos, who derive their energy from the sun's rays but would flourish more fully if they were also to eat the vegetables on their planet. The catch is that they do not realize this is the case, leading Thomson to surmise "that harm should be regarded as a type of deprivation rather than as a state of mind. It suggests that something harms us when it deprives us of the more valuable aspects of living."[50] Consequently, one could be in a state of harm without knowing it.

CONCLUSION

A fundamental need is nonderivative, noncircumstantial, and inescapable, so that the entity experiences serious harm if this need is not met. However, since this need is bound to the disposition of that entity, even in the "meeting" of this need, to *be* that being is to *have* that need regardless of inputs. Yet the entity does not have to be aware of the need or the harm she is experiencing by its being unmet for the need to be real. As far as that need is being met, the entity experiences flourishing instead of harm, but the need itself is constitutional.[51] We will now turn to the biblical accounts to see if the proposed fundamental need for a second-personal relation to God is well attested in the biblical material and to see how we see flourishing described in these texts.

49. G. Thomson, *Needs*, 16.
50. G. Thomson, *Needs*, 36. Further, he goes on to note the unsubstitutable nature of a fundamental need: "The concept of a fundamental need restricts the viable courses of action down to only one, that is seeking what we need. This is why self-alteration is impossible with regard to our fundamental needs, and why these needs are inescapable" (27–28). Less esoteric examples can also be found, such as the iodine deficiency in Aotearoa New Zealand that led to an epidemic of multiple health conditions, including goiter.
51. You may be wondering how Thomson would define flourishing. However, such a definition is not necessary for his account of fundamental need, except to speak in broad terms about well-being, health, and inescapable interests. For our purposes, defining flourishing is important because my theological presupposition is not only that God wants us to avoid harm but also that God wants us to flourish (and provides the means through which we do so).

PART 2

The Image of God

TWO

The Image of God
and Initial Humans

Now that the initial criteria are in place to determine the fundamentality of a given need, we are ready to turn to the biblical witness to see if such a need emerges across these various witnesses. Given the importance of understanding flourishing for understanding need, we will begin with some biblical scholarship on how this might be understood across the testaments before turning to the Genesis texts and asking questions about the meaning of humanness. Of course, these texts reveal far more about God than about humanity, which is something of the point. By looking at the biblical material's claims about flourishing, we can then return to questions of human constitution and whether any need is implied.

Flourishing in Scripture: A Brief Overview[1]

New Testament scholar Jonathan Pennington has focused on human flourishing and helpfully frames how this concept would have likely been understood across both testaments.[2] While his work examines the Sermon on the Mount,

---

1. The literature defining flourishing, especially across disciplines, is immense. Further, the causes of flourishing and the constitution of flourishing are often conflated. Since such discussion could take us far afield, for my purposes we need a working definition of how Scripture might frame a "universally valuable end," and Pennington's treatment of flourishing provides such a definition.

2. Pennington, *Sermon on the Mount*. The next several citations of this work are in the text.

he provides a rich backdrop for how first-century listeners would have heard this teaching from Jesus. Further, he claims that this sermon "is Christianity's answer to the greatest metaphysical question that humanity has always faced—How can we experience true human flourishing? . . . I would suggest that this question is at the core of the entire message of Scripture" (14). At the time that Jesus preached this sermon, two primary worldviews were in play for his audience, Greco-Roman and Jewish. Across the Greek and Roman philosophical systems, the question of what makes people flourish was both practical and focused on virtues (31). For the Jews, this flourishing was tied to a covenant relationship with YHWH. However, this relationship could also be characterized by virtuous alignment with God (37). Thus, Pennington notes that adherents of both worldviews recognized that "human flourishing will only be realized through a person's virtue or wholeness, experienced both individually and communally" (36). To summarize Pennington's argument, flourishing, on a biblical picture, is a wholehearted orientation toward God (73–78).[3]

To make these claims, he turns to Greek terms used in the Sermon on the Mount and then backfills their content in both Jewish and Greco-Roman contexts. He begins with *makarios* (plural, *makarioi*), often translated as "blessed," and explains that this word "ascribes happiness or flourishing to a particular person or state" (42). Instead of bestowing blessing or divine favor, however, it is a pronouncement of what is already true of that person (42). Macarisms were widespread in the ancient world, and Jesus utilized them to make some powerful theological claims about what flourishing looks like before the full realization of the kingdom of God. While *shalom* (peace)

---

3. As we saw in the first chapter, this wholehearted orientation toward God would be compatible with *shalom* and with union with God, because without this wholehearted orientation toward God, *shalom* and union would be thwarted. One might say that this orientation would be characterized by love of God and love of neighbor. In fact, as I completed the final edits on this manuscript, I attended a panel for the Society of Christian Philosophers in which theologian Sameer Yadav defined the flourishing life in those terms. In the essay he was speaking from for this panel, "Toward an Analytic Theology of Liberation," he goes into more detail on this view. He states, "Essentially constitutive of our flourishing qua images, therefore, is our capacity of mediate divine care in our mutually dependent relations with one another, and in our cooperative nurture of land and non-human life. The human 'Fall' interrupts not only human life but introduces a breach in the created order, one that involves a devolution and aberration of our relationship with God. This broken relationship is evidenced primarily by our failure in mutual dependence on and cooperation with one another and our consequent abuse of one another, land, and non-human creatures." Sameer Yadav, "Toward an Analytic Theology of Liberation," 63. Yadav's points resonate with the importance of union, *shalom*, and orientation toward God—all of which have vocational outworkings. Given the scope of this current work, the ethical, communal, and ecclesial implications will not be adequately addressed here but will have to await future work.

is the largest concept from the Hebrew Bible for describing flourishing, the closest parallel to the macarism is *ashre*.[4] *Ashre* is concentrated in the Wisdom literature, with thirty-four out of forty-five occurrences appearing in Psalms and Proverbs. Across these books, it typically describes the flourishing state of a person who lives wisely, and wise living is closely tied to walking according to the covenant of YHWH (47).[5]

Returning to the Greco-Roman worldview, we find that *makarios* is often used synonymously with the Greek philosophical word *eudaimonia* (flourishing/happiness) (46). Especially for Aristotle, this word connoted flourishing and the truly good life. The role of wisdom and becoming virtuous thus finds resonance with the meaning of *ashre* for those from a Jewish worldview. However, an important distinction for the Jews was that

> one can only flourish fully as a human when one is in a covenantal relationship with the creator God, which includes both ancient notions of what it means to flourish *and* a necessary orientation to God's revelation. Thus, when the Psalms speak of the *ašrê* state of the one who meditates on Torah (God's covenantal instructions), such as in Ps. 119, this is simultaneously a claim that this God-oriented person is in a state of flourishing precisely because he or she is experiencing the most direct means of grace that God has ordained to effect favor upon his people—meditation on God's self-revelation, or in short, knowing God (50).[6]

For our purposes, based on this account, flourishing is bound up with a wholehearted orientation toward God. In Scripture, such an orientation would often be evidenced by meditation on Torah and virtuous living in accordance with that revelation.

From this load-bearing word in the Sermon and across the testaments, Pennington turns to *teleios* as another important term for understanding a biblical and ancient conception of flourishing. *Teleios* and *telos* are closely related but distinct terms. *Teleios* means perfect and refers to a condition in which the *telos* (goal) "has been achieved" (76). So, *teleios* indicated completion, while the *telos* was the goal that was aimed at. For Aristotle, that which is *teleios* is pursued by living a life of contemplative virtue, thereby producing *eudaimonia*. This "virtue entails or necessitates an intentional wholeness of person (*teleios*)" (77). In the Sermon, Jesus tells his listeners, "Be *teleios*,

---

4. Pennington makes this case based on the Septuagint translation (the Greek version of the Hebrew Bible), which consistently renders *ashre* as *makarios*. Such consistency of translation is atypical. *Sermon on the Mount*, 46.

5. See also Charry, *God and the Art of Happiness*, 170.

6. Here Pennington is also teasing out the distinction between *makarios* and blessing.

therefore, as your heavenly Father is *teleios*" (Matt. 5:48). While this language is strongly allusive to Leviticus 19:2, 20:26, and Deuteronomy 18:13, Jesus changes *hagios* (holy) to *teleios*. Based on what we have already seen as it relates to *makarios*, Pennington argues that the call to *teleios*-ity in the Sermon is the same as the call to holiness in the Hebrew Bible. This "being perfect" is "not moral perfection but wholehearted orientation toward God" (78). As we will see, being *teleios* (complete) is the *telos* (goal) of humankind, and yet completion still includes "meditation on God's self-revelation," a revelation of God's personal presence (50).

While Greco-Roman philosophies stressed virtuous living as a means to *eudaimonia*, such a paradigm did not require knowing God or having a whole-hearted orientation to God. Nor did this Greco-Roman paradigm understand the corporate and cosmic dimensions of the flourishing intended as the *teleios*. Pennington points to N. T. Wright's perspective here: "The early Christians did not abandon the framework of shaping one's life based on the *telos* or goal, but they did replace the Aristotelian goal with a different one. The goal is, according to Gen. 1–2, what humans were made for in the first place, and according to Exodus, what Israel is called to—'It is the task of being the "royal priesthood," worship and stewardship, generating justice and beauty'" (297).[7] Consequently, returning to the story of the initial humans, we see that what is *teleios* is given alongside the creation account of this curious creature, as well as a context in which these human beings could flourish. They could live virtuously (by not eating the forbidden fruit and by being priestly stewards of creation) and know God second-personally.

Genesis 1:26–27

If a term's frequency reveals its importance, "image of God" might not register on the scale of theological weightiness. However, frequency is not the only determinant for conceptual significance.[8] The opening creation narrative states: "Then God said, 'Let us make humankind in our image, according to our likeness'" (Gen. 1:26a). Immediately following, God says, "and let them have dominion over" the rest of creation (1:26b). After stating this intention and function, God carries out the statement: "So God created humankind in his image, in the image of God he created them; male and female he created them" (1:27). Before moving on to the other three human-associated uses of image or likeness in the Hebrew text, we must examine these verses to

---

7. Emphasis original; Pennington quotes Wright, *After You Believe*, 82–83.
8. Barr, "Image of God in the Book of Genesis," 12; Harland, *Value of Human Life*, 208.

understand what they say and do not say.[9] First, *tselem* (image) and *demuth* (likeness) probably refer to the same concept, working as synonyms. While "likeness" may be explanatorily narrowing the meaning of "image," what exactly the "likeness" is remains unclear from the text.

It does not seem that these terms are addressing two different matters but instead the same concept.[10] This conceptual similarity finds support in the lack of a conjunction between these words, which would have indicated a stronger distinction between them (1:26); and the lack of "likeness" language in the subsequent verse (1:27) functions as if the "image" language already has "likeness" assumed in its meaning.[11] Later, in Genesis 5, these words will be inverted, supporting their semantic overlap due to their interchangeable use. Though the meanings of image and likeness will be explored in more detail below, *tselem* and its cognates "are primarily used in the literal sense of three-dimensional objects which represent gods, men or animals."[12] Therefore, an *image* has a connotation of materiality.

Second, although the Genesis text does communicate that the human creature is set apart from the rest of creation as unique, with the charge to have dominion, it does not say that this dominion is the content of the image, but rather that it is the *consequent* of being in the image of God. Peter Gentry and Stephen Wellum insightfully argue that the "cohortative followed by imperfect marks purpose or result." Such a grammatical construction influences the interpretation, yielding the following translation: "Let us make humankind [*adam*] in our image, according to our likeness so that they may rule." This reading exegetically supports the distinction between the constitution of the image and the consequence of being in the image of God.[13] Notably, the charge of having dominion connects to the divine presence. L. Michael Morales provides helpful insight here: "The primary blessing of being created in God's image is in order to have

9. Whether one takes the creation narrative literally or literarily, the theological points regarding the nature of humanity still remain. Also, while the scholarly consensus is that Genesis 1–3 was composed by two (or more) authors, discerning their differences is not the focus of this work. The first chapters of Genesis were especially significant to the Jewish community and believed to be inspired by God regardless of how many human agents were involved or when, exactly, this was written. To borrow a phrase from Richard Bauckham, at issue here is the "imaginative theology" of the origin account. Bauckham, "Incarnation and the Cosmic Christ," 48.

10. While not "'semantic equivalents' they may be more or less 'interchangeable.'" McDowell, *Image of God*, 125.

11. The Septuagint does insert *kai* (and) between them, which influenced the understanding of these words as communicating two different things. Cf. Harland, *Value of Human Life*, 184.

12. Harland, *Value of Human Life*, 178. McDowell, *Image of God*, 125.

13. Gentry and Wellum, *Kingdom through Covenant*, 188. For support for this grammatical argument, see Garr, *In His Own Image and Likeness*.

fellowship with the Creator in a way the other creatures cannot. . . . [The commands] should be directed to this chief end and highest goal—*ha adam* is to gather all creation into the life-giving Presence and praise of God."[14] In Morales's interpretation, being in the image of God is a unique status of humanity that results in a unique function. Claus Westermann follows a similar tack: "The Creator wants to create a being analogous to himself, to whom he can speak, who will listen and speak to him. . . . By virtue of being created, it bears a responsibility; human dignity and responsibility are inseparable."[15] Accordingly, both status and function link to the divine presence.

However, *nowhere* in the Hebrew Scriptures is the content of the image explicit. Accordingly, throughout my analysis, I will guard against conflating the content and consequence of being in God's image.[16] As many scholars have noted, the actual content of the image is not clear from these early texts, and, surprisingly, this lack of clarity may have been intentional. The image-likeness language is operating as a placeholder that states the mere minimum of what it means to be "in the image of God."[17] The reason for this ambiguity is unclear, but given the alternative language that could have been used instead, such ambiguity points to intentionality.[18] P. J. Harland suggests, "Either the significance of the image was well known or the writer did not want to be specific."[19] Even without being specific, this language did have content, however, and many have suggested it includes some type of representation of God.[20] This understanding gains support when the use of *tselem* in Genesis

---

14. Morales, *Who Shall Ascend*, 46–47. Further, as J. Richard Middleton notes, only humanity is directly addressed by God in the text; see Middleton, *Liberating Image*, 289. I am thankful to Andrew Picard for highlighting this additional scholarly support.

15. Westermann, *Genesis*, 10.

16. A significant pragmatic concern with this conflation is that when the content of the image is such that it can be degreed, this leads to degreed understandings of human dignity and, typically, to a subjection of those deemed "less" in the image of God under those who are "more" in the image of God. As the content of the image is not clear from these early texts, using these texts as a justification for acts of domination oversteps the minimalism of the text.

17. For instance, Ellen F. Davis refers to this phrase as "open-ended" in *Scripture, Culture, and Agriculture*, 55–56, and Barr states this view explicitly: "There is no reason to believe that this writer had in his mind any definite idea about the content or location of the image of God." "Image of God in the Book of Genesis," 13.

18. Barr, "Image of God in the Book of Genesis," 13.

19. Harland, *Value of Human Life*, 177.

20. Harland states directly that *tselem* "means concrete representation," and further, "[Humankind] is created as the representation of God. God is the prototype of the image who represents him. [Humankind] is not a simple copy of God but rather is in some way a representation of him." *Value of Human Life*, 180.

is compared with uses of this language outside the Hebrew text, which will receive more detailed treatment below.

Third, the Genesis text does not say that humans *are* the image of God. The way the Hebrew grammar works—using a phrase translated "in our image"—signifies in whose image humankind is to be created.[21] The Hebrew prepositions *bet* and *kaph* are consistently used in the Hebrew text, and a similar grammatical structure will also become evident when we look at the New Testament texts. Such consistency of these prepositions, glossed as "in," "after," and "according to," likely communicates something of a derivative nature.[22] This derivative aspect does not mean that the initial recipients of these words would have had even less content to understand the image. Catherine McDowell proposes that the rhetoric would have given the audience plenty of information with which to work. Focusing on Genesis 1:11–12 and 21–25, she notes that the phrase "according to its/their kind" occurs ten times in only seven verses. So, when the creation of humans is announced, instead of their being created according to their kind, they are created "in the image" and "according to the likeness" of God. Such a comparison "suggests that the author was drawing a sharp distinction between humans and the other created beings."[23] Further, and even more incredibly, while animals were created according to their kinds, "humans are made, at some level, according to *Elohim's kind*, although not literally born of God."[24] Keeping the prepositions would seem essential to preventing the collapse of humanity into some form of divinity. However, this language puts humankind in the closest relationship possible to the divine without being divine—what McDowell terms a "royal sonship."[25]

Had the text said "Let us make humankind to be our image" or "as our image," and if these prepositions were absent from later uses of image-likeness associations, such a detail would be less significant. Given that this could have been framed as an image of equivalence, it is significant that these prepositions consistently appear, and they are therefore relevant to

21. The same can be said for "according to" and "our likeness."

22. Macaskill, *Union with Christ*, 197. McDowell, upon examining both Hebrew uses and Aramaic cognates of *tselem*, concludes that these words "typically refer to a concrete object made of metal, painted stone, or human flesh which is a representation, likeness, or copy of an original." *Image of God*, 119.

23. McDowell, *Image of God*, 132.

24. McDowell, *Image of God*, 133.

25. McDowell, *Image of God*, 133–34. She dedicates much of her monograph to arguing this point. As the focus of this book is to show the significance of the divine presence for understanding theological anthropology, the entire argument does not need to be rehearsed; I need only to show that humans are not the divine presence themselves but do have the high calling of intimately relating to this presence and participating in its expansion.

understanding this concept. Gordon Wenham, James Barr, Phyllis Trible, Claus Westermann, Grant Macaskill, and McDowell concur in finding these prepositions significant.[26] Barr finds the usage of *bet essentiae* to be atypical to the author's style (he holds to later dating of Genesis 1 and to the view of Priestly authorship) and finds that this preposition "seems to indicate a property of the subject, and not of the object, of the verb."[27] On this account, the clear distinction between humans and God is maintained. In further support of this reading, Phyllis Bird and Westermann argue that these prepositions help protect against identification, making the image a possession of the human being.[28] Instead, the humans are patterned after the image.

In her monograph *The Image of God in the Garden of Eden*, McDowell also argues against the *bet essentiae* reading, asserting that "the author seems to use these prepositions as a way to avoid divinizing humankind."[29] However, she takes something of a mediating position that *bet* could be understood as "serving as," especially when it comes to how humankind is meant to rule over creation on God's behalf.[30] Since she argues that the relational aspect of image and likeness is primary, the value of the prepositions is that they strengthen her argument that humanity is created as God's children. They are not God, but they are intimately related to God.[31] She makes a compelling case contrasting Genesis 2:5–3:24 to other Mesopotamian and Egyptian divine statue animation rituals. While those rituals conclude with the manifestation of the divine presence, for the man and the woman, the order is reversed: "Rather than dwelling in the divine presence for which they were created, they would have to survive apart from it, with animal skins for clothing instead of divine glory, and without a constant supply of

26. However, some scholars have favored a reading of equivalence via the *bet essentiae* interpretation. Middleton, Clines, and others support a *bet essentiae* reading in which the preposition denotes equivalence instead of derivation. In other words, humankind *is* the image of God as opposed to God patterning humanity after the image. For instance, Clines argues, "Humanity takes the place of God on earth," and the preposition *bet* should be read as a "*beth* of essence." Clines, "Image of God," 427.

27. Barr, "Image of God in the Book of Genesis," 16–17.

28. Westermann, *Genesis Account of Creation*, 214; Bird, "Male and Female He Created Them,'" 138n22. For other scholars who also stress the importance of the prepositions, see Barr, "Image of God in the Book of Genesis," 17; Mettinger, "Abbild oder Urbild?," 406; Wenham, *Genesis 1–15*, 29.

29. McDowell, *Image of God*, 118, 137.

30. McDowell, *Image of God*, 137n110.

31. She thus argues against an exclusive *bet essentiae* reading but wants to maintain the significance of humanity's uniqueness in serving as God's images: "The author compares humankind to a divine statue while framing the divine-human relationship in filial terms." McDowell, *Image of God*, 207.

easily accessible food."[32] This contrast enunciates the tragedy that begins the Hebrew narrative. This tragedy is what the rest of the Pentateuch and even the Hebrew Bible and New Testament aim to remedy. When humans are in the personal presence of God, there is abundance and blessing. When humans reject God's ways, personal presence is withdrawn, and there is scarcity and hardship.

Fourth, the Genesis text does say that both male and female persons are made in God's image.[33] However, like dominion, being sexually differentiated is not necessarily the content of being in the image of God.[34] Even weaker than the role of dominion, maleness and femaleness may not even be the consequence of being in the image since maleness and femaleness find continuity with nonhuman creatures.[35] The command in 1:28 to "be fruitful and multiply" supports that maleness and femaleness are not expressly the image's content. God gives this command to other creatures not explicitly made in God's image (to birds and fish in Gen. 1:22). Knowing that throughout church history Christians have tended to link the image to sexual differentiation, Kilner examines Genesis 1:27 and summarizes the problem of asserting this link. This passage consists of three lines, with the first two speaking of the image without mention of maleness or femaleness. However, the third line does refer to biological sex. "As many have observed, there is little exegetical support for concluding that this third line is a statement of the same idea for the third time," especially since the third line in Hebraic poetry typically introduces a new idea.[36] At the same time, sexual differentiation is explicit as it relates to humanity, while it remains implicit as it relates to the rest of creation.[37] Though significant, adjoining the *content* of the image with sexual differentiation presses the text too far.

32. McDowell, *Image of God*, 176–77. Her arguments regarding ancient Near Eastern practices will be taken up again below.

33. The emphasis on maleness and femaleness does not mean that persons born intersex are not in the image of God. See DeFranza, *Sex Difference in Christian Theology*. For further explications of the full participation of women in the divine image, see Bird, "'Male and Female He Created Them,'" 129–59; Trible, *God and the Rhetoric of Sexuality*; Horowitz, "Image of God in Man."

34. Regarding *tselem* and *demuth*, these "seem to define, in the biblical author's estimation, the *essence* of human identity, not in terms of the male-female relationship or in terms of knowledge, as Schüle claims, but in terms of *humanity's relationship to God*." McDowell, *Image of God*, 18.

35. What seems to be unique to the male-female bond in the text is that it is marital.

36. Kilner, *Dignity and Destiny*, 225. See the Psalms: most are written in couplets (e.g., Ps. 3), and typically the third line introduces a new concept (e.g., Pss. 7:6; 10:5; 11:4).

37. For more discussion of the role of sexual differentiation in the creation narrative, see McKirland, "Image of God and Divine Presence."

Instead, being male and female is how humans in the image of God can multiply via sexual reproduction, whereby more humans in God's image can continue to fill the earth.

Gentry and Wellum make a compelling syntactical argument that supports the strength of dominion as one consequence of being in the image of God over and against being male and female.[38] This argument comes from recognizing the chiasm through which maleness and femaleness connect with being fruitful and multiplying, while dominion is syntactically bound to the image itself.[39] Gentry and Wellum propose the following chiasm:

A: in the image of God he created him
  B: male and female he created them
  B′: be fruitful and increase in number and fill the earth
A′: and subdue it and rule over the fish/birds/animals[40]

The first chiastic couplet (A and A′) suggests that having dominion is a consequence of being in the image of God. Thus, the textual proximity of maleness and femaleness to *tselem* is insufficient to bind sexual differentiation to the content of the *tselem*. The declaration of intent "Let us make humankind *so that* they may have dominion" finds reinforcement through the execution of this intention, further connecting the image with a function while not collapsing the image into a function.

Fifth, the text states that all humankind receives the commission to have dominion over the rest of the creation. Dominion is not the purview of the male person only, and if dominion is a consequence of being in the image of God, it applies to females as well as males. Additionally, as will be discussed in chapter 4's comparative study of ancient Near Eastern contexts, dominion is strongly associated with the representation of God, since the charge to rule is an extension of God's rule and of how God's presence expands into all the earth. Such a reading affiliates both royal (related to dominion) and priestly (related to divine presence) functions with both the man and the woman. According to Wilson, God allows "his power to be displayed through those creatures he has graciously chosen to extend his authority into the world."[41]

38. One of the most vocal advocates of maleness and femaleness being the constitution of the image is Karl Barth. He focused on the "I-Thou" relationship between God and humanity and also the male-female relationship. He states that the male-female relationship constitutes the image of God and is the "definitive explanation given by the text itself." Barth, *Church Dogmatics* III/1, 195.

39. Gentry and Wellum, *Kingdom through Covenant*, 189.

40. Gentry and Wellum, *Kingdom through Covenant*, 189. This is their own translation.

41. Wilson, *Psalms*, 1:207.

This authority is coterminous with God's presence, as the image of the deity communicated that deity's presence in a space.

Finally, the contrast between these creatures being made "in the image of God" and the other creatures being made "according to its/their kind" strongly implies that "at some level, humans belong to the divine class or species, that is, humanity's *kind or type is God*."[42] Whether or not the strong claim that humanity's kind is God can be made, a weak claim that humanity has a unique relation to God over and against the rest of the created world seems to be a justifiable minimum.

Other Uses in Hebrew Texts

The next occurrence of image-likeness language is Genesis 5:1. Again, reiterating the synonymous nature of *tselem* and *demuth*, this verse gives shorthand for humanity's unique origin: "When God created humankind, he made them in the likeness of God."[43] As it follows the entrance of sin into the narrative, Genesis 5:1 implies that being in the image-likeness remains true of human beings. This premise gains support later in Genesis when being in the image is the undergirding reason for not committing murder (9:6).

Just after this text, a reference to both words occurs in 5:3 as Adam fathers Seth. The same words from Genesis 1, as well as the prepositions of derivation, appear: literally, "He became the father of a son in his likeness, according to his image." Switching the prepositions seems to emphasize the continuity of derivation and the conceptual relation between image and likeness. Again, as in the first chapter of Genesis, image and likeness are a single concept, yet the content remains too ambiguous to assert dogmatically. Reiterating the final minimum parameter regarding humanity's unique relation to God, we may infer that Seth is in his father's image-likeness through relation. Nothing special about Seth merits his being in his father's image. He has yet to carry out a function, and Seth, in his entirety, is in the image-likeness of his father. As Wenham notes, "This verse makes the point that the image and likeness of God which was given to Adam at creation was inherited by his sons. It was not obliterated by the fall."[44] McDowell argues that Genesis 5:1–3 introduces some kind of correspondence between God and humanity by an analogy of a parent to a child.[45]

---

42. McDowell, *Image of God*, 132–33.

43. Wenham, *Genesis 1–15*, 119.

44. Wenham, *Genesis 1–15*, 127. That only Seth is mentioned as a son does not mean that women are no longer in the image of God, but that only the sons receive explicit mention in this patriarchal genealogy.

45. McDowell, *Image of God*, 125.

She explains that in the context of birth and creation, *tselem* and *demuth* have a strongly relational meaning, such that they "define humanity's identity in relation to God as a child to its father/parent. Humanity's function—the royal commission to rule and have dominion over the earth and creation—comes as a result of being the child of the Creator, Elohim."[46] In Genesis 1, as in Genesis 5:1, 3, the "relational aspect" of image and likeness is central.[47]

The final explicit reference to this language with human associations in the Hebrew text is in Genesis 9:6: "Whoever sheds the blood of a human, by a human shall that person's blood be shed; for in his own image God made humankind." This passage returns to the vertical relation between humankind and God while also indicating how this relation affects the horizontal relation. Again, the image's content remains unclear but seems to include the whole person and hinges on some type of relation to God via the consistent use of the preposition. Absent from this passage is any appeal to a function that would substantiate the value of human life. The human life has value because it is created in God's image, regardless of what this person has done that would cause someone to want to kill him or her.[48] This passage occurs after the story of the flood and God's lament over the wickedness of humanity. Despite how evil humankind has become, their being in the image of God persists as the justification for prohibiting murder.

Consequently, being in the image-likeness of God is not destroyed or lost.[49] Finally, and again reinforcing the unique relation of God to humanity noted above, McDowell argues that Genesis 9:6 establishes God as the blood avenger for the victim who has lost her life at the hands of another human. Such a reading finds justification because "he is humanity's *nearest kin*. Human beings are members of his clan and are, therefore, kin to one another. . . . Furthermore, to murder one's kinsman is to slay a member of *God's* family."[50] While this relation does not negate the radical ontological difference between God and humanity, the special dignity of humankind as beings in unique relation to God seems clear. Consequently, the designation "in the image of God" finds its grounding in the divine life, extending unconditional relationship to this novel creature. Moreover, such a designation communicates a status or identity to humankind externally conferred by God and thereby non-degreed.

---

46. McDowell, *Image of God*, 137.

47. McDowell, *Image of God*, 137.

48. Harland, *Value of Human Life*, 162.

49. Harland makes this point explicitly in his work on the value of human life especially as it relates to the flood. *Value of Human Life*, 207.

50. McDowell, *Image of God*, 121 (emphasis original).

The fixity of this unique relation finds further support in Psalm 8, which uses the language of human transcendence and uniqueness. While the actual words of image or likeness do not appear, this passage presupposes them. Several scholars see this Psalm as a commentary on Genesis 1:26–27, recognizing the value of human life and the vocation of giving glory and honor to the Creator, especially through the function of dominion.[51]

Finally, how need is understood here is concomitant with identity and function—what something is and what it is meant to do. Humanity is made "in the image of God," which is immediately linked to "having dominion" (Gen. 1:26–28). By "dominion," the passage does not refer to domination, since "the sort of power or rule that humans are to exercise is generous, loving power. It is power used to nurture, enhance, and empower others, noncoercively, for their benefit, not for the self-aggrandizement of the one exercising power."[52] As we will see, humanity was meant to relate second-personally to God, unhindered, faithfully serving in a royal priestly capacity to expand God's presence and reign in all the earth.[53] When humans sinned, they were no longer allowed in God's personal presence, so God set up a new way for humans to be in this presence. While they remained in the image of God, how they understood themselves and their function as it related to God's presence was derailed. Utilizing the covenants, God set up a relationship with a special people, Israel, whereby they could be in God's presence through the tabernacle and temple and Torah keeping. As a nation, they were meant to find their identity through this relationship and function as a holy nation.

Tentative Boundaries and Historical Views

Based on these six passages, there are seven tentative boundaries for understanding the image-likeness: (1) humanity is *in* the image-likeness of God; (2) being in the image-likeness is not contingent on a specific function or sexed embodiment; (3) being in the image-likeness is not lost due to the entrance of sin; (4) being in the image-likeness includes the entire person; (5) one consequence of being in the image-likeness of God is dominion; (6) this consequence of dominion is stated in a charge given to both male and female

51. For examples of this view, see Watson, *Text and Truth*, 295; Barr, "Image of God in the Book of Genesis," 11; Gentry and Wellum, *Kingdom through Covenant*, 184, 196; Harland, *Value of Human Life*, 196.

52. Middleton, *Liberating Image*, 294–95.

53. Such an identity and vocation connects Israel with original humanity: "Set apart as a royal priesthood, Israel's covenantal relationship embodies God's original purpose for humanity." Morales, *Who Shall Ascend*, 118.

persons; (7) as beings in the image-likeness of God, humans are uniquely related to God in a different way than other created beings are.[54]

How do these boundaries line up with the historical views from interpreters in years past? Historically, theological thinking about the image of God posited how humans are most like God and most unlike animals. Such a theological anthropology has resulted in degreed understandings of the image in that someone could possess more or less of the image depending on what attributes she manifested. If reason constitutes the image, and someone has less ability to reason than someone else, then the less reasoned person is perceived as being less in the image of God. Injustices throughout church history have resulted from this theology, from slavery, to the Holocaust, to the pervasive subordination of women.[55] Such a view also disenfranchises disabled people, as evidenced by appalling statements from significant church figures.[56] Due to the lack of clarity about the exact nature of the image of God and based on the word "likeness," theologians have often relied on concept proximity and speculation in defining what this likeness means. Specifically, substantival, functional, and relational views have broadly captured historical interpretations of the image of God.

These historical views identify the image with a particular capacity, on the substantival view; a particular activity, on the functional view; or particular relationships, on the relational view. The multifaceted view proposes some kind of combination of these.[57] Given the tentative boundaries proposed above, it seems hard to argue that the *constitution* of the image is substantival or functional. There are no indicators textually about what the capacities would be, and the function is a consequence of being made in God's image. However, this does not undermine the importance of those two categories for understanding human nature, especially given the significance of an entity's constitution and *telos* for understanding flourishing. Instead, it seems more reasonable that being made in the image is best described relationally regarding the image itself. Humankind is made *in* the image *of* God, and this

---

54. As important as the image of God is for providing a biblical precedent for understanding human uniqueness, this should not require a theological anthropology that is anthropocentric. David L. Clough recognizes the dangers here in his *On Animals*, vol. 1.

55. Surveys of this ideological consequence abound, but Kilner provides a summary, as does DeFranza. Kilner, *Dignity and Destiny*, 3–51; DeFranza, *Sex Difference in Christian Theology*, 186–237; McDowell, *Image of God*, 126–31.

56. E.g., Martin Luther promoted drowning a twelve-year-old boy because the latter's mental abilities were so low. He interpreted the boy's condition as a corrupted reason and corrupted soul. Kilner, *Dignity and Destiny*, 188.

57. For thorough overviews of these views, see Cortez, *Theological Anthropology*; Farris and Taliaferro, *Ashgate Research Companion to Theological Anthropology*.

is intimately related to knowing God second-personally and expanding God's presence in the world. Given the unique relationship humans are meant to have with God, human ontology must be such that they need to relate to God's second-personal presence to flourish. This capacity to flourish is deepened in Christ, who is the true image, as we will see later in our exploration of Kathryn Tanner's participatory account.

Thus, these boundaries do not deny the importance of human substance and function related to human nature, but they do cause us to query their being used to identify the content of the image itself. The relational view holds the most promise pertaining to the image of God and fundamental need in that God chooses to relate to humankind differently than God relates to the rest of creation. Whether or not human beings recognize God's desire for a relationship, they were intended to relate to God in a particular way.

CONCLUSION

All humans are made in the image of God and, as such, are intended to commune with the divine life. As they do, the functional outworkings of this communion will proceed from being in the image of God even if the relational status of being in the image of God is fixed and immutable. However, humans need to be a certain kind of creature to respond to God relationally. For that reason, certain human capacities are important, even if they span a range of development and actualization. Thus, the relational designation that humans are "in the image of God" applies to all human beings, conferring a special dignity, even if the image's content is not entirely clear. This overview also sets up a foundation for the concept of the image of God, as its content is clarified in the New Testament and through understanding its ancient Near Eastern backgrounds. Such clarification binds the image of God to the personal divine presence in such a way as to supply more support for a fundamental need for a second-personal relation to God.

THREE

The Image of God
and Jesus Christ

We will now see if the seven minimalistic boundaries for understanding the image of God from the Old Testament will hold throughout the entire canon. Further, we will see if the understanding of the *imago Dei* is developed in the incarnation of Jesus Christ. In this chapter, I will argue from biblical scholarship that the Son is, in fact, the teleological prototype toward which God desires all humankind to progress. If Jesus is the prototypical human, then the fundamental need for a second-personal relation to God must also characterize his humanity, a theme to which we will return in chapters 6 and 8.

The New Testament and Septuagint Use of Image or Likeness

In the New Testament, the explicit language of image and likeness appears again but within a new, Christ-oriented context—with Jesus identified as the embodiment of Israel's God and the true image. Jesus is also directly associated with the temple, which communicated God's localized presence. Through Jesus's atoning work, all humanity receives an invitation into becoming like this image, which is the end for which it was already intended.[1] Responding to this invitation requires divine enactment by the Holy Spirit,

---

1. By atoning work, I mean the life, death, resurrection, and ascension of Jesus Christ, which somehow opens the way for communion with God, in light of overcoming and defeating human sin and death.

enabling becoming like the image of God as a member of the royal priest-hood. Further, such an invitation extends to even being the temple of God, both individually and corporately, as the Spirit of God now dwells within the believer (1 Cor. 3:16–17; 6:19; 2 Cor. 6:16; Eph. 2:21; 1 Pet. 2:5). The golden thread running across the canon pertains to this unique invitation to relate to the divine presence.

Lastly, the true image of God is both the fullness of God's presence (as God) and the ultimate expression of reliance on God's presence (as a human being), so tracing the significance of this presence has direct anthropological bearing. In Jesus, we see the ultimate ongoing meeting of that need for God's personal presence in human form. However, since there is only one true image and prototype for all humanity, anthropology and Christology cannot col-lapse into one another. Thus, to understand this human need most fully, we will make Jesus Christ central to our investigation.

Image and Likeness Exceptions

Before addressing the christological emphasis of the New Testament image-likeness language, I should mention the exceptional uses of this term. These exceptions include a use applicable to all humanity (James 3:9) and then a use that states a relation of equivalence between the image and men, to the seeming exclusion of women (1 Cor. 11:7).

In James 3:9, James comments about the tongue that "with it we bless the Lord and Father, and with it we curse those [*anthrōpous* = humans] who are made in the likeness [*homoiōsin*] of God." Again, like the Hebrew Scriptures, this text fits within the minimum parameters stated in chapter 2 above. Like Genesis 9:6, this text underscores the stability of humanity's being in the likeness of God even after sin. Further, since in the Genesis text one would presumably want to murder a despicable human being, and likewise, one would only want to curse someone who has done something shameful (James 3:9), the persistence of humans being in God's image, even in a sinful state, is supported. Being creatures in God's image brings with it a moral injunction—not to murder and not to curse other humans, even if they are despicable or do something shameful.[2]

While the James text is exceptionally inclusive for the New Testament, the text in 1 Corinthians 11 seems exceptionally exclusive for the *entire canon.* The text of most relevant interest is verse 7: "For a man [or "husband"] ought

---

2. David C. Allison finds parallels to these texts regarding the injunction to treat an image well in 2 Enoch 44.1–2 and Alexander of Aphrodisias, *In Aristotelis Metaphysica commentaria* 710; see Allison, *James,* 554. Cf. McKnight, *Letter of James,* 294.

not to have his head veiled, since he is the image and reflection [*doxa*] of God; but woman [or "wife"] is the reflection [*doxa*] of man [or "husband"]." This section is notoriously challenging to interpret, given the difficulty in reconstructing what was so culturally egregious in what the Corinthians were doing with head coverings. Part of the ambiguity stems from the terms *anēr* and *gynē*, since these could refer to husband-wife relations in the assembly or man-woman relations in the assembly.[3] Finally, the central point of these ethical injunctions is "because of the angels" (v. 10), and speculation about the role the angels are playing in Paul's corrective is varied.[4] For my argument, two major concerns are pressing: Is Paul overturning the precedent of image derivation present in the Scriptures up to this point (including in his own writing), and are women no longer fully in the image of God?

Scholars, both biblical and theological, reject that Paul undermines women's creation in God's image.[5] Paul states that Christ is the true image, but this does not mean that Paul understands men/husbands to be the image of God equivalently or exclusively. If he were to be introducing this new way of envisioning the image of God—that humans are the image of God and only male humans are the image—such an understanding would need further articulation.[6] Instead, Paul is reminding his audience of their unique relation to God, not positing a new constitution of the image. The creation story of Genesis 2 functions as a moral appeal for men not covering their heads based on their relation to God, which is one of imaging and reflecting God to the world. How they act in the Corinthian assembly reflects poorly back on their source and ground of being: God.[7] In the same way, when women/wives act in a shaming way, they reflect poorly on their source and ground of being, which, according to the creation story, is the man. Given the reputation of the gospel of Jesus Christ being a critical concern for Paul, such a poor reflection

3. Massey, "Gender versus Marital Concerns."

4. BeDuhn, "'Because of the Angels.'"

5. In fact, Lucy Peppiatt argues that Paul is quoting his opponents' views in 1 Cor. 11:7–9 in order to argue against them later in the same chapter. See Peppiatt, *Rediscovering Scripture's Vision for Women*, 66–67; Peppiatt, "Man as the Image."

6. Of course, someone could argue that the distinction between being the image itself and being in the image is artificial. Such an objector would need to be able to account for the consistent prepositions used as well as how this comports with the image of God being explicitly equated with Jesus Christ (and the philosophical problem that something cannot be numerically identical to x without being x, and x is the divine-human person Jesus Christ). My thanks to Jonathan Rutledge for pointing out this identity problem.

7. Amy Peeler makes the relationship between "creating life," glory, and the image of God explicit in "Imaging Glory," 158–59. She concurs that there is no hint of Paul's redefining the image to be exclusively male and that the glory reflecting done by humanity is both corporate and interdependent.

by both men and women required forceful redress.[8] Therefore, the reference to the man being the image of God is likely Paul's shorthand referring his audience back to the Genesis accounts, and not his stating an identity between men and the image of God, nor negating the woman's identity of being made in the image (cf. 1 Cor. 15:49).[9] Thus, it is highly unlikely that Paul is positing "men" as the new constitution of the image of God or that women are not also made in God's image.

Image as Christ

Moving on from these exceptional uses of this term, *eikōn* (image) takes a christological turn in the New Testament. Paul uses this term to classify the new humanity—those in Christ—and describes Christ himself as the actual image. The key passages for the equation of the Son with the image itself are 2 Corinthians 4:4 and Colossians 1:15. The author of Hebrews also picks up on this shift in the exposition of the image in 1:3 and provides even more context for the idea of a heavenly reality determining earthly realities.[10]

In 2 Corinthians 4:4, Paul uses the phrase "the gospel of the glory of Christ, *who is the image of God*," within the context of removing the veil over the gospel. George Guthrie notes that "Jesus's identity is revealed by his glory, and that glory is directly related to the image of the Father."[11] As will be seen even more clearly in the next chapter, the glory of God was typically a visible manifestation of the localized presence of God. As such, this glory is often associated with the Spirit of God, and here, it is associated with Jesus himself—the one full of the Spirit and the visible manifestation of God's self. Throughout the Hebrew Bible and the New Testament, "God's glory is closely related to his divine presence, . . . [as is] the fundamental significance of the Spirit for the person and work of Jesus."[12] Notably, Pauline Christology and anthropology are inextricably linked. Such a linkage is clear in the language

---

8. We can ascertain as much even without knowing precisely what head coverings meant for men and women during that time.

9. L. Ann Jervis argues that "when Paul says that woman is the glory of man (v. 7b), he explains this regarding the second creation account (vv. 8 and 9). While the first story of creation (upon which the Corinthians' practice and attitude are based) may not speak of a differentiation between the genders, through a midrashic recombination of the first story with the second, Paul is able to bring out what he considers to be the meaning of the stories: men and women are distinct and that distinction is good." Jervis, "'But I Want You to Know . . . ,'" 243.

10. The true temple in the heavenly plane may preexist the copy that comes to exist on the earthly plane (Exod. 25:40; cf. Heb. 8:4–5; 9:1–11).

11. Guthrie, *2 Corinthians*, 242.

12. Cortez, *ReSourcing Theological Anthropology*, 114. Regarding "glory," he cites Aalen, "Δόξα," 44–52.

he uses for Christ and in what language he does not use. As Ben Witherington notes, Paul omits "Son of Man" language but instead uses "second Adam" terminology.[13] This second Adam—or last/eschatological Adam—theology "is about the humanity of Jesus and about the believer being conformed to his human image."[14] Concerning 2 Corinthians 4:4, Gordon Fee concurs with Witherington that the "second Adam" is "the one who first of all in his humanity is the perfect image-bearer of the eternal God."[15] With Christ, there is an apparent shift from the prepositional buffer that has characterized humans as *in* the image of God to references to Jesus *as* the image of God.

The same equivalence appears in Colossians 1:15: "He [the Son] *is the image* of the invisible God, the firstborn of all creation." N. T. Wright notes that here the text refers to "the exalted man, but identifies him with the pre-existent Lord."[16] Wright goes on to say that "from all eternity Jesus had, in his very nature, been the 'image of God,' reflecting perfectly the character and life of the Father. It was thus appropriate for him to be the 'image of God' as man: from all eternity he had held the same relation to the Father that humanity, from its creation, had been intended to bear."[17] Douglas Moo seems to accept Wright's reading, recognizing the creation account as the background for this passage and acknowledging that Christ is the image "in accordance with which human beings are formed."[18] Additionally, we see the priority of the Son as the image of God—he, not the man and the woman, is the *prōtotokos* (prototype; Col. 1:15 NRSV: "firstborn"). While in history, the Son was the last Adam; he was before the first Adam in logical priority.

Though not likely Pauline, Hebrews 1:3a has conceptual overlap with 2 Corinthians 4:4 and Colossians 1:15: "He is the reflection of God's glory and the exact imprint of God's very being, and he sustains all things by his powerful word." This text communicates "that the Son is the 'representation' (i.e., the 'image') of the Father," and this "stands as a confession of direct identity."[19] While this text does not use image or likeness language explicitly, it indicates that Jesus is the *charaktēr* (character) of the nature of God—the imprint or exact representation of God's nature. This text seems to be offering a fusion of Hebrew concepts as the author conflates multiple themes of

13. Witherington, *Indelible Image*, 1:238.
14. Witherington, *Indelible Image*, 1:238.
15. Fee, *Pauline Christology*, 487.
16. Wright, *Colossians and Philemon*, 69.
17. Wright, *Colossians and Philemon*, 70.
18. Moo, *Letters to the Colossians and to Philemon*, 117.
19. Guthrie, *2 Corinthians*, 242.

Word, wisdom, image, and glory.[20] And yet, as F. F. Bruce asserts, "While our author's language is that of Philo and the Book of Wisdom, his meaning goes beyond theirs."[21] Given that this is the only occurrence of *charaktēr* in the New Testament and that *eikōn* would have been the more common word to use, the author may be flagging something significant about the Son. Kilner proposes that *charaktēr* works in contradistinction to Philo's use of the term. For example, Philo argues that "God is *aneu* [without] *charakteros*" since "nothing can be an exact imprint of God's very being."[22] Consequently, the author of Hebrews may have been making a polemical point in that the Son is the *charaktēr* of God.

Whether the Hebrews and Colossians texts are referring to the incarnate Son or the eternal Son is ambiguous. Looking at both Colossians and Hebrews, Cortez notes the authors' lack of concern about moving from preincarnate Son to the incarnate Son. Drawing from Moo's work on Colossians, Cortez recognizes that *eikōn* may be pointing to both the eternal Son and the incarnate Son at the same time.[23] For the author of Hebrews, the association with the Son's humanity is apparent, since "rather than focusing our attention immediately on the eternal reality of the Son, the author locates this discussion in the context of the Son's revelatory work in the incarnation (1:1–2a)."[24] The author then moves into works regarding redemption and glorification

20. Thiselton, *First Epistle to the Corinthians*, 834. He cites the following as passages where those themes are conflated: John 1:1–3; 1 Cor. 8:6; Col. 1:16–17. The early Christian personification of Wisdom as a "bridge to understanding Christ as God's image (cf. Col 1:15; Jn 14:9)" is also attested in Keener's work, *1–2 Corinthians*, 174. Cf. Wright, *Colossians and Philemon*, 67, and Moo, *Letters to the Colossians and to Philemon*, 112. For those who would see Wisdom as the dominant concept in Colossians instead of the image of God (e.g., Dunn, *Epistles to the Colossians and to Philemon*, 87–90; Lamp, "Wisdom in Col 1:15–20"; Beetham, *Echoes of Scripture*, 175–77), it is entirely possible that Paul is referring both to the image of God and to the wisdom tradition. Cortez endorses this mediating position, articulated by Moo: "On the one hand, the Son is the incarnate one who has come as the perfect *imago Dei* through whom God will truly manifest his presence in the world, and, at the same time, the Son is the eternal Wisdom through whom God created the universe and who entered the world to enlighten God's people. The former is a more purely anthropological frame of reference, locating the Son in the story of God's image bearers; the latter more properly emphasizes the eternal relationship between the Son and the Father, which is then worked out in creation. If Moo is correct, the language of the *eikōn* is sufficiently evocative to allow readers to hear echoes of both ideas in the same passage." Cortez, *ReSourcing Theological Anthropology*, 120.

21. Bruce, *Epistle to the Hebrews*, 48.

22. Kilner, *Dignity and Destiny*, 67.

23. Cortez, *ReSourcing Theological Anthropology*, 120; Moo, *Letters to the Colossians and to Philemon*, 118. See also O'Brien, *Colossians–Philemon*, 42–44; Thompson, *Colossians and Philemon*, 29. The reading that this applies to both the preexistent Logos and the incarnate Logos is also affirmed in Gareth Lee Cockerill's commentary on Hebrews, *Epistle to the Hebrews*, 95.

24. Cortez, *ReSourcing Theological Anthropology*, 121.

(1:3b–4) that Jesus accomplishes in human history. So, even in a text that "clearly emphasizes the eternal, divine nature of the Son, we actually have what appears to be a mixed set of statements that refer to both the eternal and the incarnate states at the same time."[25] Cortez's summary statement seems helpful for moving forward theologically from this exegetical ambiguity: "I will suggest that the best approach is to conclude, without rejecting the idea that the Son is consubstantial with the Father from all eternity, (1) that the *imago Dei* refers specifically to the humanity of the Son in the incarnation and (2) that the *imago Dei* is still an eternal truth about what it means to be human."[26] Further, the meaning of *charaktēr* has the semantic range to include the object stamped (the coin or a wax seal) or the object doing the stamping.[27] This word leaves open the interpretation of Christ as the prototype of humanity.[28] By referencing Psalm 2 and Psalm 110, the author of Hebrews pictures this prototype as the royal Son and the royal Priest, and even the Wisdom of God.[29]

Finally, the author's use of Psalm 8 in Hebrews 2:6–9 "interprets the psalmist's universal anthropology Christologically," thereby connecting universal humanity with the individual humanity of the Son, Jesus of Nazareth.[30] In William L. Lane's commentary on Hebrews, he recognizes the author's intentional connection of Jesus with all humanity and how this points forward to a consummated reality yet to come in that "the writer leads his readers to contemplate Jesus in his solidarity with humankind."[31] The language of "glory" is also significant to this text. Regarding this passage in Hebrews, G. Walter Hansen argues that "the glory of God expresses the being of God."[32] The Son is the perfect reflection of God. He simply is God's glory. Furthermore, while the glory of Christ is intrinsic to him, the term "glory" remains significant when we turn to the use of the image-of-God concept concerning

25. Cortez, *ReSourcing Theological Anthropology*, 122.

26. Cortez, *ReSourcing Theological Anthropology*, 101.

27. Kilner, *Dignity and Destiny*, 67; cf. Bruce, *Epistle to the Hebrews*, 48; Cockerill, *Epistle to the Hebrews*, 94.

28. Cortez puts it this way: "The *imago Dei* is true of the Son in virtue of the incarnation *and* that the *imago Dei* is eternally true in virtue of God's eternal decree to become incarnate in Christ." *ReSourcing Theological Anthropology*, 129. This would be the view of Karl Barth, though scholars interpret his position along a spectrum: from the view that he identifies the eternal Son with the incarnate Son (the strong position) to the view that he understands both an ontological and a logical distinction between the two (weak position). See Cortez, *ReSourcing Theological Anthropology*, 129.

29. Lane, *Hebrews 1–8*, 18; Johnson, *Hebrews*, 69.

30. Grenz, "Jesus as the Imago Dei," 618.

31. Lane, *Hebrews 1–8*, 49–50.

32. Hansen, *Letter to the Philippians*, 138.

those who follow Christ and take part in this glory, even though this glory is not intrinsic to them.[33]

In each of these cases, the two Pauline and one Hebrews uses, the prepositions disappear and thereby communicate equivalence between the Son and the image. When "image" is used to refer to followers of Christ, the true expression of the image makes possible the progression from being in the image to becoming like the image.

Identity and function are taken up by those of the new covenant, on the heels of the embodiment of the divine presence in the person of Jesus of Nazareth. Due to his life, death, resurrection, ascension, and ongoing ministry in the heavenly realm, those who now follow him receive the gift of the Holy Spirit. Willie Jennings expounds on this identity and proposes that "just as Torah formed Israel's identity, establishing human life in the presence of God, so Jesus intends the formation of a new humanity in his presence, listening to his speaking through the Spirit."[34] This now internal, personal divine presence of the Spirit establishes his followers' identity as members of a new spiritual family and their function as royal priests under the new covenant. They share their identity with Christ, and their function is now to be his body on this earth, expanding the kingdom/presence of God as representatives of God's personal presence. Since Christ's identity (as the image of God) is intended for all humanity's conformation (as beings in the image of God), the very constitution of human flourishing is bound to the incarnate Logos. Simultaneously, flourishing is bound to the Spirit, because Jesus is the embodiment of the divine presence, the giver of this divine presence, and also dependent on the divine presence, himself.

Image and Humankind

The language of a new family shows this progression that Jesus inaugurated through the Holy Spirit's indwelling. Romans 8:29 states this expressly, that "for those whom he foreknew he also predestined to be conformed to the image [eikonos] of his Son, in order that he might be the firstborn [prōtotokon] within a large family." Again, Christ has always been the intended *telos* to which humanity will conform. Such an intention seems to predate the beginning of the world, as is announced in other texts revealing the preexistence of the Son (Eph. 1:4; Heb. 4:3; 1 Pet. 1:20; Rev. 13:8). Haley Goranson Jacob's monographic treatment of Romans 8:29 makes a compelling case that the Son is the true image of God. Connecting Romans

---

33. Cf. Ferguson, *Holy Spirit*, 139–40.
34. Jennings, *Christian Imagination*, 272.

8, Psalm 8:5–7, and Genesis 1–3, she argues that "glory" refers to the status of rulership that all humanity received but failed to enact. Hence, "as those with the unique image-bearing vocation, humans share in the glory of God as they rule over his good creation."[35]

In 2 Corinthians 3:18, Paul contrasts the glory that shone from Moses's face (which he veiled, and which faded) after beholding the glory of God to the glory that Christ-followers now have access to and that will not fade: "And all of us, with unveiled faces, seeing the glory of the Lord as though reflected in a mirror, are being transformed into the same image [*eikona*] from one degree of glory to another; for this comes from the Lord, the Spirit." What seems to be occurring here is a supernaturally initiated transition into the likeness of the true image, accompanied by varying degrees of glory. The variation is significant because the only "degreeing" that is happening is with regard to glory, not in terms of being in the image of God.[36] Moving from being in the image to becoming like Jesus results in varying degrees of glory.[37] Paul Barnett says that "the One who is the end of our transformation ('the Lord') is also its means and provider (through 'the Spirit')."[38] Thomas Smail reinforces the varying degrees of glory, saying, "The copy is made by exposure to the original. It is by beholding his glory that we begin to be changed into his likeness."[39] Guthrie's commentary is also insightful here, as he notes that "Christ himself radiates the Shekinah glory. And we experience this glorious observation through the presence and work of 'the Lord,' the Holy Spirit."[40] This interpretation is affirmed by Michael Horton in that "the Spirit shapes creaturely reality according to the archetypal image of the Son."[41] It seems clear that an observable change is occurring, which is due to the work of the Spirit and manifests God's glory in an unfading way for those who are now in Christ.

Colossians, which already explicitly equated the Son with the image of God and the *prōtotokos* of humanity (1:15), affirms that the image now extends to the believer's transformation. In 3:10, Paul reminds the believers, "[You] have clothed yourselves with the new self [*anthrōpon*, inferred

---

35. Goranson Jacob, *Conformed to the Image of His Son*, 76.

36. Kilner brings out this point in *Dignity and Destiny*, 62–63.

37. Therefore, Paul Barnett can attest that "Paul's christological goal of transformation ('to be conformed to the image of [God's] Son'—Rom 8:29) is unparalleled." Barnett, *Second Epistle to the Corinthians*, 207. Cf. Joseph A. Fitzmyer, "Glory Reflected on the Face of Christ," 630; Lambrecht, "Transformation in 2 Cor 3,18."

38. Barnett, *Second Epistle to the Corinthians*, 208–9.

39. Smail, *Reflected Glory*, 25.

40. Guthrie, *2 Corinthians*, 227.

41. Horton, *People and Place*, 21.

by NRSV from its use in 3:9], which is being renewed in knowledge according to the image [*eikona*] of its creator." Given the establishment of the Creator's image earlier in the letter, this "new self" now seems to give the believer access to greater capacities for knowledge, or to some type of renewal of the mind, due to this metamorphosis (Rom. 12:2). In terms of the claim that sin has not destroyed the image of God, I. Howard Marshall notes that this passage implies "knowledge was lost or corrupted at the fall," which is a more consistent conclusion than saying the image was lost or corrupted at the fall.[42] Also, this knowledge is being renewed "*according to* the image of the creator" (Col. 3:10, emphasis added), since this image is the standard for perfect knowledge, which is now accessible by putting on the new self.[43] To borrow the language of Kilner, Jesus is the "standard" for what humanity is meant to be, even as the "status" of being in the image of God is constant. This status is based on humanity's identity of derivation—of being creatures patterned after the true image.[44] Macaskill elaborates:

> It is noteworthy that the preposition used is κατά [*kata*], reflecting Genesis 1:27 and the Jewish resistance of a direct identification of humans with the divine image. Believers are restored 'according to' the image of the creator. By contrast, Jesus 'is' the image of the invisible God (1:15). Again, the image of clothing requires us to speak in different terms of the intrinsic identity of Christ and the derivative identity of the believer. The work of the Spirit, though, ensures that the derivative identity of the believer is a real one, outworked in that person's life.[45]

The Christocentricity of the image and the invitation for humans to join into Christocentric conformity are connected through the mechanism of the image of God in Colossians.

Finally, a passage that seems to connect the Son as the image and humans as those patterned after the image is 1 Corinthians 15:49: "Just as we have [worn/]borne the image of the man of dust, we will also [wear/]bear the image of the man of heaven." This section of text compares the first man and the second man based on the chronological sequence of the creation narrative and the life of Christ. There is again a distinction of images, but instead of using prepositions to distinguish these images, the language of earth and heaven

42. Marshall, "Being Human," 63.

43. "At last, in Christ, human beings can be what God intended them to be." Wright, *Colossians and Philemon*, 138.

44. Kilner, *Dignity and Destiny*, 62–63.

45. Macaskill, *Union with Christ*, 197.

comes to the fore. Adam's image is one of derivation from the true image of the Second Adam. The true image is the eschatological *telos* of humanity. Cortez recognizes the significance of this text for anthropology and argues that the juxtaposition of Adam and Christ illustrates Christ's superiority in the kind of life that he gives. Whereas Adam was "a living being," a *psychē* (1 Cor. 15:45)—the text calls to mind the Septuagint translation of Genesis 2:7—Jesus became "a life-giving Spirit," *pneuma*.[46]

Likeness and Christ

If the Hebrew Scriptures communicate that humans are *in* the image of God, the New Testament Scriptures now communicate who that image is— Jesus Christ—and that Christ-followers can be conformed to this image (cf. Rom. 8:29; Phil. 3:21; 1 John 3:2). Such an interpretation gains strength when we examine the uses of "likeness." Whereas this term expresses humanity's being in the likeness of God in the Hebrew Scriptures, the New Testament uses this word to indicate the Son's becoming like humanity by becoming enfleshed (except for James 3:9, already discussed above). These texts include Romans 8:3 and Philippians 2:7: "For God has done what the law, weakened by the flesh, could not do: by sending his own Son in the likeness [*homoiōmati*] of sinful flesh . . ."; "but [Christ Jesus] emptied himself, taking the form of a slave, being born in human likeness [*homoiōmati*]." In the same way that humans are made in God's image and likeness, God takes on human flesh as the likeness of humanity, opening the way for them to become like God themselves. Colin Kruse comments on how "likeness" functions in Romans 8:3, throughout Romans (1:23; 5:14; 6:14), and in Philippians 2:7, noting that "Paul's usage of 'likeness' indicates that it may denote either similarity with certain distinctions, or real identity."[47] The Son—in whose likeness humans are meant to become—deliberately became like humans in every way, thereby granting access to this transformation. Philippians 2 communicates theologically that "even before his incarnation, as the one existing in the form of God he was already the divine original for the creation of humanity in the image of God. . . . By his incarnation, death, and exaltation, Christ opens the way for humanity to share in the glory of the original."[48] So, while "the parallel with Adam has been illegitimately pressed by some writers, . . . there is an undeniable network of associations between Philippians 2 and Genesis 1–3 (mediated by such passages as Rom. 5:19; 8:29;

46. Cortez, *ReSourcing Theological Anthropology*, 38.
47. Kruse, *Paul's Letter to the Romans*, 326. Cf. Wright, "Romans," 578.
48. Hansen, *Letter to the Philippians*, 142.

1 Cor. 15:41; 2 Cor. 3:18; 4:4; Phil. 3:21; Col. 1:15; 3:10)."[49] The Son is the divine original who is perfectly manifest in Jesus of Nazareth, after whom all humanity is patterned.

One more illuminating use of this language deserves mention even though it is not directly related to humanity. The author of Hebrews uses *eikōn* in a way that also supports the idea of a greater reality than the earthly reality via a heavenly prototype: "Since the law has only a shadow of the good things to come and not the true form [*eikona*] of these realities, it can never, by the same sacrifices that are continually offered year after year, make perfect those who approach" (10:1). In this case, the point is to show the lesser ability of the law to "make perfect" those who attempt adherence to its precepts. In so doing, however, the author here recognizes that the law functioned anticipatorily to point to a greater reality. As the rest of Hebrews attests, this greater reality is Jesus Christ as the perfect high priest and the perfect sacrifice entering the perfect heavenly temple on humanity's behalf. N. W. Porteous affirms this reading in that the opening statement in 1:3 "governs [the author's] conviction throughout his letter that in Christ reality had come to take the place of shadow."[50] Therefore, it seems a possible parallel that this Second Adam opens access to God that even the First Adam, like a shadow, did not have. Since Jesus is the prototype of humankind, anthropology thus proceeds from Christology and ends with Christology, giving us a christological anthropology.

For a Christian theological anthropology, the idea that anthropology should take christological shape is not an original concept.[51] How and to what extent one connects anthropology and Christology is another matter, as is how one connects anthropology and pneumatology, which is far less commonly addressed.[52] Such a reading would still fit within a relational understanding of the image of God. Christ is uniquely related to God as the true image of God and shares this relationship with us as creatures made in his image.

49. Silva, *Philippians*, 102. Cf. Ridderbos, *Paul*, 68–78.

50. Porteous, "Image of God," 684.

51. This line of thinking can be found in Irenaeus, Athanasius, Gregory of Nyssa, Maximus the Confessor, Julian of Norwich, Martin Luther, John Calvin, John Owen, Søren Kierkegaard, Hans Urs von Balthasar, Friedrich Schleiermacher, Karl Barth, etc. Marc Cortez draws this out convincingly in his *Christological Anthropology in Historical Perspective*. Other examples of current theologians who support a christological anthropology include Anderson and Speidell, *On Being Human*; K. Tanner, *Christ the Key*; Treier, "Incarnation"; Vanhoozer, "Holy Scripture"; Crisp, "Christological Model of the Imago Dei," 39; Erickson, *Christian Theology*, 752–53; Watson, *Text and Truth*, 277–304; Kreitzer, "Christ and Second Adam in Paul."

52. This will be the focus of chap. 8.

─────────────── CONCLUSION ───────────────

Having looked at every passage about humans in the Hebrew Bible, Greek New Testament, or Septuagint that uses "image" or "likeness," we can see that the minimum boundaries from the Hebrew Scriptures continue to apply in the New Testament, while the New Testament also adds a critical layer of content to "image" and "likeness" due to the incarnation. Christ is the image itself, and the people of God have a calling to become like this image as seen in the human person Jesus Christ.[53] The image of God serves as a viable mechanism connecting the general *status* of every human being (who is made *in* the image of God) to the new *standard* of becoming like Christ (who *is* the image of God). The content of the image is Jesus Christ.[54]

If the New Testament can be used to "fill out" and even reinterpret the Hebrew Scriptures, it seems right to understand the image of God as Jesus Christ. There is only *one* image of God, which humanity is patterned after and from which it derives its unique status. Such an interpretation corresponds with the minimum boundaries regarding the image's content, based on the Hebrew Scriptures, adding an eighth minimum: Jesus Christ is the true image of God, the one into whose likeness humanity is meant to be transformed by the Holy Spirit. Consequently, these minimum parameters distinguish between the image of God and humanity while keeping the image and humanity closely linked. So, in looking at Jesus, one sees the pattern after which all other humans are formed.[55] While all humans are made *in* this image in an unimpeachable, non-degreed way, they are not the image themselves. Nevertheless, according to the New Testament, God desires that all humans become like the true image. Such a *telos* has an immediate bearing on what sort of creature humans are, since such an intention requires certain capacities to pursue this aim. However, these capacities do not *constitute* the image of God; rather, they enable the pursuit of humanity's unique *telos* of likeness to Jesus Christ.

Whereas this chapter has focused on the biblical scholarship to show the tentative boundaries for understanding the image of God, added contextual

---

53. "Jesus as Son of Man, therefore, presents a glorified picture of human destiny, showing humanity eschatologically transformed to fulfill the destiny that God intended for it 'in the beginning.'" Marcus, "Son of Man as Son of Adam," 370.

54. Regarding the temple specifically, Richard Hays comments, "*For John, Jesus is not only the Temple—the place where we meet God—but he is also himself the God who meets us and rescues us by gathering us into union with him.*" R. Hays, *Reading Backwards*, 82 (emphasis original). The language of status and standard was coined by John F. Kilner in his article "Humanity in God's Image."

55. At the same time, this was still a full flourishing in a fallen context. Determining the extent of flourishing that is possible in the eschaton is thus highly speculative.

evidence from ancient Near Eastern cultures, including how temples and images functioned for them and for Israel, will further unpack the meaning of this phrase. Consequently, the implicit association with the divine presence established thus far will become explicit in the next chapter, laying the foundation for the centrality of relating to God's personal presence as the content of a human fundamental need.

FOUR

The Image of God
and the Temple

The import of the image of God, as examined in chapter 2, frames the uniqueness of humanity and justifies the significance of the image of God in theological anthropology. Further, the New Testament's elaboration of this concept to ground the constitution of the image in Jesus himself underscores its
heft. This chapter further contextualizes the *imago Dei* concept by drawing on
the Jewish cosmology of Eden as temple, the later tabernacle construction, the
ongoing temple motif throughout the Hebrew Bible and the New Testament,
and ancient Near Eastern understandings of images as idols. Such contexts
tacitly but consistently link God's personal presence and the image of God.[1]
The personal divine presence is so pervasive that later themes, as significant
as temple and covenant, serve as overarching means for human creatures to
commune with the divine presence.[2]

1. The closest parallel to this attempt is found in Meredith G. Kline; however, instead of
moving from Christ as prototype to human as prototype, his argument is that the "theophanic
Glory was present at the creation and was the specific model or referent in view in the creating
of man in the image of God." *Images of the Spirit*, 13, 17.
2. Regarding the connection between the divine presence and covenant, Morales states, "The
divine desire to dwell with humanity, the goal of both creation and redemption, is the essence
of covenant theology." Morales, *Who Shall Ascend*, 103.

Temple and Creation

God desires to dwell with humanity and for humanity to expand the divine presence, and these desires continue even after humans sin. While God wants to dwell among humanity uniquely, this does not mean God does not extend this presence into the rest of the created world (Num. 14:21; Ps. 72:19; Jer. 23:24; Isa. 6:3; Hab. 2:14). Here, words referring to God's glory and those referring to God's presence seem to function synonymously even though they may not be interchangeable in all instances. Morales makes a similar point associating the glory, or Shekinah (unique to the intertestamental literature), with God's presence. He explains, "When the Shekinah, the visible manifestation of God's immanent Presence, fills the tabernacle, therefore, the scene represents a new creation filled with the glory of God."[3] Thus, Israel's cosmology and ancient Near Eastern understandings of temples and idols will help us understand the backdrop for the association of images with divine presence. Israel's cosmology contains consistent temple associations and contributes to a novel understanding of how the *imago Dei* functions and how it later develops in the New Testament. In Israel and throughout the ancient Near East, sacred spaces functioned as carefully crafted contexts intended for divine engagement with humanity, and within these spaces, images or statues of the commemorated deity played a prominent role. To see whether Genesis reveals a fundamental need for a second-personal relation to God, we need to examine the centrality of the divine presence east of Eden.[4]

The language of the image of God appears in the opening narrative of the Pentateuch, then occurs in a cluster of early passages that would have been formative for the people of Israel. Though this exact language does not appear explicitly after Genesis, it undergirds Psalm 8 and also connects with the motif of temple and tabernacle, which is woven throughout Israel's history.

---

3. Morales, *Who Shall Ascend*, 117.

4. Morales, *Who Shall Ascend*, 209. Carey C. Newman proposes that glory means the "visible and mobile presence of Yahweh." *Paul's Glory-Christology*, 24. However, it should be noted that glory does not always indicate God's presence, though it does often accompany God's action. Haley Goranson Jacob provides a compelling case that *doxa* often denotes the "honor, esteem, power, or governing status of God as a result of his identity as Creator and King. And in reference to humanity, δόξα [*doxa*] and δοξάζω [*doxazō*] primarily denote the honor, esteem, power, and governing status of people as a result of their identity as renewed humans in the new Adam." This does not mean that glory does not indicate God's presence. As Goranson Jacob goes on to argue, "Put another way, the visible splendor of God does not connote the presence of God but the presence of a particular God with particular attributes and who acts in the world in particular ways (aka the Ruler rules). Whether functioning literally or symbolically, the glory of God identifies who God is, and who God is includes both his person (ontology) and his activity (function)." *Conformed to the Image of His Son*, 47.

Morales recognizes the tendency of some interpreters to downplay the opening chapters of Genesis, and he argues that "the fundamental plotline of the
Pentateuch (and redemptive history) is often missed precisely from the failure
to discern the ultimate goal of creation, namely *for humanity to dwell with
God*."[5] This kind of dwelling is making a home with them. God's intention to
dwell with humanity is the uniqueness that sets this "kind" of creature apart
from the rest of creation and revolves around access to and reliance on that
personal presence as the progressive meeting of that need.

The very first use of image language in the Genesis account pictures humanity with unfettered access to God. While the text is unclear as to whether
the man and woman could approach God of their own volition, since God
comes to them, they appear to enter the presence of God without mediation.
They have conversations and relate second-personally to God. Considering
this unmediated access to God and other features articulated below, many
scholars have been quick to associate Eden with a temple, especially given
the parallels with other ancient Near Eastern cultures that also have origin
stories of gods carrying out world building as temple building.[6] Such a motif
ratifies the importance of divine presence because there is substantial evidence that the temple motif is present and because temples were the places
of divine-human encounter.

In Israel's cosmology, the cosmos was viewed as God's temple, with Eden
as the sanctuary. According to J. D. Levenson, this primordial world "was
conceived, at least in Priestly circles, as a macro-temple, the palace of God
in which all are obedient to his commands."[7] On this understanding, God
has ultimate dominion as the creator-ruler of the cosmos and interfaces with
the created world through heaven-and-earth intersections. Eden may have
served as the connecting point of heaven and earth. This bond is a common
theme in ancient Near Eastern contexts, as evidenced by the specific names of
temples, such as "the bond of heaven and earth," at Nippur, Larsa, and likely
Sippar.[8] Serving as an interface of heaven and earth, Eden is, at the very least,
functioning in a temple-like way. There does not appear to be a holy of holies
or a throne, so Eden may not have been understood as the most holy place

---

5. Morales, *Who Shall Ascend*, 40 (emphasis original).

6. There is broad consensus on this point. For a few examples, see Alexander, *From Paradise
to the Promised Land*; Beale, *Temple and the Church's Mission*; Middleton, *New Heaven and
a New Earth*; J. Walton, *Lost World of Genesis One*. More specifically, Walton argues that "the
temple is a microcosm, and Eden is represented in the antechamber that serves as sacred space
adjoining the Presence of God as an archetypal sanctuary" (83).

7. Levenson, "Cosmos and Microcosm," 235.

8. Burrows, "Some Cosmological Patterns in Babylonian Religion," 28. Gary A. Anderson
makes a similar point in this same volume, in "Cosmic Mountain," 373, 377.

in the temple, but it was still part of the temple.[9] According to other Hebrew texts, the throne remains in the heavenly realm, seemingly in the holy of holies (Ps. 11:4; Isa. 6:1; cf. Pss. 47:8; 103:19; Isa. 66:1).[10] The garden of Eden, on the other hand, "is the initial core location of God's presence on earth."[11] John Walton concurs with this reading by seeing Eden as "the antechamber" and seeing the veil of the earthly holy of holies as functioning like the firmament, which separated God's presence from human habitation.[12] Regardless of whether Eden functioned as the holy of holies, God could "walk" in the garden (Gen. 3:8) and dwell in this earthly space without inhibition, since this was a sacred space.[13]

The Hebrew understanding of delineated sacred space influences later elements of Israel's tabernacle and eventual temple. The Edenic temple themes find symbolic representation and parallels as the tabernacle represents a microcosm of the macrocosmic temple. Evidence of those parallels is eastward entrances to both the temple and Eden; cherubim guarding the entrances of both; the lampstand outside of the holy of holies paralleling the tree of life; and God's holy presence characterizing both.[14] Also, the importance of water is apparent, seen in the fertilizing rivers flowing from Eden—representing the divine presence and implying that Eden is an elevated place since water flows downhill.[15] Eden, in this way, represents a cosmic mountain. Gary Anderson

9. Dumbrell, *Search for Order*, 23–26; Dumbrell, *Covenant and Creation*, 34–35. The argument against Eden as the holy of holies is twofold; exegetically seeing it as "temple-like" is stronger than delimiting it to a codified space, especially given other prevailing Jewish cosmologies; theologically, the image of God would be in the innermost sanctum, and as derivative images, the man and the woman may not have had access to that level of sacred space even in their state of incorruption.

10. According to Beale, the holy of holies is associated with this heavenly throne room, while the holy place included the heavens, and the outer court included the rest of the habitable world. Beale and Kim, *God Dwells among Us*, 52. Kline concurs with this reading in *Images of the Spirit*, 21.

11. Middleton, *New Heaven and a New Earth*, 164.

12. J. Walton, *Lost World of Genesis One*, 82–83. Bartholomew also holds to the Eden-as-sanctuary reading. Bartholomew, *Where Mortals Dwell*, 28.

13. However, the fact that God can walk somewhere does not necessarily mean it is a "temple." According to Philip Jenson, since God can be present anywhere, such a place does not necessarily need to be holy. Jenson, "Genesis 1–3 and the Tabernacle." This point strengthens the overall case for the importance of humanity being in the divine presence regardless of the mode of space as temple. Arguably, "temple" is a conditioned reality due to sin. Had sin not occurred, perhaps all space would have been the temple, and thus the statement that the world is the temple or a part of the temple would have functioned as a sort of truism.

14. Beale and Kim, *God Dwells among Us*, 18–19; cf. Meyers, *Tabernacle Menorah*.

15. Gentry and Wellum also note, "In the ancient Near East, temples were situated on mountains because that is where the heavens meet the earth. In Ezekiel 28:13–14, Eden is also described and portrayed as a mountain sanctuary. . . . The future new Jerusalem/Zion is likewise

argues compellingly for the association of the mountains of Eden, Sinai, and Zion.[16] Not only does this association of significant mountains proceed from the biblical text (cf. Ezek. 47; Rev. 22), but they also appear in later Jewish thought in Jubilees (chap. 4) and early Christian writings: Ephrem the Syrian's *Hymns on Paradise* (1.4), and as a theme in the anonymous Cave of Treasures. Anderson goes so far as to claim that an "appreciation of how Eden functions as an archetype for the cosmic mountain in Israel and why it is identified with pre-exilic and eschatological Zion is absolutely necessary for a proper understanding of what the Rabbis and the early Christians do with the narratives of Genesis 2–3."[17] Eden thereby becomes a "hermeneutical device" that helps to interpret the entire biblical canon.[18]

As a hermeneutical device, Eden echoes throughout the biblical witness, continually pointing the reader to the Creator's original intentions. The purpose of this Edenic space was to provide a temple context for God to dwell with humanity and the rest of the created world. The temple was also a space for humanity (and the rest of creation) to respond in priestly service to their Creator. Given the command to "be fruitful and multiply," this initial pair is meant to grow, with later generations also charged with representative dominion and priestly tasks.[19] The linguistic overlap of temple-specific language evidences such priesthood. The verb for the "walking" that God is doing in the garden is the same verb used for the presence of God walking in the tabernacle in Leviticus 26:12, Deuteronomy 23:14, and 2 Samuel 7:6–7.[20] This walking underscores the second-personal presence: "And I will walk among you, and will be your God, and you shall be my people" (Lev. 26:12); "Because the LORD your God travels along with [or "walks in the midst of"] your camp . . ." (Deut. 23:14). Curating a space for this kind of presence, God gives humanity the same duties in Genesis 2:15 as were given to the Levites as ministers and priests in the sanctuary, as seen in the use of "to work" and

---

a mountain sanctuary (Isa. 2:2–4; 4:5; 11:9; 25:6–8; 56:7; 57:13; 65:11, 25)." *Kingdom through Covenant*, 212–13.

16. Anderson, "Cosmic Mountain," 377.

17. Anderson, "Cosmic Mountain," 387.

18. Anderson, "Cosmic Mountain," 388.

19. Alexander, *From Paradise to the Promised Land*, 25. Alexander recognizes this connection in saying that even though "it is not stated, the opening chapters of Genesis imply that the boundaries of the garden will be extended to fill the whole earth as human beings are fruitful and increase in number."

20. Alexander, *From Paradise to the Promised Land*, 123; cf. Gentry and Wellum, *Kingdom through Covenant*, 212–13. Dumbrell concurs with Wenham's verbal highlighting of "cultivate/work," "serve," and "guard" with priestly service in the tabernacle (Num. 3:7–8; 8:25–26; 18:5–6; 1 Chron. 23:32; Ezek. 44:14; see also Isa. 56:6). Dumbrell, *Covenant and Creation*, 59.

"to keep/guard."[21] According to T. Desmond Alexander, "Because they met God face to face in a holy place, we may assume that Adam and Eve had a holy or priestly status. Only priests were permitted to serve within a sanctuary or temple."[22] Whether they had a formal priestly status or not, they did have a second-personal relationship with God in the Edenic place, the kind of relationship that was always intended and that later covenants seek to restore and even deepen.

Later covenants help establish a "place" for the people of Israel.[23] Craig Bartholomew's work on place is helpful here, for comprehending both what sort of place Eden is described to be and what kind of place the covenants intended to cultivate. Human persons are people of place.[24] Bartholomew notes the association of place with the image of God in that humans are embodied, and as such, "humans are always dated and located, that is, placed. As a metaphor, the *imago Dei* alerts us to the similarities and differences between God and us, and our placedness is one of the differences."[25] Bartholomew also connects emplacement with identity, in such a way that being displaced is central to God's judgment in Genesis 3.[26] The place where the man and woman could meet with God, Eden, was where they knew who they were. They were creatures made in God's image and charged with a specific task. After sin enters the story, they experience displacement from this place, and their access to God's presence requires further intervention.

Consequently, God initiates a covenant with Abraham that includes a promise of worldwide blessing for people and a blessing of place in the form of land. Later, in the covenant at Sinai, God covenants to meet with his people in the place of the tabernacle—a place patterned after the prototype in heaven. The through line appears to be God's intention to relate to humanity through

---

21. Gentry and Wellum, *Kingdom through Covenant*, 212–13; Alexander, *From Paradise to the Promised Land*, 123.

22. Alexander, *From Eden to New Jerusalem*, 25.

23. Regarding the centrality of this placedness for Israel's identity, Craig Bartholomew argues: "Just as Israel is the center of the nations in Genesis 10, so Yahweh, living in the tabernacle, is the center of Israel's life, and the camp boundaries mark the limit of life under his reign and the wilderness and chaos that threatens outside." *Where Mortals Dwell*, 70.

24. For a powerful theological treatment of this fact, see Jennings, *Christian Imagination*.

25. Bartholomew, *Where Mortals Dwell*, 131. Furthermore, "From this perspective place is never fully place without God as a co-inhabitant" (29).

26. Bartholomew, *Where Mortals Dwell*, 29. While place and presence do not explicitly connect, since the presence was localized in the sacred place, they go hand in hand. Thus, Morales can say: "This expulsion from the divine Presence is the central tragic event that drives the history of redemption, determining and shaping the ensuing biblical narrative. Indeed, all of the drama of Scripture is found in relation to this singular point of focus: *YHWH's opening up the way for humanity to dwell in his Presence once more*." Morales, *Who Shall Ascend*, 55 (emphasis original).

God's own presence, which must be related to by emplaced persons. This circumscription exists not because God cannot be everywhere but because humans are embodied and, therefore, emplaced.

Heavenly Patterns, Earthly Copies

While other ancient Near Eastern cultures did not have the same origin story or covenant history as Israel, the theme of creation correlating with temple building evinces interesting overlap. The idea of an earthly copy of a divine prototype can be found in other ancient Near Eastern texts, as early as Sumerian writings, in which the earthly temple is "the likeness of the dwelling of the god in heaven."[27] The Enuma Elish (6.113) creation myth of Babylon discusses a similar patterning of the earthly temple of Marduk after the heavenly counterpart.[28] The earthly temple in Eden is an extension of the cosmic temple, the actual antechamber. Then, the tabernacle at Sinai and the temple at Jerusalem are cosmic microcosms of a heavenly prototype.[29] Such a view requires that a heavenly reality of the true temple preceded the earthly reality, which the text does not make clear. However, if Israel's cosmology was functioning like her neighbors', it is possible that in Israel's cosmology, the heavenly prototype informed the earthly reality. Even if this may be less clear in Eden, later tabernacle and temple constructions clarify the earthly patterning of the temple after a heavenly prototype.

Beyond the importance of associating the temple with God's personal presence, this patterning after a prototype is significant because such patterning sets an interpretive precedent for the Israelite community.[30] The earthly temple has a heavenly prototype, and likewise the earthly image has a heavenly prototype. Paul-Eugène Dion, Gordon Wenham, J. D. Levenson, T. N. D. Mettinger, and James Barr make this connection explicit in that the idiom of "making A patterned after B" follows Genesis 1:26 and Exodus 25:40.[31]

27. Burrows, "Some Cosmological Patterns in Babylonian Religion," 39, 38–44. Burrows also references the preexistence of the heavenly city and the tabernacle in Wisdom 9:8 and Apocalypse of Baruch 4.2–6.

28. Beale, *Temple and the Church's Mission*, 51; J. Walton, *Genesis*, 151; Alexander, *From Paradise to the Promised Land*, 123; Weinfeld, "Sabbath, Temple and the Enthronement of the Lord," 150–51.

29. Rowland and Morray-Jones, *Mystery of God*, 338.

30. This does not mean that ancient Israelites would have expected the true image to one day be revealed; I'm arguing, rather, that they had an incipient conceptual backdrop to understand the incarnation of the prototype, even as radical as it was.

31. Dion, "Image et ressemblance"; Barr, "Image of God in the Book of Genesis," 16–17; Wenham, "Sanctuary Symbolism Story"; Block and Cassuto, *Commentary on the Book of*

Such a connection closely ties the creation of humanity, made in the image of God, to the tabernacle itself. Furthermore, the vocation of humans as bringers of the divine presence directly corresponds with the teleological messages in Israel's temple. Such a *telos* contrasts with other ancient Near Eastern designs. This forward-focused trajectory is evident in that "Israel's temple pointed to the end-time goal of God's presence residing throughout the entire cosmos. . . . The pagan temples had no such eschatological purpose as a part of their symbolism."[32] The temple of Israel was forward pointing, since God's presence and rule were always intended to "fill the earth." For all things to be whole, to become *teleios*, has always required a divine input.

Cast against this temple backdrop, the Genesis story dignifies the whole cosmos. This cosmic temple is not a stagnant locale, but a dynamic locale intended to expand through the stewardship of the man and the woman, those who are in the image of God. Through their relationship to God, they are meant to expand YHWH's presence throughout the earth. Through humanity's filling of the earth, God intended that God's reign would spread throughout the created world as a vocational consequence of man and woman being made in the image of God. This presence expansion was their act of worship as archetypal rulers and priests. Consequently, the imperial and priestly role of images and idols in Israel's cultural context strengthens the relationship between humanity and the divine presence.

Images and Idols

We can now attend to the role of images within these religious spaces, given the evidence of a strong connection between the heavenly temple and the earthly temple for both Israel and other ancient Near Eastern cultures. The similarities and differences between Israel and these other cultures illuminate how images would have functioned within this sacred space even if the Genesis usages are not an exact parallel. For instance, the prevailing religious practice of ancient Near Eastern cultures was to honor each god with a statue or image and to place it in the innermost part of the temple.[33] Given these concrete forms of the deity, their location, and their inscriptions, the majority view among scholars for the Hebrew Scriptures and these cultures is that

---

Exodus, 476; Kearney, "Creation and Liturgy." Mettinger makes this most explicit: "Both man and the tabernacle are made according to the heavenly pattern; man is created according to a divine prototype." However, Mettinger sees man as resembling both God and angels. See Mettinger, "Abbild oder Urbild?"

32. Beale, *Temple and the Church's Mission*, 60.

33. Beale, *Temple and the Church's Mission*, 89.

the image was a physical representative of the deity, often used to establish the authority of that god.[34] In other words, the image was a representation of the deity's *presence*.[35]

However, the strength of the association of identity between the deity and the idol was a primary difference for Israel. To examine this, we should especially attend to the Mesopotamian and Egyptian "washing" or "opening of the mouth" rituals known as *ms pî ps pî* and *wpt-r*.[36] Four stages made up this ritual. First, the craftsman would form the idol/image in a workshop associated with the temple district, even though the worshiping community recognized the deity as the true creator of the image. Associated with this same act of creation was the first mouth opening in which the worshipers understood the god to be putting his or her breath into the image, vivifying it. Second, the image would be led down to the river after passing through a wilderness-type land to arrive at a garden. Third, once the idol was at the garden, worshipers opened the image's mouth several more times. It remained in the garden overnight and spent time in the presence of the gods, becoming the "bodily appearance of a God, the very medium through which he enters the world of created life and, correspondingly, through which he can be addressed by prayer, worship and sacrifice."[37] However, the ritual remained unfinished until the accomplishment of the fourth stage. Although the image was fully fashioned, it was not in the right place. The final stage of the ritual was its emplacement within the deity's holy of holies.

While these rituals seem to postdate the Genesis texts, the overlap with the Hebrew origin accounts remains interesting.[38] The themes of the temple, garden, God breathing into the human, and the image represent the deity's presence in the world, and all seem to overlap with the opening chapters of the Pentateuch. Most significantly, these parallels support the special relationship between the

34. J. Walton, *Genesis*, 130–31. While the image was physical, it did not have to bear physical likeness to the god it represented, although it could bear physical resemblance.

35. Gentry and Wellum, *Kingdom through Covenant*, 192. Gentry and Wellum provide a clear example of this through the archaeological discovery of an inscription from the Karnak temple "marking the triumph of Thutmoses III at Karnak, c. 1460 B.C. . . . In the thirteenth century B.C., Pharaoh Ramesses II had his image hewn out of rock at the mouth of the Kelb River, on the Mediterranean just north of Beirut. . . . In the ancient Near East, since the king is the living statue of the god, he represents the god on earth. He makes the power of the god a present reality."

36. McDowell, *Image of God*; Schuele, "Made in the 'Image of God,'" 11–12; Beale and Kim, *God Dwells among Us*, 45.

37. Schuele, "Made in the 'Image of God,'" 12.

38. Even the latest estimates for the writing of Genesis 1–3, putting them contemporaneous with prophetic literature, predate this by a few centuries. Schuele, "Made in the 'Image of God,'" 2.

deity and the image as it correlates to divine presence and function.[39] In other words, the image of a deity is the physical manifestation of the divine presence in created reality, and because of the ontology of the image as a conduit of the divine presence, its function was practically inseparable from its being.

Andreas Schuele makes these similarities explicit, especially as they relate to dominion and kingship, since rulers were often understood to be images of the divine.[40] J. Richard Middleton concurs with these findings, recognizing a parallel between how images were understood through the *ms pî ps pî* ritual and how Mesopotamian kings were recognized as unified with the divine, becoming the deity's rightful authority as representative of that deity on earth.[41]

However, as significant as these similarities are, the differences may prove even more pertinent to understanding the *imago Dei* in the Genesis narratives. In her monograph on the meaning of the image of God, especially in light of the Mesopotamian and Egyptian mouth-washing and -opening rituals, Catherine McDowell recognizes that perhaps the most striking dissimilarity between them and the Genesis accounts is that in Genesis, "humans were not created *to be* gods."[42] Even more significantly, worshipers believed these ceremonies "to be the means by which *a particular divine manifestation of a pre-existent god* was brought into being."[43] In her conclusion, she proposes that the Genesis author's comparison between humankind and divine images is meant to "introduce an innovative understanding of the divine-human relationship."[44] While the Mesopotamian and Egyptian rituals crescendo at the installation of the divine statue in the temple, the Eden narrative reverses the order. Her observations are worth quoting at length:

> Adam and Eve dwelt in the divine presence at creation, having been placed and perhaps installed in the garden of Eden, which may have been a temple-type of Yahweh. Fruit was provided in abundance, and they may have even been

---

39. Further support for the association of identity and function can be found in the eighth-century-BCE statue of King Hadduyiî from Guzana in which the image is a material object that both links the king to his deity and also has the special function of making "the king present in the face of his god, while he himself might be absent. . . . The image is part of the person of the king, not just some well crafted art object which is essentially detached from what it expresses." Schuele, "Made in the 'Image of God,'" 10.

40. Schuele, "Made in the 'Image of God,'" 5. See also, McDowell, *Image of God*, 137.

41. Middleton, *Liberating Image*, 137. Cortez, a theologian who has thoroughly engaged with this literature, especially as it relates to anthropology, also endorses this parallel in "Idols, Images, and a Spirit-ed Anthropology," 275–79.

42. McDowell, *Image of God*, 169 (emphasis original).

43. McDowell, *Image of God*, 205 (emphasis original). At the same time, this idea is quite interesting as it relates to the description of Jesus as the image of God. More anon.

44. McDowell, *Image of God*, 176, 204, 207.

'crowned' with the very glory of Yahweh himself. All of this was lost, however, when their eyes were opened. Rather than dwelling in the divine presence for which they were created, they would have to survive apart from it, with only animal skins for clothing instead of divine glory, and without a constant supply of easily accessible food. Now only by hard labor would they have enough food to eat (Gen. 3:19).[45]

The ancient Near Eastern rituals end with the impartation of the very presence of the deity through the god's inbreathing, yet the Eden text begins with the inbreathing while also maintaining the distinctiveness between God and humans.[46] Instead of becoming divine (as evidenced by the prepositional buffers argued in chapter 2), humankind begins with a special relation to the divine that is bound to relating second-personally to God's presence and representing God's presence in the world. Upon sinning, human beings forfeit the benefits of this relationship, even while the divine intention that they relate to the divine presence and represent it remains. Thus, God's personal presence remains available to human persons, even if now difficult to access.

Something distinctive is going on with presence in the ancient Near Eastern rituals. They are about "bringing images *to life*," and at the conclusion of their rituals, the statues become "divine manifestations." However, Adam is animated at the beginning of the second creation account, and upon rebellion, "he and his wife are no longer royal figures in the garden of God but mortals, now in decay, void of glory, forced to live out their days in pain and toil isolated from the divine presence."[47] The second Genesis account begins hopefully but ends in tragedy, and all because of how human beings initially related to God's personal presence and then were exiled from the place of that presence.

Further contrasts appear when we compare the Eden accounts even more broadly to narratives in surrounding cultures. Kings were images of their deities with the sole purpose of serving their gods. Whereas pagan gods created humanity to meet their needs, YHWH creates Eden to suit the needs of humanity, including access to the divine presence.[48] The Enuma Elish epic "presents the destiny of humans in terms of providing food for the gods, [whereas] Genesis ascribes to people a divinely given royal authority to rule over the earth."[49] Israel's origin story is an identity story.[50] As creatures made in the image of God, humans are meant to be royal representatives of YHWH,

45. McDowell, *Image of God*, 176–77.
46. McDowell, *Image of God*, 177.
47. McDowell, *Image of God*, 177
48. J. Walton, *Genesis*, 134.
49. Alexander, *From Paradise to the Promised Land*, 124.
50. J. Walton, *Lost World of Genesis One*, 70.

living in God's presence and expanding God's rule in all the earth. While kings would have had this unique identity in ancient Near Eastern contexts, such an identity would have excluded the rest of the people.[51] This exclusive image-bearing right was especially dominant in Egypt and Mesopotamia, which understood that "the king (like the cult statue in the temple) is the official mediator of the presence and will of the gods on earth," and in this way, the king acted much like a priest, and this was an exclusive role.[52]

In Genesis, these roles are given to the Edenic man and woman, who represented the ruler of the universe by exercising dominion and serving a priestly role by tending to the temple-garden. The democratization of this vocation differed starkly from the exclusive status of kings as images of deities in surrounding cultures. Instead, all humanity shared this vocation of representing the divine presence in the world. A further contrast to the surrounding nations was the prohibition of having any carven images of YHWH.[53] A carven image could not capture the fullness of YHWH, even as humankind was deemed a creation "in the image of God" (Gen. 1:27). Furthermore, other cultures were polytheistic and required multiple temples for multiple gods, whereas Israel had one God and one temple, and—as has been proposed thus far—only one true image.[54]

By recognizing the distinctions and similarities, McDowell's account helps keep the boundaries set up in chapter 2 and implies some new parameters for discussing humans as creatures made in God's image. McDowell makes this explicit as she continues her argument that the Eden authors were conveying something innovative about humanity through the context and the choice of the words *tselem* and *demuth*. She summarizes this innovation into three points: humans have a unique status as those in a "filial relationship with God"; humans have a unique function of ruling over creation; and instead of using

---

51. Schuele, "Made in the 'Image of God,'" 6. Schuele further notes the contrast to Israel's anthropology in that "Adam, the creature of the sixth day, does not occur in the role of the servant, but is himself associated with the image. It is not for >pragmatic< reasons that humans are created, they rather assume divine dignity in that they represent God in the created world as the cultic image would do" (punctuation original).

52. Gentry and Wellum, *Kingdom through Covenant*, 192–93; Harland, *Value of Human Life*, 181–82. These scholars also note the significance of the Tell Fekheriyeh statue inscription (Akkadian-Aramaic bilingual text), dated to the ninth century BC, which uses both terms of image and likeness for a governor-king and reiterates the representational and royal nature of these terms. Middleton, *New Heaven and a New Earth*, 43. See also Beale and Kim, *God Dwells among Us*, 30; Alexander, *From Paradise to the Promised Land*, 125; von Rad, "εικών [εικōn]," 392.

53. Kilner, *Dignity and Destiny*, 88. Yet there is one exception from a Tenth Dynasty wisdom text from Egypt, where "it is *humanity in general* that is defined both as the image and the offspring of the creator-god." McDowell, *Image of God*, 135, 137 (emphasis original).

54. Regarding these differences, see Beale, *Temple and the Church's Mission*, 59; Middleton, *New Heaven and a New Earth*, 43.

statues, the deity has made humans to be derivative images "created to dwell in the divine presence."[55] The first two innovations McDowell highlights have significant overlap with the minimum parameters already stated above. The third, however, adds a parameter that, especially in light of the temple context, seems reasonable—namely, that by using the language of "image," the biblical authors are making a strong association between being human and dwelling in the divine presence. McDowell asks why the author of this account would draw so clearly from these ceremonies and proposes that the author did so "in order to offer a new framework for understanding the divine-human relationship: humankind was designed to dwell in the divine presence, that is, with God in his most holy place."[56] Despite the contrasts, the centrality of humanity's relating to the divine presence—albeit differently than how humanity related to such presence in Egypt and Mesopotamia—was essential to this author's thinking.

An added and significant contrast between the Genesis account and ancient Near Eastern rituals is that the latter identified the physical image or idol with a deity's presence, especially once the image had received the breath of the deity. If you have ever seen Disney's animated film *Hercules*, recall the statue of Zeus being "zapped," with Zeus himself becoming the statue. Zeus then talks to Hercules as the statue because he is the statue. The language in the Hebrew Bible, in contrast, keeps some distance between deity and image while still maintaining a strong association between the image and the divine presence.[57]

Such a case can be based on two reasons. First, humans are not the only creatures in the Genesis account with the breath of God. Wenham makes this explicit in his commentary on Genesis when he interprets the use of "breath of life" to describe God's vivification of other creatures: "It is not man's possession of 'the breath of life' or his status as a 'living creature' that differentiates him from the animals. . . . Animals are described in exactly the same terms."[58] Breath more strongly associates with a vivifying or animating effect than any personal reception of the divine Spirit.[59] Second, the use of the prepositions supports a distinction between the image and the human persons as derivative images. They are not the image itself.

55. McDowell, *Image of God*, 141.

56. McDowell, *Image of God*, 208.

57. According to José Faur's understanding of the ancient Near Eastern rituals, these communicated "the identification of a god with his idol." "Biblical Idea of Idolatry," 7, quoted in Cortez, "Idols, Images, and a Spirit-ed Anthropology," 277.

58. Wenham, *Genesis 1–15*, 61.

59. Such an interpretation also comports with McDowell's study. *Image of God*, 177. However, whether more can be said theologically will be addressed in later chapters. The roles of the Spirit and Word will thus be revisited in Kathryn Tanner's work, wherein this kind of vivifying presence could be termed "weak participation."

Without conflating Israel's understanding of the image with the ancient Near Eastern understanding of the image, Cortez concludes, "The image is inherently pneumatological since the Spirit is precisely the one who manifests divine presence in the world throughout the Old Testament."[60] Even though the human creatures receive the vivifying breath of God, this does not necessarily equate their being in the image with being the divine presence themselves. However, the close parallels between the Genesis account and these pagan rituals make the association between an image and the divine presence unavoidable. Thus, it is reasonable to adopt a minimalistic reading in which we take the ancient Near Eastern background seriously but do not map the Genesis account onto this background in a one-to-one relationship. Human beings are intended to dwell in God's presence and function as representatives of the divine presence—especially through a function of dominion—in light of being creatures made for a special relationship with God. The question of whether this special relationship reached its zenith before sin is underdetermined in these texts. However, this does not compromise the pneumatological centrality of being in the image of God, since we see God intending that humankind dwell in God's presence and play a special role in expanding this presence.[61]

This pneumatological centrality is reinforced through the vocations of rulership and priestly service that flow from the text, even if many scholars do not separate the constitution of the image from the consequence of being in the image.[62] If the content of the image of God is the Second Person of the Trinity, then the derivative image of humanity may be better understood as an identity for humanity.[63] Such an identity finds its source in the divine intention of becoming like the true image through relying on God's personal presence. This identity is relationally constituted.

Spirit, Presence, and Glory in the Hebrew Bible

While temples were designated sacred sites, God's presence is not circumscribed by the boundaries of these locations. Instead, God's presence is everywhere, even if it is experienced more intensely at certain times and in

60. Cortez, "Idols, Images, and a Spirit-ed Anthropology," 277.

61. For this reason, Cortez can make the strong claim "that divine presence is fundamental for understanding the image of God." *ReSourcing Theological Anthropology*, 29.

62. A formidable case for this interpretation of "image" is given by Middleton in *Liberating Image* and *New Heaven and a New Earth*; cf. Merrill, "Image of God," 442; Williams, "First Calling," 80, 97.

63. For a persuasive monograph arguing to this effect, see Peterson, *Imago Dei as Human Identity*.

particular places. This intensity of God's presence is evident in the way that the Spirit, as God's presence, and glory are intertwined. Even though God's presence may not have been formally categorized as "Spirit" until later in Israel's history, the nation recognized that YHWH was personally present with them, leading them.[64] This retrospective recognition was especially tangible in their desert experience. Gordon Fee makes this connection explicit when he argues from Isaiah 63:9–14 that "the divine presence in the Exodus narrative was specifically equated with 'the Holy Spirit of the Lord.'"[65] There is a conceptual evolution in Israel's later history when Isaiah's authors recount the exodus and postexodus experiences, recognizing God's ongoing, identifiable presence with Israel. Regarding glory, repeatedly, the "glory of God" indicates the presence of God through a visible manifestation of God's supernatural presence (Exod. 16:10; 33:12–20; Deut. 5:24).[66] Notably, Israel's eschatological hopes were bound to this glory-presence filling the final temple: "The glory of God in the Old Testament signified the manifestation of the presence of God (e.g., Num. 14:10; Ps. 26:8; 102:16; Jer. 17:12; Ezek. 10:4). The glory cloud covered the Tabernacle when it was first erected (Exod. 40:34), and 1 Kings 8:10–11 records that during the dedication of Solomon's Temple, 'the cloud filled the house of the Lord.' Furthermore, even though the presence of God's glory had departed from the city (Ezek. 11:23), the glory of God would once again dwell in the end-time Temple (Ezek. 44:4)."[67] When God was present in this identifiable way, it was often indicated by the "glory cloud," which signified the localization of God's Spirit. Consequently, when God's presence came on a specific place (typically, the temple) there would be visible manifestations of this presence (known as "glory") and this became progressively associated with God's Spirit.

---

64. Fee, *God's Empowering Presence*, 114. This presence being understood as personal is especially supported by the use of language referring to God's face, *panim*, as synecdoche for God's presence. This is the "central term used extensively for the presence of God throughout the OT." Duvall and Hays, *God's Relational Presence*, 93.

65. Fee, *Paul, the Spirit, and the People of God*, 14.

66. As McDowell states, "The glory of Yahweh is described in the Bible as a physical manifestation that is visible and audible to humans. It has substance and mass, it is mobile, and it has a sanctifying effect." *Image of God*, 164. James Arcadi also argues this point in "God Is Where God Acts." Though focused on Ephesians, Andrew Lincoln's commentary on Ephesians notes "the force of the OT notion of *kābôd* as the mode of God's being and activity, which lies behind the designation here. 'Glory' denotes the splendor of the divine presence and power. In fact, in Paul 'glory' and 'power' can be synonymous in terms of God's activity (cf. Rom 6:4 and 1 Cor 6:14 with reference to his activity in raising Christ)." *Ephesians*, 56. As noted above, while glory can also mean God's reputation and renown, this does not negate the frequency of God's glory indicating God's personal presence in the world.

67. Um, *Theme of Temple Christology*, 154.

In this way, the glory-presence of God indicated the divine presence in Israel's midst, often appearing in a cloud, thereby making God's invisible presence visible. Such a manifestation also induced fear. According to Schuele, the *kavod* required containment "in order to avoid its potentially detrimental effects"; thus the tabernacle and the temple, each with its differing chambers, provided a "kind of graded access to the *kābōd*" to enable humans to draw closer to the divine presence (Exod. 40:33–38).[68] The tabernacle and temple allowed people access to the living God, with God going to great lengths to establish this portal.[69] At the same time, Israel was also meant to respond with covenant faithfulness so that God's presence could dwell among them in the tabernacle and temple. This presence, as holy, could only come to a purified place, and the laws that God gave to Israel to follow enabled the people and the tabernacle to be clean before beholding God's holiness as the presence of God filled the tabernacle with glory.[70] The reception of such glory was the unique purview of Israel, since they were and are God's special possession and chosen people. In this way, Israel's keeping covenant with YHWH was the necessary prerequisite to God's presence dwelling among the nation.

The association of the covenant with divine presence and glory persists under David's kingship and line. For example, when Israel or her kings failed to keep the covenant, God's glory and presence could be withdrawn. Macaskill notes this trajectory as it relates to the Davidic line and Zion, especially noting the contingent nature of God's glory and presence: "The glory of the Davidic line and of Zion is not a property inherent to those things; rather it is an alien property, communicated to them and contingent upon the presence of God."[71] Macaskill argues that with the presence of God comes a transference of God's glory into the human domain. This transference would also hold for holiness in that humans cannot make themselves glorious or holy; a divine agent must make them so.[72] Being in God's presence enacts such a transference, but it is conditional and therefore temporary. Glory-presence can be lost.

68. Schuele, "Spirit of YHWH and the Aura of Divine Presence," 22.

69. While the temple was the centralized point of access, this does not mean that the Spirit did not empower individuals, since the Spirit clearly did so. Given that this book is seeking an inescapable fundamental need and given that the Spirit's empowerment does not seem to have been given to all faithful Israelites, this particular form of Spirit endowment does not establish the fundamental human need for a second-personal relation to God, even if it is one manifestation of it. For more elaboration on this special Spirit endowment, see M. Turner, "Jesus and the Spirit in Lucan Perspective," 37.

70. Macaskill, *Union with Christ*, 263.

71. Macaskill, *Union with Christ*, 112.

72. "Israel's call to holiness may be grasped in a twofold manner. First, the *need* for Israel's holiness is rooted in the essential nature of God—in his own utter holiness. . . . If there is to be any intimate relationship with him, that is, if the goal of the covenant and telos of creation

After sin and humanity's excision from the presence of God, the most common geographical space in which to encounter YHWH's presence was the tabernacle and temple, the main site of Jewish culture.[73] This language of the temple, signifying a space where God's presence could become visible and apparent, remains significant in referring to Jesus. He is the one who "tabernacles" among humanity (John 1:14), who calls himself the temple and enables postresurrection disciples themselves to become temples of this personal divine presence.

Tabernacle, Temple, and Covenant

The garden narrative portrays a temple sanctuary, a place where God's presence could dwell among humans without any hindrance. After the account of human rebellion, humans could no longer live in the divine presence. Separation from the divine presence became central to their deterioration when they were cast out of the garden. However, God remains actively involved in bringing about a context in which human relation to this presence can be realized once more. As Morales summarizes, "The tabernacle cultus is presented as a mediated resolution to the crisis introduced in Genesis 3 with humanity's expulsion from Eden."[74] As such, the tabernacle and later temple implicitly communicate God's intention to commune with Israel and, ultimately, with all of humanity.

Furthermore, the presence of God and humanity's dwelling with God are central to Israel's identity. Morales goes so far as to claim: "The primary theme and theology of Leviticus (and of the Pentateuch as a whole) is YHWH's opening a way for humanity to dwell in the divine Presence."[75] Thus, the covenants are God-initiated actions to create this context again. God's undergirding reason for initiating the covenants seems to be his will to be accessible—and, arguably, eventually more accessible than in the garden originally. As Edward Malatesta observes, "In the OT the Law, like the Temple, is an answer to the problem of the presence of God."[76] The man and the woman lost access to

---

will ever be realized, Israel's character must steadily be conformed to YHWH's." Morales, *Who Shall Ascend*, 208–9 (emphasis original).

73. It also occurs on significant mountains, which were thought of as connecting points of heaven and earth and thus connoted temple significance.

74. Morales, *Who Shall Ascend*, 75.

75. Morales, *Who Shall Ascend*, 23. Morales continues: "The essence of that *way* and the heart of the Pentateuch's theology is the Day of Atonement" (38).

76. Malatesta, *Interiority and Covenant*, 74. Also, the association of Wisdom with temple and Torah seems to provide another connection with divine presence. However, given the scope of this book, this association cannot be explored in depth. See Terrien, *Elusive Presence*, 473.

God's immediate presence, and God intervenes through the covenants that restore and mediate this access.[77]

The idea that God would dwell among the human community—specifically, Israel—runs throughout the Hebrew Scriptures.[78] In the Hebrew texts, these dwelling spaces "draw their significance not from their physical structure but from the fact that God is present in them, relating to his people who come to worship him."[79] From Eden to the tabernacle and then the temple, God's intent for fellowship with humanity is abundantly clear.[80] In the Hebrew Bible after Eden, the actual presence of God is often localized to these circumscribed spaces.

Before this access could begin to match what humanity first experienced, it was given to a special people, the people of Israel.[81] Exodus 19 tells the story of God's invitation to Israel to be a "kingdom of priests and a holy nation." They were all meant to represent the nations to God and see God's presence expand into all the earth—like the first man and woman were meant to do under the original mandate. However, unlike the access that the first humans had at the beginning of humanity's origin story, the opportunities for contact with God in the nation of Israel were exclusive and became more and more so the closer one came to the presence of God, reaching a crescendo in the holy of holies, where only the high priest could stand in God's presence, or glory, once a year. Affirming the centrality of God's presence, Morales writes: "At the heart of the Pentateuch, then, one finds humanity's deepest penetration into the divine Presence—this by way of the cultic means opened by YHWH. . . . However, the book of Leviticus holds out the prospect of deeper

77. "Covenants" here includes the new covenant, though I recognize that the new covenant introduces a new extent of human flourishing.

78. To say that God desires to include all humanity is not to suggest a replacement theology of the church as the new Israel. Due to space constraints, the role of Israel after the inauguration of the new covenant cannot be discussed here, but I should register agreement with T. F. Torrance in that "the Christian Church must not forget that it has no independent existence, for through Christ it is grafted on to the trunk of Israel, nor must it imagine that God has cast off his ancient people or that the promises made to Israel as a people of divine election and institution have only a spiritualized fulfilment." *Theology in Reconstruction*, 198. For a stringent critique of the supersessionist tendency, see Jennings, *Christian Imagination*.

79. J. Hays, *Temple and the Tabernacle*, 10.

80. As Dumbrell notes, "In the context of Genesis 2:15, the meaning of 'abad' is 'till' or 'cultivate,' but the regular use of the verb as 'worship' later in the OT imports into the Genesis 2 context the aspect of human response in what seems to be this sanctuary, where the presence of God is directly experienced." *Covenant and Creation*, 59.

81. This book will assume that regeneration and the indwelling of the Holy Spirit are separable and that there were regenerate persons in the various historical periods described in the Hebrew Bible but that they could still lose the Spirit (cf. Ps. 51). For a full defense of this view, see Hamilton, *God's Indwelling Presence*.

communion with God, through the Day of Atonement, but also beyond it."[82] The temple cultus was not a permanent solution to the "problem of the presence of God."[83] Such a solution would require a new priesthood, a new temple, and a new covenant.

Samuel Terrien, in his work on Isaiah, also notes the significance of the relationship of presence to the covenant. He recognizes that "covenant" language is absent in Isaiah, which "only strengthen[s] the opinion that the motif of divine presence may well be more important than that of Covenant for the understanding of the Hebrew religion and the formulating of a truly biblical theology."[84] W. J. Phythian-Adams, while not articulating the priority of presence to covenant, nonetheless urges their pairing, claiming, "The Covenant-People and the Covenant-Presence are inseparable in the religious thought of Israel: where one is, there the other must be, not temporarily but for ever."[85] God's covenant establishment with Israel is meant to instantiate the context for God's presence to be among all people once again. This presence, especially in its corporate dimensions, becomes evident in the book of Exodus and remains a theme throughout the Hebrew Bible. According to Fee, "The most prominent way God's presence is experienced in the Old Testament is in the tabernacle and the temple. Such a presence motif, culminating in God's glory descending on the tabernacle, is the structural key to the book of Exodus."[86] The presence motif in Exodus is especially important since the events of that book continue to color Israel's identity as the people of God through much of the Hebrew Bible.[87] Furthermore, the glory-presence is also intrinsically relational, since it is a special initiative of the Creator God to be with humanity.[88]

In Ezekiel—as well as in the prophetic literature more broadly—the speaker prophesies about a new era, a new covenant, which is to come, in which the

---

82. Morales, *Who Shall Ascend*, 32.

83. Morales, *Who Shall Ascend*, 74.

84. Terrien, "Proclamation and Presence," 568; Terrien, *Elusive Presence*.

85. Phythian-Adams, *People and the Presence*, 17. Malatesta confirms this interpretation, given that "the very name of God revealed to Moses in Ex 3,14 is a pledge of saving presence." *Interiority and Covenant*, 65.

86. Fee, *Paul, the Spirit, and the People of God*, 11. Richard Bauckham supports this understanding as well, stating that God "gives himself a localized presence in the temple, where he is accessible to those who know him by name. In this self-identification of God as Israel's God he, in a sense, particularizes himself and does so by identifying with a worldly reality." "Incarnation and the Cosmic Christ," 32.

87. For a book-length argument detailing this case, see Estelle, *Echoes of Exodus*.

88. Um concurs with this view in that "the Temple and other types of sanctuaries (e.g., tent of meeting, tabernacle) represent Yahweh's desire to dwell with his people." *Theme of Temple Christology*, 147.

Spirit of God will enter the hearts of God's people (Ezek. 36:27). Here "God's Spirit means the presence of God himself, in that by putting 'my Spirit within you . . . you shall live' (Ezek. 37:14)."[89] The presence that had occupied the temple made of wood and stone would one day occupy human hearts.

Of unique significance is the dependence that Israel, as a nation, was meant to have on YHWH. God's special presence was meant to set Israel apart as a nation of priests as they brought light to the nations (Exod. 19). While individual Israelites were expected to obey the stipulations of the covenant given at Sinai, the choices of these individuals collectively affected the whole and whether God's presence remained among them. God could also bring divine presence back to Israel under the leadership of individuals, as seen in the monarchical period of Israel's history. However, this presence could be lost if Israel was unfaithful. Eventually, a time would come when this presence would dwell in the human person. The strength of this divine intention becomes more evident when we trace the significance of divine presence through Israel's scriptures and the New Testament.

Creation, Temple, and Divine Presence in the Gospel of John

Texts that associate creation, temple, and divine presence would seem to shed more light on the interpretation above that the creation account of Genesis 1–2 is inextricably bound to sacred space and that Exodus 25 alludes to Eden in the tabernacle construction. However, whether such connections are incidental or would have been discernable and appropriated by first-century Jews is another question. Fortunately, evidence that these connections were recognized and theologically interpreted does exist. Such texts are present especially in Johannine writing.[90]

The Gospel of John weaves an especially unique tapestry of creation, temple, and divine presence by narrating the story of Jesus.[91] Opening the book with the same linguistic introduction as the book of Genesis, this Gospel presents Jesus as the fulfillment of God's creational purposes.[92] Coinciding with this presentation is the personal role of the Holy Spirit, which enunciates this new creation reality embodied in Jesus. Throughout John's Gospel, Jesus is the new temple, the new location of God's presence. Consequently,

---

89. Fee, *Paul, the Spirit, and the People of God*, 16.
90. The treatment of these texts in this chapter will not be comprehensive but will simply serve to illustrate the significance of these themes in the New Testament as well.
91. For more detail concerning their connection, see Coloe, "Theological Reflections on Creation in the Gospel of John."
92. Cortez, *ReSourcing Theological Anthropology*, 46.

theologians such as Cortez rightly assert that this Gospel recognizes "the central role that pneumatology must play in any christological anthropology," due to the significant role of the Spirit throughout John's Gospel.[93] Morales also recognizes the centrality of pneumatology in an intrinsically trinitarian way: "The Spirit brings us into the Son, and the Son unveils to us the Father."[94] Jesus is the essential link for connecting humanity with the Spirit, and thereby to the Father.

John's prologue and the Gospel's concluding chapters connect Jesus with the new creation. Cortez recognizes the association of John 20:22 and Genesis 2:7 in that "just as humanity came into existence when God breathed the Spirit into his creatures, John portrays Jesus as the one who inaugurates new humanity by breathing the Spirit into his followers. This was almost certainly intended as well to bring to mind texts that refer to the life-giving Spirit in new creation contexts."[95] Such an interpretation finds broad scholarly support, as many have argued that Jesus comes to complete what was only begun in creation.[96] Since Jesus is the true image, the true temple, and the new creation, those who wed themselves to him take on a new, though originally intended, identity.

CONCLUSION

Having examined the tentative boundaries for the image of God in chapters 2 and 3, and now the contextual backdrop of temple and images linking anthropology to the divine presence, we return to Wolterstorff's category of *intended manifestational revelation*. While the text nowhere explicitly states something like, "Understanding humanness is only possible by understanding how it relates to God's second-personal presence," such a revelation is plausibly true based on the intended manifestational revelation examined thus far.[97]

From the very beginning, God uniquely dignifies humanity by creating it in the divine image. The Hebrew Scriptures do not expand on the content of that divine image but suggest that the consequence includes expanding the

93. Cortez, *ReSourcing Theological Anthropology*, 27.

94. Morales, *Who Shall Ascend*, 267.

95. See Isa. 44:3–4; Ezek. 36:25–28; 37:9; Joel 2:28–29; Cortez, *ReSourcing Theological Anthropology*, 47.

96. R. Brown, *Gospel according to John I–XII*, 908. See also Andrew Lincoln, *Gospel according to Saint John*, 498; J. Brown, "Creation's Renewal in the Gospel of John," 285–86; Cortez, *ReSourcing Theological Anthropology*, 38.

97. This is another way of speaking of abduction.

reign and presence of God in all the earth. Therefore, within creation is an embedded *telos*—a built-in intention for further development—insinuating that goodness does not mean lacking nothing. Humanity's identity is to be in a unique relationship with God, to be bringers of God's presence into the world, and to be in this presence themselves. As utter gift, God wills humanity's absolute best, that people be in relationship with Godself, perpetually experiencing God's personal presence (which is goodness itself). When humans rebel, God makes an explicit covenant with Israel, and later, with the church. The same identity is in play; however, the human creatures need renewal to take part in their divinely given identity. Such an identity is bound to their need for a second-personal relation to God.

The New Testament theme that God wants humanity to further expand the divine presence and deepen humanity's connection to this presence tacitly affirms that human beings are to become like the true image. The ambiguity regarding whether the archetypal humans were able to *enter* God's presence at will, even though they could be in God's presence, may communicate a contrast between their being *in* the image and Jesus's *being* the true image. Comparatively, Jesus can enter God's presence (Heb. 9–10) and is the divine presence (argued below). Further, the possibility that Eden was not itself the holy of holies, but that the holy of holies has always remained in the highest heavens, suggests that the true image may also reside in this most holy place. While these archetypal humans are deemed "very good," the New Testament raises the question of whether the man and the woman are the prototype for humanity, given that the express content of the *imago Dei* is the preexistent Logos, referred to as the incarnate Second Adam.

Communicated by the mechanism of the *imago Dei*, the triune God invites humanity to become like Christ, the true image, through dependence on the Holy Spirit. Whereas the first Adam was created as "a link between above and below," the second Adam is the preexisting connection of above and below—he is where heaven and earth meet.[98] It seems reasonable that Jesus Christ is the prototypical human being and that humans are made in his image, given the significance of (1) Eden as a temple-like space, (2) humanity's implicit lack of access to the holy of holies (throne room), (3) the precedent of the temple as the heavenly reality after which the earthly temple was patterned, (4) the common practice of keeping the image in a temple's innermost sanctum, (5) the parallelism between the grammatical structure of the account of humanity's creation and the account of the tabernacle's construction, (6) the consistent use of prepositions referring to humanity as

98. Fishbane, "Sacred Center," 392.

"in" the image of God, and (7) the statement of equivalence between Jesus and the image. Further, this combination of significant factors leads us to conclude that we cannot understand humanity apart from its relation to God's personal presence.

On this view, human sinfulness in no way corrupts the image of God, since that would mean the corruption of the preexistent prototype. Neither does sin corrupt the status of all humans being *in* the image of God, nor does it corrupt the divine intention that humanity becomes like the true image. What sin affects includes the capacities of human beings to pursue their unique end. Humanness entails the unique *telos* of becoming like Christ through reliance on the divine presence (the Spirit), and thus Christology, anthropology, and pneumatology intersect. What is clear so far is that God desires to dwell with humanity personally and that humanity expands the divine presence. These two divine desires continue even after humans sin. God's pursuit of a relationship with humanity, as well as God's ongoing provision for their need to relate to God's self, reveals these intentions.

PART 3

Divine Presence

*Temple, Bread, Water, Sonship,
Firstborn, and Adoption*

FIVE

Divine Presence in the Old Testament

The Significance of Bread, Water, and Sonship

A Jewish Messiah invites gentiles to fully participate in Israel's story. Because of this, how God's personal presence functioned by meeting Israel's needs, specifically for bread and water, is significant. The intuitive centrality of bread and water for human survival and flourishing indicates Israel's need for God's personal presence.[1] Further, being a part of a divinely originated family, a kin group, was central to the identity and function of Israel, providing more evidence for the importance of YHWH's personal presence.[2] How bread, water, and sonship functioned in Israel's history will again take us through one stage of human experience of this fundamental need. This context will also illuminate how Jesus uses these terms to refer to himself and how later biblical writers apply those terms to the new covenant community.

---

1. Given that we have just addressed Israel's understanding of the temple in the prior chapter, we will not rehearse those details here.

2. Israel is not replaced but reconfigured. Willie Jennings summarizes this well: "The children of Israel must choose to form a new family in Israel. Jesus will challenge the very foundations of social life by challenging the power of the kinship network, which organized the central social, economic, and geographic realities of life in Israel. Jesus entered fully into the kinship structure not to destroy it but to reorder it—around himself." *Christian Imagination*, 263.

Bread

The metaphor of bread for God's presence is most clearly evinced with the provision of bread from heaven in the form of manna during Israel's wilderness wanderings.[3] According to Israel's narrative history, God supplied their bread daily for forty years. By way of striking contrast, in Deuteronomy 8:3, the author notes that the life-giving bread from heaven was insufficient for sustenance and that life proceeds, instead, "by every word that comes from the mouth of the LORD."[4] The larger context of this passage describes God as the one who provides Israel with both food and clothing. YHWH is called "your God" (8:2, 6, 7, 10), and the speaker parallels God's actions to Israel in the wilderness with those of a father to his son (8:5). Yes, YHWH disciplines them, but YHWH also brings them into a fruitful land without scarcity (8:9). The point of the discipline is to remind them to keep God's commandments (8:6). Amos 8:11 communicates a similar thought: "The time is surely coming, says the LORD God, when I will send a famine on the land; not a famine of bread, or a thirst for water, but of hearing the words of the LORD." By listening to the voice and obeying the instruction of YHWH, Israel would prosper (cf. Isa. 55:2; Prov. 9:5). Hearing God's voice required remaining in God's presence or following the law of the covenant—God's voice in written form. These words, the bread, could be equated with God's presence, which sustained Israel so long as they maintained covenant faithfulness.[5] Bread also played a substantial role in the tabernacle and temple beyond the associations of bread as a daily necessity, which faithfulness to YHWH ensures.

While bread was a common element necessary for life, it also represented fellowship in sharing a meal with YHWH. Beale explains that twelve loaves of bread were baked each week, and the Aaronic priests would enter the holy place every Sabbath to eat them in God's presence (Lev. 24:5–9).[6] Even before this, on the holy mountain of Sinai, the seventy elders and Moses entered God's presence to drink and eat (Exod. 24), as an analogue of the temple that would be built.[7] As they gathered there, "they saw the God of Israel" (Exod.

---

3. Exod. 16:31–35; Num. 11:6–9; Deut. 8:3–16; Josh. 5:12; Neh. 9:20; Ps. 78:24.

4. And as early as the patriarch Jacob, provision for fundamental needs, such as bread, is associated with YHWH's presence (Gen. 28:20).

5. There are other associations of God's presence with bread in Neh. 9:30; Pss. 37:25; 78; 105; 132:13–18.

6. Beale and Kim, *God Dwells among Us*, 55.

7. Beale and Kim, *God Dwells among Us*, 55. Beale notes that "this occurred at the middle section of the Sinai mountain temple, which corresponds to the middle part of Israel's temple, the Holy Place." Morales confirms this reading as well. *Who Shall Ascend*, 96–97.

24:10). Subsequently, Exodus 25 provides some of the instructions for the tabernacle offerings, wherein the bread of the Presence first appears. After the inaugural event (Exod. 24), when the priests ate the bread of the Presence, they recalled this moment—a symbol of God's intention to dwell with people in a personal way—as fellowshipping with them.[8]

Biblical scholars Brant Pitre and Roy Gane have written extensively on cultic practices in the Hebrew Bible, and their work on the bread of the Presence adds depth to Beale's view.[9] Pitre recognizes the importance of the fellowship but makes a stronger connection to the enacted *memorial* of the priests' weekly ritual of the bread of the Presence.[10] Contra Gane, Pitre argues that the flagons and bowls on the golden table (Exod. 25:25–30) were not empty but contained wine that the priests would drink as they ate the bread of the Presence (cf. Num. 4:7; 15:5–7; 28:7).[11] If recalling the banquet of the seventy is indeed what is going on in the earthly holy of holies, then the consumption of the bread *and* wine would seem likely for humans dining before God, as both would have been consumed at that meal.

Concerning the bread, Pitre contends that the Hebrew phrase means "the bread of the face."[12] Given the use of this same language in similar contexts, these words "strongly suggest that the bread is a visible sign of God's presence."[13] The use of bread offerings was not unique to Israel, as "in the ancient world, cakes of bread that were offered in temples (and later, in churches), were often stamped with some symbol of the deity (cf. Jer. 7:18; 44:19)."[14] What is unique to Israel is that this presence was highly covenantal, first in its original associations with the covenant given at Sinai, and second in the overall content of the covenant enacting a place where God's presence could dwell. Therefore, this ritual communicated the personal nature of God's relationship with Israel. The temple was meant to be a place of God's rest and an invitation for Israel to enter this rest by relying on YHWH's sustaining

---

8. Psalm 41:9 reiterates the intimacy of sharing bread with someone, since it is incredible that a friend with whom one had shared bread would then "lift his heel" against the bread giver.

9. Gane, "'Bread of the Presence'"; Pitre, *Jesus and the Last Supper*, 125. While this is similar to Beale's view, Pitre argues, further, that the priests are reenacting this banquet in the bread-of-the-Presence ritual.

10. Pitre, *Jesus and the Last Supper*, 122.

11. Pitre, *Jesus and the Last Supper*, 123. Pitre believes it to be more likely that the wine was drunk by the priests, finding support from Haran, *Temples and Temple-Service in Ancient Israel*, 216–17. Since this is significant for the broader argument Pitre makes regarding the connection of this ritual to the Last Supper, he argues for the wine's consumption.

12. Pitre, *Jesus and the Last Supper*, 125; Bartholomew, *Where Mortals Dwell*, 61. For parallel use, see Exod. 33:11, 20, 23.

13. Pitre, *Jesus and the Last Supper*, 125.

14. Pitre, *Jesus and the Last Supper*, 125.

presence. Therefore, the bread served as symbol and sacrifice—a memorial of divine-human fellowship and a bloodless sacrifice offered on behalf of the twelve tribes of Israel.[15]

According to Gane, the bread ceremonies of Israel were distinct from those of the surrounding cultures. Unlike the belief systems of the surrounding nations, Israel's deemphasized the anthropomorphism of YHWH. While libation vessels were present, drink offerings were not a part of the bread-of-the-Presence ritual. This lack of drink offering contrasts with Mesopotamian rituals, where "food was placed in front of the image, which was apparently assumed to consume it by merely looking at it, and beverages were poured out before it for the same purpose."[16] The assumption was that the gods required daily food and drink, which their human subjects loyally provided. However, in the bread-of-the-presence ceremony, the priests would not place the bread on the altar, since YHWH only received the incense.[17] The lack of consumption by the deity was significant, since the bread's sole consumers were the priests, the ministers of God's presence. They need food. YHWH does not.

Within the extensive worship practices of Israel, this is the only object referred to as "of the Presence." Further, Gane notes that the bread is the only human food offered within the tent (180). The word for "presence" (*panim*) referred to the actual location of "the divine presence residing above the ark behind the *pārōket*-veil" (180). The emphasis is not on the bread but on the proximity of the bread to the actual presence of YHWH, so that this special bread "belongs to the inner, more intimate sphere of the theocentric cult" (182). So important was this bread that it was the sole offering that would have been moved with the rest of the tabernacle when Israel broke camp (199). Both Morales and Wenham remark on the relation of the bread to the lampstand in that the lampstand's light intentionally shone forth onto the twelve loaves of bread, which represented the twelve tribes of Israel (Exod. 13:21–22; Lev. 24:5–9).[18] This light and fire symbolized God's life-giving personal presence and blessing, which is why Aaron would adjust the lamps to shine on the showbread.

Consequently, "this arrangement portrayed visually God's intention that his people should live continually in his presence and enjoy the blessing mediated by his priests," and thus God's presence is linked with God's mediated

---

15. Pitre, *Jesus and the Last Supper*, 127–28.
16. Oppenheim, *Ancient Mesopotamia*, 190–92, quoted in Gane, "'Bread of the Presence,'" 190.
17. Gane, "'Bread of the Presence,'" 196–97. The next several citations are in the text.
18. Morales, *Who Shall Ascend*, 16; Wenham, *Numbers*, 106–7.

blessing.[19] The Creator-Israel relation is thus highly personal, and it makes sense that this offering is the only one designated an *eternal* covenant (Lev. 24:8).[20] As such, this ritual uniquely symbolized "the relationship itself between YHWH and his people, not serving merely as an instrument of that relationship."[21] The twelve loaves support this covenantal symbolism, as the priests represent Israel as the responding party in this covenant.[22]

While this ceremony communicated the special covenant relationship with Israel, it also signified the special relationship between the people in whose midst YHWH dwells.[23] Unlike the daily offerings outside the tent, this bread was only arranged once a week, on the Sabbath. The weekly, Sabbath-day observance linked this ceremony with creation.[24] Since the first instance of the Sabbath rest was believed to have occurred at creation, and thus in a temple space, the association of Eden and Sabbath is important for Israel even after the garden is inaccessible. Sabbath consistently serves as a distinctive marker of time for Israel, so that even the account of Genesis 2:1–3 underscores the uniqueness of humanity's participation in God's rest, and, by implication, in God's presence. Bartholomew makes this explicit: "Polemically 2:1–3 establishes a calendar contrary to the Mesopotamian practice of a Sabbath related to the day of the full moon. The Israelite calendar is connected not to heavenly bodies but directly to the creator God. In contrast to the Akkadian and Ugaritic narratives, in which the god's rest is achieved at the expense of humankind, who were created to relieve the gods of manual labor, the Genesis account of creation represents humans as intended to participate in God's rest."[25] Consequently, the bread represented "the concept that YHWH is Israel's resident Creator-Provider who, unlike other ancient Near-Eastern deities, acknowledges no dependence upon human food."[26] YHWH is self-sufficient and self-sustaining. Therefore, even the concept of rest is human-conditioned. An all-sufficient God does not need to rest, just like an all-sufficient God does not need to eat or drink. However, in order to bless humanity, YHWH offers both food and rest to those entering the divine presence. By contrast, other gods required provision for their needs, including drink offerings. The lack of explicit libation rituals accompanying

19. Morales, *Who Shall Ascend*, 16 (emphasis omitted).
20. Gane, "'Bread of the Presence,'" 192.
21. Gane, "'Bread of the Presence,'" 192. Gane footnotes, by way of contrast, the bulls of Exod. 24:5, which are examples of a covenant instrument.
22. Gane, "'Bread of the Presence,'" 193.
23. Gane, "'Bread of the Presence,'" 194.
24. Gane, "'Bread of the Presence,'" 202.
25. Bartholomew, *Where Mortals Dwell*, 14.
26. Gane, "'Bread of the Presence,'" 179.

the bread ritual further supports Gane's assertion that this cultic practice of Israel was distinctive.[27]

The bread from heaven, the words of God as greater than bread, and the bread of the Presence all connect with YHWH's presence in some way. Those who fellowship with YHWH and obey YHWH's commands will be provided for and flourish. From the power of God's personal provision during Israel's wanderings to provision of the covenant that would enable God to dwell among Israel, to the symbol of this covenant as a welcome into fellowship with God's presence, bread is used as a powerful indicator of the significance of God's personal presence for Israel.

Water

Similar to the need for food (indicated by bread) is the need for water. Just as bread was associated with God's presence to Israel, water imagery is also highly significant in Israel's history as it relates to God's presence. Stephen Um's extensive monograph *The Theme of Temple Christology in John's Gospel* focuses primarily on water imagery in both the Hebrew Bible and the New Testament to make his argument concerning John's Gospel. Given his close reading of this metaphor, he confidently asserts that the water metaphor indicated the Spirit in the Hebrew Bible.[28] He goes on to illustrate the significance of this image across both testaments. Water is fundamentally necessary to survival and flourishing and points to the necessity of divine presence in the human life.

Regarding the life-giving associations with water, Um observes that "the river which flowed out of Eden clearly suggests that the water was the source of life among the plants in the garden. Yet, this physical life parallels the spiritual life in the garden before the presence of God (3:8)."[29] God's presence is intrinsically life-giving for the whole person, and water is the best means of communicating this point. He argues later that "whether literally, metaphorically, or symbolically, water conveys ideas of refreshment and power, hence God was understood to be the 'fountain of living waters' (Jer. 2:13)."[30] The

27. Perhaps Gane and Pitre can find common ground here in that the libation rituals are, at most, implicit. Whether they were drunk (Pitre) or not (Gane), they are not emphasized like they would have been in other ancient Near Eastern contexts.

28. Cf. Isa. 32:2, 15; 44:3; Ezek. 36:25; Um, *Theme of Temple Christology*, 166.

29. Um, *Theme of Temple Christology*, 27. McDowell also associates water with the divine presence in that the garden has astonishing lushness and fertility, and its abundant supply of water suggests both divine blessing and divine presence." McDowell, *Image of God*, 38.

30. Um, *Theme of Temple Christology*, 50.

"fountain" communicates the abundance of this water while the modifier "living" emphasizes its dynamism. Both words are descriptively rich when it comes to being in a second-personal relation to YHWH. This is not a trickling and stagnant relationship but an abundant and dynamic relationship. We also see that "a 'river of life' flowing from the throne of God ('the holy place of the tabernacle of the Most High,' Ps. 46:6b) in the end-time temple (Ezek. 47:1–12), signified to the Israelite community that water was a source of abundant life."[31] Again, that God is life-giving, as represented by water, is enunciated by abundance and overflow. Dripping water does not represent the divine presence, but a river of life does. It is reasonable to pair water and God's presence together, given that the places where this water freely flows are also places of God's personal presence. God's presence is life-giving and enables the flourishing of humankind.

The strength of this association is reinforced by the way water and divine presence are said to pertain to God's sanctuary. As Um observes in Ezekiel, "The stream of water, which started as a trickle, was flowing down from the very presence of God."[32] Since water connoted a source of life, especially given the desert context of much of Israel's history, the thought that the sanctuary of God's presence would also be a source of life and blessing comes out pervasively in Psalm 65:10; Isaiah 33:21; Ezekiel 47:1–12; Joel 3:18; and Zechariah 14:8.[33] In Ezekiel 47:1–12, we see a reminiscence of Genesis 1 wherein there is new creation, a paradise on earth "perpetually nourished out of Zion."[34] The trees produce fruit every month, revealing the abundance that is associated with God's presence.

Though imaged through a tree and its fruitfulness, the water in Psalm 1:3 and Jeremiah 17:7–8 is also implicitly significant. The tree's reliance on the water determines its fruitfulness. Jeremiah connects this explicitly with trust in the Lord: "Blessed are those who trust in the LORD, whose trust is the LORD. They shall be like a tree planted by water, sending out its roots by the stream. It shall not fear when heat comes; and its leaves shall stay green; in the year of drought it is not anxious, and it does not cease to bear fruit." We see that water is a "potent metaphor for the Spirit," and those relying on it not only survive but also flourish.[35]

From the garden temple of Israel's origin story through to the end of the Hebrew Bible, God is the giver of life due to humanity's reliance on God's

---

31. Um, *Theme of Temple Christology*, 55.
32. Um, *Theme of Temple Christology*, 148.
33. Um, *Theme of Temple Christology*, 150.
34. Ryken, Wilhoit, and Longman, *Dictionary of Biblical Imagery*, 930.
35. Ryken, Wilhoit, and Longman, *Dictionary of Biblical Imagery*, 806.

personal presence. Thus, Um can assert, "This source of life in early Jewish traditions, both biblical and post-biblical, is usually associated with God (e.g., Jer. 2:13) who is the giver of life (cf. Ps. 36:10; 65:10), but the Temple, which symbolizes his divine presence, is also viewed as the source of eschatological life."[36] The life-giving presence of God is, therefore, meant to be tasted now but is also the hope of the eschaton.

The symbols of the bread and water depict the reality of life-giving abundance. At the same time, the contexts of tabernacle and temple are the geographical places for the experience of this reality. Thus, the special relationship with God in these sacred spaces is central to Israel's narrative as a people—those in the family of God.

Israel's Sonship

Israel's identity as the people of God stems from their self-understanding as God's son. We have already seen this to some extent in chapter 4 in the discussion of Catherine McDowell's work, but this becomes more explicit later in the text. As God's son, this identity entailed a specific vocation that was bound to God's presence. In her significant work on adoption, Erin Heim traces this theme of sonship through the New Testament while recognizing the importance of understanding Israel's relationship to YHWH in the Hebrew Bible. She states that "in the Old Testament, sonship is a model most often employed to express Israel's particular relationship to YHWH."[37] This filial bond is a relationship extended by God's gracious gift, not based on Israel's merit or righteousness.[38] YHWH calls Israel "my son" in Exodus 4:22–23; Isaiah 43:6; and Hosea 11:1, and YHWH is called Israel's father in Isaiah 63:16; Jeremiah 3:4, 19.[39] As God's son, Israel enters into the blessings of YHWH—for instance, as YHWH is the owner of the land (Deut. 10:14; Ps. 24:1) and gives the land of Canaan, a land flowing with milk and honey, to Israel as Israel's inheritance.[40]

As a people especially related to God, like sons, they can enter into their Father's presence. They are meant to keep the covenant as God's children, thereby being people of the presence for their benefit and the sake of the

36. Um, *Theme of Temple Christology*, 162–63.

37. E.g., Exod. 4:22; Deut. 8:5; 2 Sam. 7:14; Ps. 2:7; 14:1; Prov. 3:11–12; Isa. 43:6–7; Jer. 31:9; Hos. 2:1 (Masoretic Text); Mal. 3:17. Heim, "In Him and through Him," 132.

38. As seen in earlier chapters, such a filial bond can also be seen in the use of image-of-God language.

39. Ryken, Wilhoit, and Longman, *Dictionary of Biblical Imagery*, 806.

40. Ryken, Wilhoit, and Longman, *Dictionary of Biblical Imagery*, 806.

nations (Exod. 19:6). Sonship and covenant intertwine. Macaskill brings these concepts together explicitly, relating the "concept of 'adoption' to covenant: chosen by Yahweh, Israel becomes God's son (Ex 4:22–3)."[41] As children of this covenant, they enjoy a special means of access to the personal presence of God. Although God's ongoing work outside of Israel and the temple cult is evident, the provision of the temple and priesthood communicated a special intention to relate personally to Israel as a people set apart. However, the reason they were set apart was always so that they would fulfill the Abrahamic covenant, wherein God would bless all nations through Israel (Gen. 12:3).

Although God intends for Israel to relate to God's personal presence themselves and function as bringers of God's presence into the rest of the world, they struggle to fulfill this vocation. For this reason, it is vital that we return to our discussion of the person of Jesus, since he is the true representation of Israel and of humanity. As such, he is, himself, the personal divine presence, the true Temple, the Bread of Life, the Fountain of Living Water, and the Son by nature, not adoption.

CONCLUSION

While the tabernacle and temple were explicitly places wherein God's personal presence would dwell, the metaphors of bread and water and the language of sonship are not as clearly associated with the divine presence. The use of bread and water in Israel's history is closely related to what is needed continually for sustenance. Both elements are life-giving in the same way that being in God's presence is life-giving. This fellowshipping presence goes beyond the vivifying presence of God, as seen in the banquet with the bread of the Presence and the gushing fountain of waters, wherein there is abundance and consequential human flourishing. Thus, these terms are associated with flourishing and not merely existence or survival. The sonship of Israel is a special designation for those with whom God chooses to dwell personally. Unlike other nations, with whom God is still at work generally, Israel is the chosen people, through whom God chooses to bless the entire world. The way these terms of bread, water, and sonship function in the Hebrew Scriptures sets a precedent for their later use in the New Testament, reinforcing the centrality of the personal divine presence, on which all of humanity was intended to depend for our flourishing.

---

41. Macaskill, *Union with Christ*, 104–5.

SIX

Divine Presence in Jesus

The New Significance of Temple, Bread, Water, and Firstborn

Since Jesus is the fulfillment of all these metaphors, his need for a second-personal relation to God may look different from what it looks like for the rest of humanity—especially since he *is* the divine presence. However, since he is also fully human, *that* he needs God's personal presence remains true but will need to be examined.[1] After all, if Jesus is the truest expression of what it means to be a flourishing human, and if humans are intended to become like Jesus, then how we understand his need for God's personal presence is of paramount importance. Further, we can reason by abduction that if God intends for humans to rely on God's own presence to meet this fundamental need for God's second-personal presence, then the incarnate Son's humanity would align with that divine intention. Thus, if Jesus depended on the Spirit, this should strengthen the case that a second-personal relation to God is a fundamental human need. Yet, at the same time, he is human sui generis since he is also the very embodiment of divine presence—and in this way, he *cannot* be the *telos* of humanity.[2] In other words, before arguing for fundamental

---

1. We will do this in a theological key in chap. 8.

2. This warning against understanding Jesus's Spirit endowment as the same as his disciples' reception postresurrection comes across strongly in Max Turner's work. The reason the two are not the same, as Turner points out, is that Jesus is the one and only Messiah, and those who are his disciples are not. *Power from on High*, 430.

need, we must justify the continuity of divine presence for Jesus while also recognizing the distinctiveness of Jesus's being in relation to this divine presence (while also being the divine presence, himself).[3] Finally, humanity's access to the kind of dependence relation we see *in* Jesus also *requires* Jesus, since he is the one who gives the Spirit.[4]

Spirit Dependence in the Life of Jesus

Max Turner's work, *Power from on High: The Spirit in Israel's Restoration and Witness in Luke-Acts*, seeks to articulate a Lukan understanding of Jesus's Spirit empowerment. Turner's primary interlocutors are James Dunn and Robert Menzies, with Dunn advocating a relation of identity between Jesus's reception of the Spirit at his baptism and the believers' reception of the Spirit at Pentecost, and Menzies arguing that the Spirit Jesus received was exclusively a Spirit of prophecy.[5] Instead, Turner argues that the Spirit likely remained with Jesus from his birth onward. Thus, the Spirit anointing at the Jordan River focuses on his unique ministry as the one and only Messiah.

Mark Strauss, largely agreeing with Turner's work, argues in support of Jesus's dependence on the Holy Spirit. First, he argues for the intertextuality of Isaiah 11 in that "there is certainly a great deal of biblical evidence that Jesus acted in full dependence on the Holy Spirit." He supports this claim by referring to the text itself: "Isaiah 11:1–4 presents the coming messianic king as one who will live a life of complete dependence on God. He will not 'judge . . . with his eyes' or 'decide . . . with his ears.'"[6] Instead, this Messiah will trust in God for insight. Strauss acknowledges that "though Isaiah 11 is not cited explicitly in the Gospels, it provides the conceptual backdrop to Jesus' dependence on the Spirit."[7] Specifically, Luke's description of Mary's annunciation introduces Jesus as the messianic king, conceived by the Spirit, and establishes a unique relationship between the Father and Son (Luke 1:32–35). Next, the temple scene with young Jesus acknowledges an intimate

---

3. Thus, this chapter is pressing on the *extent* to which Jesus is the prototypical human, which has been raised as a concern for any Christocentric theological anthropology. See Cortez, "Madness in our Method," 20.

4. Since Jesus seems to retain his humanity even in glory, he would seem to continue to depend on the Spirit, though now without keeping latent any of his divinity. See Moffitt, "It Is Not Finished."

5. M. Turner, "Jesus and the Spirit in Lucan Perspective," 36; Turner, *Power from on High*, 209.

6. Strauss, "Jesus and the Spirit," 276.

7. Strauss, "Jesus and the Spirit," 276.

relationship with his Father. Two statements follow this scene regarding his growth in wisdom and grace with both God and other human beings (2:40, 52).[8] This context supports the idea that the Jewish expectation would have been that the Messiah would be especially wise because this wisdom came from dependence on the divine.

Second, Strauss argues that Jesus's reliance on the Spirit is evident at his baptism. In Luke's Gospel, "the divine voice from heaven alludes to Psalm 2:7 ('you are my son')—a royal Davidic psalm—and Isaiah 42:1 ('in whom I delight')." After these explicit allusions, the implicit allusions are then merged with "imagery related to the Spirit-endowed messianic king (cf. Isa. 11:1–4) and the Servant of the Lord (Isa. 42:1)."[9] By pairing these together, Luke makes explicit the coming down of the Spirit and Jesus's anointing as the Messiah.[10] We then see Jesus returning from the Jordan full of the Spirit, being led by the Spirit into the wilderness, returning to Galilee in the power of the Spirit, and reading from Isaiah 61, "The Spirit of the Lord has anointed me." He then goes on to do the things the Messiah of the Spirit would do: preach, heal, and set people free.[11]

Third, a part of this messianic anointing is ruling over the powers of darkness, which Jesus claims to do by the power of the Spirit (Matt. 12:28). Later, Luke's commentary on Jesus's actions indicates that "the power of the Lord was with him to heal" (Luke 5:17) (277). Thus, Strauss concludes, "Jesus heals not in his own power, but by virtue of the power of God at work within him."[12] Fourth, the apostles remember and preach that Jesus relied on the Spirit during his time on earth (Acts 10:37–38). Fifth, Jesus admits that his knowledge is limited on earth, implying that the Spirit mediated supernatural knowledge he possessed (Matt. 24:36; Mark 13:32). Sixth, Jesus explicitly submits to the will of the Father. John's Gospel especially indicates that Jesus's revelatory wisdom and power come from the Spirit, who is given in fullness to Jesus by the Father.

Finally, in addition to Strauss's reasons, Turner includes a seventh reason for supporting Jesus's Spirit dependence by contrasting Jesus and John the Baptist. While Luke is silent about the Spirit's activity until 3:21–22, he implies the Spirit's action in Jesus from his conception onward, because John the Baptist's knowledge of God and his wisdom are attributed to the Spirit, and it would be unlikely that the Spirit would play a lesser role in Jesus's life

8. Strauss, "Jesus and the Spirit," 276.
9. Strauss, "Jesus and the Spirit," 277–79. All six reasons are Strauss's and are summarized here.
10. Strauss, "Jesus and the Spirit," 276.
11. Strauss, "Jesus and the Spirit," 277.
12. Strauss, "Jesus and the Spirit," 277.

than he does in John's.[13] Further, "the 'fit' with the messianic portraits drawn from Isaiah 11:1–4 would encourage such an assumption."[14] None of these reasons denies Jesus's full divinity, but they support Jesus's full humanity and a willingness to depend on the Spirit. When we read the Gospels, we do not get a picture of Jesus being self-reliant, as if being fully divine negated his need to rely on the Spirit. Instead, we see an ongoing personal relationship of dependence between Jesus and God. He intentionally withdraws to pray to his Father, is led by the Spirit, and is empowered by the Spirit.[15]

While both Turner's and Strauss's reasons support Jesus's dependence on the Spirit, Jesus's uniqueness also helps establish how his disciples might have related to God's presence in an intimate way after Jesus's resurrection. Turner again brings his insight to bear regarding Isaiah 49:24–25, noting that "if the original passage refers to Yahweh's direct action, here it is performed by Jesus as God's agent, the messianic Son/servant empowered by his Spirit."[16] Therefore, a first-century Jewish audience hearing Luke 1–2 could understand "Jesus as the anticipated messiah of the Spirit."[17] While Jesus seems to depend on the Holy Spirit in his own life, the uniqueness of his dependence because of his sonship is critical for his later bestowal of the Holy Spirit into believers after his resurrection. Such an action is only possible because Jesus is the embodiment of the presence of the God of Israel in human form.[18] As Turner comments, "The key transitional passages (Luke 24:47–49 and Acts 1:1–8) mention only one power that Jesus will give from the Father that could possibly be expected to continue the saving/transforming momentum of Jesus' ministry, and that is the Holy Spirit."[19] So, while Jesus depends on the Spirit, he is also the giver of the Spirit due to his uniqueness.[20] Jesus's dissimilarity to humanity is significant, mainly because God's personal presence is now also localized in a person. But his unique status of being the divine presence does not negate Jesus's seeming dependence on the Spirit.

13. M. Turner, *Power from on High*, 161.
14. M. Turner, *Power from on High*, 161.
15. The Spirit does not constitute Jesus's divinity, contra some Spirit Christologies. This will be addressed in more detail, theologically, in chap. 8.
16. M. Turner, *Power from on High*, 208.
17. M. Turner, *Power from on High*, 428.
18. That Jesus is the divine presence will be explored in more detail below; however, Bauckham's summation is a suitable placeholder in the meantime: "Jesus, as fully human, enjoys genetic continuity with the whole human race and shares all sorts of features of the common life of humanity. But incarnation is more than that; it is the personal and intentional presence of God. It is God's unique act of loving solidarity with all people. . . . It is the most radical kind of being with." "Incarnation and the Cosmic Christ," 33–34.
19. M. Turner, *Power from on High*, 347.
20. Macaskill, *Union with Christ*, 176–77.

Given the dependence of Jesus on the Spirit during his earthly ministry, and given my argument that Jesus is the true image after which all humanity is patterned, it then follows that human beings are also intended to depend on this Spirit.[21] In other words, if the true image needs the Spirit, so do all human beings. By extension, the Holy Spirit is foundational to understanding the *imago Dei* for Jesus and all humankind. In Jesus's case, he not only needed the Spirit in order to flourish (just as we do), but also he needed the Spirit to instantiate his existence as the God-human (not like we do, because our existence is not constituted by being hypostasized to the second person of the Trinity). We will return to these claims in chapter 8, but the point remains that the Spirit, understood as the second-personal presence of God, is not an "*eschatological addendum*" but is central to what it means to be human.[22]

Jesus as the Divine Presence

Jesus depended on the divine presence, yet simultaneously he was (and is) the personal divine presence.[23] Therefore, several aspects of Jesus, as the Logos Incarnate, do not characterize the rest of humanity. Specifically, he is dissimilar because he embodies the divine presence as communicated through his identifiers as the Bread of Life, the Fountain of Living Water, and the Son by nature, not adoption.[24] However, before turning to those categories, we will be better situated to see Jesus as the bread, water, and firstborn Son by nature if we first see how he is the glory of God, the new temple, and the inaugurator of the new covenant.

Glory, Temple, and New Covenant

In addressing glory as it pertains to Jesus, we will find a brief treatment of Adam Christology helpful here. This view holds that Second Temple Jews

21. A similar line of reasoning can be found in Cortez, "Idols, Images, and a Spirit-ed Anthropology," 267.

22. This is a concern raised by Cortez regarding the significance of the Spirit for anthropology. "Idols, Images, and a Spirit-ed Anthropology," 269–70 (emphasis original).

23. Pulling specifically from Phil. 2, "a number of interpreters have defined the meaning of the form of God by referring to numerous references in the OT that indicate that the glory of God is the outward appearance of the presence and majesty of God." Hansen, *Letter to the Philippians*, 136–37.

24. While many more descriptors could be given of Jesus, those chosen here are those that span the entire biblical drama and are also applied to Israel and the church. Further, while king and priest are significant, they have already been addressed in chap. 2 and are also not metaphors but literal vocations endowed to humanity.

believed the eschatological *telos* of humanity was a restoration of what Adam had before sin—some type of glory or splendor. Dunn reads this as the context of several New Testament texts, but Macaskill and Bauckham question the plausibility of this reading.[25] Specifically, Macaskill notes the consistency with which glory is seen as a "property of God, shared with or given to human beings in the divine presence, and is not considered to be an innate property of human beings."[26] Also, that the Hebrew Bible most typically associates glory with the temple and with God's presence does not strengthen Dunn's view.[27] Another critique regards how Second Temple Jews understood the image of God, which was not seen as lost because of sin. Thus, to think that "a glory lost to Adam through sin [was] recovered by faithful believers is problematic."[28] Finally, if glory language in the New Testament is tied more to restoring what Adam lost than to gaining divine glory, then the focus becomes about restoring something intrinsic to humans instead of focusing on the divine glory as the gift of God's presence. Since nowhere does the text indicate an intrinsic glory of humanity, but only a reflected glory of God, such a reading does not seem likely.

Instead, what seems to be more prevalent in relation to Adam is death, not glory. Macaskill makes this argument, especially concerning 1 Corinthians 15. He argues that Paul uses Adam, the human of dust, and Christ, the human of heaven, to contrast death and life. Further, Adam's lost glory is nowhere to be found, although the resurrected body is glorious (1 Cor. 15:42–43).[29] The prominent contrast "portrays Adam and Christ as belonging to different realities. What is specifically transmitted by Adam is death; the glory that comes from Christ is a heavenly gift."[30] This glory is alien to humanity but gifted to it by God's graciousness.

25. Dunn, *Theology of Paul the Apostle*, 79–101, 281–92, 390–412; Dunn, *Christology in the Making*, 98–128; Macaskill, *Union with Christ*, 29, 128, 132–33, 139, 143, 197; Bauckham, *Jesus and the God of Israel*, 41, 203–7.

26. Macaskill, *Union with Christ*, 128.

27. Regarding the sources Dunn consults for his Adam Christology, Macaskill responds: "Such an idea is widespread in the rabbinic texts, though here the traditions are diverse and often contradictory: some depict Adam as inherently glorious, others depict the first couple as clothed with glorious robes lost through their sin and others present such garments as given by God at the expulsion from Eden in Genesis 3:21. We should not too quickly conflate these various strands: a glorious Adam is not the same as a gloriously garbed Adam. . . . To phrase this differently: it is not that an Adam myth influences and affects the way in which symbols of Jewish faith and piety are construed, but rather that these symbols or motifs govern the way in which Adam is described. If any of these texts do embody traditions that go back to the Second Temple period, then they suggest that the presentation of Adam may not drive but rather be driven by more central motifs of glory." *Union with Christ*, 133.

28. Macaskill, *Union with Christ*, 139.

29. Macaskill, *Union with Christ*, 247.

30. Macaskill, *Union with Christ*, 247.

Jesus's identity as the embodiment of the personal divine presence gains support from how glory is associated with him. As mentioned above, glory made visible God's invisible presence. Jesus is now the visible manifestation of God's presence, an idea that John's Gospel makes clear. According to Um and Raymond Brown: "*Shekinah* is a technical term in rabbinic theology for God's presence dwelling among his people, and the prologue reflects 'the idea that Jesus is now the *shekinah* of God.'"[31] Further, this new expression of God's presence brought about access to a new reality for those who trust in Jesus—who is the glory of God: "What was impossible for Moses, seeing the radiant glory of God (Exod. 33:20), has become possible for those who believe (John 1:14, 'we have seen his glory') since the Word incarnate has seen God (John 1:18; 3:11)."[32]

Returning to the Hebrew Bible's backdrop, the association of glory with presence reveals the contingent nature of glory and that glory is never intrinsic to the human person unless that human is the God-man. Glory is a "reflection of divine presence," which finds a stark contrast in the New Testament, where "the glory of Jesus is presented as essential to his identity."[33] Yet he needed to depend on the Spirit in his daily life just as we do. Such an understanding of Jesus also connects to him being the true image of God, which the author of Hebrews makes explicit. There, the author says that the Son comes as the "'effulgence of God's glory' (ὃς ὢν ἀπαύγασμα τῆς δόξης [*hos ōn apaugasma tēs doxēs*])," thereby identifying him "with the kavod itself, the divine presence in visible form, and hence the 'exact representation of his being' (χαρακτὴρ τῆς ὑποστάσεως [*charakter tēs hypostaseōs*])."[34] Macaskill elaborates on Jesus's embodiment of glory as the true "image" in 2 Corinthians 3:18: "The significance of εἰκών [*eikōn*] is to emphasize the place of Christ as covenant mediator in a capacity that could never be realized by Moses: not as the one who reflects glory, but as the one who embodies it."[35] Such a view reinforces my conclusions in chapter 3, that Jesus is the prototypical human after whom all humanity is patterned. Any glory humanity has is a reflection of the glory Jesus has in himself. As derivative images, humanity has a derivative glory.

---

31. Um, *Theme of Temple Christology*, 154, quoting from R. Brown, *Gospel according to John I–XII*, 33.

32. Um, *Theme of Temple Christology*, 154. Um finds support for this view from Koester, *Dwelling of God*, 102–6. Terrien, also commenting on John's prologue, states, "The presence of the encamped Logos was necessarily elusive, but it engendered a new mode of communion between God and man." *Elusive Presence*, 421.

33. Macaskill, *Union with Christ*, 124.

34. Macaskill, *Union with Christ*, 180.

35. Macaskill, *Union with Christ*, 232.

Furthermore, John's Gospel connects Jesus with the tabernacle most explicitly in the opening prologue. Um elaborates that the tabernacle was "the site of God's localized presence on earth" and that Jesus is the new living reality of God's presence on earth.[36] The tabernacle was the place where God's presence resided on earth, and Jesus is the incarnation of that presence. Moreover, the tabernacle was also the place where God's people kept the covenant. Now that there is a new tabernacle of the incarnate Son, there also comes a new covenant. Jesus makes this explicit at the Last Supper as he drinks the wine, as reported in Luke's Gospel and built on by Paul in 1 Corinthians, saying, "This cup . . . is the new covenant in my blood" (Luke 22:20; 1 Cor. 11:25). The author of Hebrews also details the institution of this new covenant and states that it required a new priesthood, replacing the old covenant (Heb. 8:13; 9:15; 12:24). Hebrews may lack the association of Jesus as the new temple; what the author "does have, however, is a thoroughgoing concept of access to the divine presence in the heavenly temple that is grounded in the ontology and history of the incarnate Son, the heavenly High Priest."[37] If we combine these themes, Jesus is the new temple, the new high priest, and the inaugurator of the new covenant.

Consequently, the access to the divine presence is greater under the new covenant than it was under the old, since "the earthly tabernacle and temple are specifically portrayed as patterned after the heavenly (8:1–5), reflecting the lesser access to God's presence made possible by the first covenant. In 8:7–13, the author cites Jeremiah 31:31–4 as warrant for speaking of the new covenant."[38] Jesus is the hinge of the entire canon, connecting divine intention for all those made in his image and all creation.

As the true high priest and the embodiment of God's glory, Jesus inaugurates a new covenant by which God's presence communes with humanity in a new way. The newness of this communion is communicated through the Hebrew metaphors already discussed, which are now appropriated by the New Testament authors.

Bread

The Gospel of John is rife with metaphorical language with deep Jewish roots. Jesus utilizes these metaphors to both define who he is and redefine messianic expectations. Some of this redefinition comes from his implication

---

36. Um, *Theme of Temple Christology*, 153.
37. Macaskill, *Union with Christ*, 186.
38. Macaskill, *Union with Christ*, 185.

that he is the superior form of these symbols.[39] In John's Gospel, Jesus makes
the superiority of the bread he is offering (which is himself) explicit:

> "Do not work for the food that perishes, but for the food that endures for
> eternal life, which the Son of Man will give you. For it is on him that God the
> Father has set his seal." . . . Then Jesus said to them, "Very truly, I tell you, it
> was not Moses who gave you the bread from heaven, but it is my Father who
> gives you the true bread from heaven. For the bread of God is that which comes
> down from heaven and gives life to the world." They said to him, "Sir, give us
> this bread always." Jesus said to them, "I am the bread of life. Whoever comes
> to me will never be hungry, and whoever believes in me will never be thirsty."
> (John 6:27–35)

Here we see Jesus's explication of the manna given to the Jewish forbears
in the desert, in which he asserts that he is "the true bread from heaven"
(6:32–33). Further, he is a superior bread, since those who eat of this true
bread will not die: "Very truly, I tell you, whoever believes has eternal life. I
am the bread of life. Your ancestors ate the manna in the wilderness, and they
died. This is the bread that comes down from heaven, so that one may eat of
it and not die. I am the living bread that came down from heaven. Whoever
eats of this bread will live forever; and the bread that I will give for the life
of the world is my flesh" (6:47–51). This allusion to bread is also significant
given the Second Temple Jewish literature regarding the role of manna in
Israel's history and regarding the future Messiah.[40] Gary Burge recognizes
this especially against the backdrop of Jewish thought about the original
feeding of the Israelites and the eventual feeding of God's people that would
accompany the Messiah's ministry.[41] However, Jesus communicates the messianic fulfillment in unexpected ways. He is the bread. He is the blessing itself.

We see this same theme in the other Gospels as well. In Matthew 4:4 and
Luke 4:4, Jesus quotes from Deuteronomy 8:3: "One does not live by bread
alone."[42] He practices what he preaches when tempted to turn stones into

---

39. The superiority of Jesus as the bread itself is confirmed by the grammatical analysis
of J. C. Hutchison, in that "predicate nouns as a rule are anarthrous. Nevertheless the article
is inserted if the predicate noun is presented as something well known or as that which alone
merits the designation (the only thing to be considered)." "Vine in John 15," 73.

40. For more detail on Jesus's fulfillment of Israel's cultus in John, especially as it relates
to Israel's feasts and covenants, see Yee, *Jewish Feasts and the Gospel of John*, 59–64 (though
I would not use language of "replacement" in terms of what Jesus is doing with the feasts);
Wright, *Jesus and the Victory of God*.

41. Burge, *John*, 197.

42. In Matthew Jesus continues, "but by every word proceeding from the mouth of God."
According to J. Palmer, Luke presupposes those words. "Bread," 84.

bread to satisfy his physical hunger. Jennings insightfully narrates Satan's temptation of Jesus to turn stones into bread: "Every people, every nation wants to be self-sufficient, to feed its own, to turn its stones into bread. And Jesus was told to enter this self-sufficiency, to allow the urgency of need to determine his course of action, his obedience. . . . His response, however, builds from the central truth of Israel in the land. They are not sustained simply in the face of any urgency by the land but by the words of God."[43] Jesus reveals that there is more to life than only physical survival: "Life is more than food (Matt. 6:25 par. Luke 12:23). Alternatively, by using bread as a symbol for what sustains spiritual/eternal life, a similar point is made (John 6:27)."[44] At the same time, we still see Jesus exhorting prayer for daily bread. The need for the Bread of Life does not negate the need for daily bread. However, it does reprioritize it.

Jesus draws not only on the bread-from-heaven imagery but also the bread-of-the-Presence imagery. Pitre points out that Jesus connects the ritual of the bread of the Presence with an understanding of this as a sign of the new covenant. Given the multiple parallels, Pitre argues:

> Just as the bread of the presence was connected to the twelve tribes of Israel, so Jesus celebrates the Last Supper with the twelve disciples, symbolizing the nucleus of eschatological Israel. And just as the bread of the presence was offered with wine as a sign of the "everlasting covenant," so too Jesus couples his offering of bread with the wine that he ties to the establishment of the new "covenant," spoken of by the prophets. And just as the bread of the presence was an unbloody sacrifice offered as a "remembrance" of the covenant at Sinai, so too Jesus commands the twelve to offer this bread—which he identifies as his body—as a "remembrance" of the sacrifice of his own flesh, which will be given in order to establish the new covenant.[45]

The strength of Pitre's argument comes from the parallel language, which convincingly associates the Jewish ritual of the bread of the Presence with what would become a new Christian ritual of the Eucharist.[46]

---

43. Jennings, *Christian Imagination*, 260.

44. Palmer, "Bread," 84–85.

45. Pitre, *Jesus and the Last Supper*, 129.

46. This reading does not negate the significance of the Passover meal but highlights the overlap of the bread-of-the-Presence ritual with the Last Supper. For other engagements with the Lord's Supper as a unique way in which God is personally present to us, see Stubbs and Witvliet, *Table and Temple*; Arcadi, *Incarnational Model of the Eucharist*. For a strongly symbolic perspective that still recognizes the significance of this presence in Holy Communion, see the first volume of Tom Greggs's *Dogmatic Ecclesiology*, 202–45.

Water

Just as the metaphor of bread is applied to Jesus, so too is the metaphor of water. In John's Gospel, Jesus's references to living water are best understood in relation to Israel's eschatological temple imagery and the divine presence. Macaskill, in his reflection on Jesus's call to worship in spirit and in truth, observes, "Whether or not 'in spirit' is immediately a reference to the Holy Spirit, or to the subjective participation of the human spirit in worship, the fellowship of the human with the divine presence requires the indwelling presence of the Fount of Living Water."[47] This fellowship is only possible through a relationship with Jesus Christ, since he is the only one who can offer access to this presence. Such ideas are especially clear from the story of the woman at the well (John 4). Um explains that "the Samaritan woman understood the expression to mean fresh, running water, but Jesus offered her more, eschatological life mediated by the Spirit."[48] While the water represented the very presence of God, Jesus can give this presence, himself: "Jesus said to her, 'Everyone who drinks of this water will be thirsty again, but those who drink of the water that I will give them will never be thirsty. The water that I will give will become in them a spring of water gushing up to eternal life'" (John 4:13–15). Jesus reiterates this message when he is back in Jerusalem:

> On the last day of the festival, the great day, while Jesus was standing there, he cried out, "Let anyone who is thirsty come to me, and let the one who believes in me drink. As the scripture has said, 'Out of the believer's heart shall flow rivers of living water.'" Now he said this about the Spirit, which believers in him were to receive; for as yet there was no Spirit, because Jesus was not yet glorified. (John 7:37–39)

According to Um, Jesus can offer this because he "is the new Temple from which the living waters flow."[49] While not explicitly connected with water, John 10:10b encapsulates who Jesus is and what he has come to do: "I came that they may have life, and have it abundantly." George Beasley-Murray notes that this verse expresses the message of this Gospel: "Jesus has come that all in the world may have life in its fullest sense—the eternal life of the kingdom of God."[50] The identification of Jesus as the embodiment of the personal divine presence, the temple, is closely related to the life-giving water that flows

---

47. Macaskill, *Union with Christ*, 177.
48. Um, *Theme of Temple Christology*, 161.
49. Cf. John 1:14; 2:19–21. Um sees this as primarily referencing Ezek. 47:1 and secondarily Zech. 14:8. Um, *Theme of Temple Christology*, 157, 162–63.
50. Beasley-Murray, *John*, 171.

from the eschatological temple in Israel's narrative (Ezek. 47). Yet the fact that he is and does all of these things proceeds from his unique relationship to YHWH, and this brings us to Jesus's sonship by nature.

Son by Nature

Not only is Jesus the divine presence, the glory of God embodied, but he is also the means by which humanity might be adopted as permanent sons of God.[51] Erin Heim examines one of the quintessential adoption passages of Romans 8 and highlights how it emphasizes Jesus's uniqueness as a human being while also upholding his full continuity with humanity. Paul's unwillingness to use the term "firstborn" for anyone besides Christ reveals this uniqueness. Jesus is a son by nature, whereas the rest of God's children are adopted based on God's loving-kindness.[52] Furthermore, the cultural practice of adoption eschewed the adoption of more than one son, since this would lessen the firstborn's inheritance. Counterculturally, "the Father is willingly extending the inheritance to any son who possesses the Spirit of adoption, while the passage simultaneously affirms and upholds Christ's status as firstborn."[53] Jesus's unique sonship brings about a kinship relation for those who are part of God's spiritual family.[54]

Macaskill has also recognized the significance of adoption, given his emphasis on union with God. Looking at Galatians 3:27, he observes that the grammar and syntax emphasize the "clothing metaphor depicting the transfer of Christ's identity onto those who are located in him: his appearance becomes theirs. The link between his identity as 'son' (4:4) and the adoption of believers is, therefore, vital."[55] Further, in 1 John, adoption, as Malatesta stresses, is being made perfect and is progressive.[56] The Spirit seals the adoption of believers, but the Son constitutes it.[57] Such adoption is possible because Jesus

51. The language of sonship is significant, especially rhetorically, in Rom. 8. However, this becomes "children" later in that text.

52. "In this passage [8:29], there is a subtle shift here from the metaphor of adoptive kinship predicated of believers (whether Jew or gentile) to a metaphor of biological kinship (*prōtotokos*) predicated of Christ that must be recognized." Heim, "In Him and through Him," 134–35.

53. Heim, "In Him and through Him," 134–35.

54. However, again, "Jesus does not intend the destruction of Israel, only its rebirth in him." Jennings, *Christian Imagination*, 263.

55. Macaskill, *Union with Christ*, 222.

56. See Malatesta, *Interiority and Covenant*, 242–43, regarding 1 John 3:2.

57. Macaskill, *Union with Christ*, 223. This seems supported by Heim's observation: "Ephesians 1:4–5 presents Christ as the locus of adoption. The children of God are chosen 'in him [Christ] before the foundation of the world,' 'destined for adoption,' and the Father lavishes his blessings on his children (1:6–7), chief among them the seal of the Spirit, which is the promise of their future inheritance (1:13–14)." Heim, "In Him and through Him," 136.

is not a Son by grace but is a Son by nature, willingly sharing his inheritance with those adopted into his family.

CONCLUSION

As we have seen, the Hebrew Bible consistently uses the metaphors of bread, water, and sonship to communicate humanity's relationship with the divine presence saliently. Each of these takes on new significance in the New Testament both for Jesus and for those who follow him, strengthening the continuity between the Hebrew Bible and New Testament while also developing the distinctive interiority of divine presence that seems to develop over time.[58] Such an interiority of the divine presence in the life of other human beings is only possible due to Jesus's reliance on God's personal presence. This interiority is contingent on him being, in himself, the embodiment of God's personal presence. Thus, while Jesus is unique in his humanity (as the only human hypostasized to the divine nature of the Second Person of the Trinity), continuity still exists between his humanity and the rest of humanity as it pertains to the relationship with God's presence as Spirit.

These metaphors communicate the centrality of Jesus for understanding God's presence under this new covenant era while also communicating that he is the source of life and flourishing. As Terrien poignantly claims, "At the dawn of the Roman Empire, a handful of Jews hailed from their own ranks a new prophet through whom they discerned a radically new mode of divine nearness. A man became for them the bearer of the presence."[59] Jesus's need to depend on the divine presence in his own life does not negate his full divinity. Instead, he models what a human being is meant to look like by perpetually needing the divine presence in his own life while also providing for our need in himself.

58. Interiority denotes that the divine presence was consistently exterior to the human person, and sometimes interior, but impermanently. However, under the new covenant the divine presence is can be consistently within the human person.

59. Terrien, *Elusive Presence*, 405.

SEVEN

Divine Presence in the New Covenant Community

The Ongoing Significance of Temple, Bread, Water, and Adoption

The temple language and bread and water metaphors extend beyond Christology to the new covenant community that is introduced in the New Testament and described with the language of adoption. This chapter explores the New Testament's expansion of these terms to include anyone with faith in Christ, then returns to Thomson's rubric and the theological benefits of speaking of humanness in terms of fundamental need. We see in the New Testament that a second-personal relation to God now has the dimension of faith in Christ, who is the embodiment of that second-personal presence.

The Spirit in New Covenant Believers

Those who are deemed "in Christ" experience the presence of God in a way that is new but not completely dissimilar to the way those who have believed in YHWH before them have experienced it. Comprehending Paul's view of the Christian life requires understanding his Hebraic view of God's presence.[1]

1. According to Terrien, *Elusive Presence*, 478n18. For an argument that this is made possible because of Jesus, see chap. 6 above (cf. John 1:16).

Consequently, for Paul, the work of God in the special people of Israel continues even as it expands.[2] The temple, bread, water, and adoption concepts all continue to indicate the ongoing significance of God's presence. The temple as a place and water and bread as metaphors also entail a new dimension to this presence—indwelling by God's very Spirit. There is a close relationship between 1 John and John's Gospel, and Malatesta notes that "just as Jesus' own union with the Father was mediated by the gift to Him of the Holy Spirit (see John 1:32–33; 3:34), so too the disciples of Jesus enter into communion with Jesus and the Father only through the mediation of the Spirit."[3] This gracious gift of union requires the Spirit, and the Spirit's coming necessitates a new covenant.

The New Testament records the divine presence transitioning from dwelling with people to dwelling in people. Such indwelling was an anticipated reality, given that the most significant texts of the Hebrew Bible "mention the theme of interior renewal."[4] Specifically, Ezekiel has a promise of a new heart and spirit, and the "composition of Jeremiah 31 (LXX 38), 31–34 highlights three elements of the New Covenant: an interiorization of the Law, knowledge of God, and forgiveness of sins."[5] While whole theologies address the new covenant, the main point here is that the newness of this covenant centers mainly on the innovation of access to the divine presence, which the faithful experience more deeply. This new depth is both christological and pneumatological. Morales states this deepening eloquently: "The result of this outpouring is union with the ascended Christ—that is the goal, and everything else follows from this bond. God's people are raised with Christ and, together with him—in him— form the household of God and the house, the living temple, of God. But also, the Spirit is the taste of—and down payment on—the eschaton, because in a manner of speaking he is the eschaton."[6] The new covenant, building on the old, opens a unique experience of God's presence—God's indwelling presence. This new interior reality of the divine presence, which Malatesta explores in detail in 1 John, would have been discernable from Jeremiah 31 and Ezekiel 36. These texts prophesied a new covenant, including a law written on the heart, a new heart, and God's indwelling Spirit. In light of this interior change, the new covenant institutes a new belonging for the people of God and an increased intimacy of love and faith.[7] Thus, the new covenant inaugurates a new era.

---

2. Jennings, *Christian Imagination*, 252, 256, 259, 260–65.

3. Malatesta, *Interiority and Covenant*, 323.

4. Malatesta, *Interiority and Covenant*, 69. He lists these passages, including a Deuterocanonical text: Deut. 30:1–10; Jer. 24:5–7; 31:31–34; 32:37–41; Ezek. 11:14–21; 16:53–63; 36:22–35; 37:21–28; Bar. 2:29–35.

5. Malatesta, *Interiority and Covenant*, 69–70.

6. Morales, *Who Shall Ascend*, 282. Cf. Vos, "Eschatological Aspect."

7. Malatesta, *Interiority and Covenant*, 23.

This new era is not only inseparable from the personal divine presence but also inseparable from the embodiment of the divine presence—Jesus himself.

Temple, Glory, and Holiness

Jesus is the new temple (John 2:21; cf. 1:14), and his temple identity extends to those united to him by the Spirit. Being united with Jesus includes being indwelt with God's presence as the Spirit. This temple identity now includes the believing community, whose members are both individually and corporately called to be the temple of the Holy Spirit (1 Cor. 3:16–17; 6:19; 2 Cor. 6:16; Eph. 2:21; 1 Pet. 2:5). Ultimately, this temple identity will be consummated in the eschatological garden, when the new heaven and earth are the temple (Rev. 21:22), and God's presence dwells with God's people in its fullness (22:1). Again, we find "temple" acting as the means for communion with the living God. For this reason, Fee says, "God's presence . . . is the crucial matter for Israel's existence (Exod. 33:15–16). God's presence, first in the tabernacle and later in the temple in Jerusalem, distinguishes God's people from all the other peoples on the earth."[8] Now that this living God has revealed the new temple of Jesus Christ, new covenant believers are included as part of this temple through their communion with Jesus and the indwelling of God.[9]

Gordon Fee has studied the role of the Spirit across several of his works, and he recognizes 1 Corinthians 3:16–17 as essential to understanding Paul's view of the believing community as "a people of the Spirit."[10] Like Israel, who could also have this moniker, they are meant to have God in their midst. However, unlike Israel (though still derived from this people), those under the new covenant are intended to have access to a deeper union with the Spirit of God, since the Spirit will permanently dwell *in* them. Thus, "what made them God's alternative [to Corinth's religions and vices], his temple in Corinth, was *his own presence* in and among them!"[11] Fee goes on to make similar observations about 1 Corinthians 6:19–20, observing that the individual believer's body now "houses the presence of the living God by his Spirit."[12] Concerning

---

8. Fee, *Paul, the Spirit, and the People of God*, 114.

9. New covenant participants are recognized as part of the temple as well as being individual temples, depending on the context. The main point of continuity, however, is that no matter the context, they are indwelt by God's presence.

10. Fee, *Paul, the Spirit, and the People of God*, 113. For more on the Spirit from Fee's perspective, see his tome *God's Empowering Presence*. Macaskill also affirms the importance of this text in his own study of the believer's union with Christ while restating the transference of a glory alien to the human person. *Union with Christ*, 156.

11. Fee, *Paul, the Spirit, and the People of God*, 116 (emphasis original).

12. Fee, *Paul, the Spirit, and the People of God*, 136.

2 Corinthians 2:16–17, Fee notes the Spirit's role in establishing people as members of God's family, because the Spirit "is the experienced expression of the divine presence who also creates and guarantees membership in God's family."[13] Thus, some of the metaphors of the divine presence in Israel's history begin to mix into this new creation reality.

Another mixed metaphor occurs in Ephesians 2:19–22 with the recognition of the corporate people of God as a temple—but a temple that is organic and grows. Contextually, this temple imagery pairs with the body metaphor and describes believers' relation to one another and to Christ, the head. The Spirit unifies them and allows them "common access to God's presence."[14] In conjunction with this text, 1 Peter 2:5 seems to be communicating a similar message but differently. Instead of using "temple" language, the author uses the language of "a spiritual house." Most likely, this is "a metaphor for the community where the Spirit of God dwells."[15]

While Jesus is the true tabernacle and temple, he extends this identity to those who follow him as his disciples. Those who do so themselves become a tabernacle of the living God while also becoming the temple of God collectively. Tellingly, those associated with this new dwelling are also given a renewed function as priests (1 Pet. 2:5). The vocation that the man, the woman, and then Israel were given, as bringers of God's presence into the larger world, is now bestowed on all who follow Jesus. This function is reiterated in the symbol of the bread of the Presence now offered to the priesthood of all believers.

Bread

The bread of the Presence and the bread from heaven return to the narrative of those following the one who is the divine presence and the true bread from heaven. Pitre insightfully recognizes the radically new use of bread symbolism, which is simultaneously rooted in ancient Jewish rituals. He asks a provocative question: "Where did Paul ever get the idea that bread could effect 'communion' with a person?"[16] He responds by noting that there is no precedent for this being understood symbolically through the Passover or other Torah sacrifices. Instead, the bread of the Presence is the fertile soil out of which the symbolism of this language grows. As seen in Pitre's arguments above, this bread was intimately associated with the personal presence of God and fellowship in God's presence. The Lord's Supper, wherein the bread of Jesus's body is consumed, is a special

---

13. Fee, *Paul, the Spirit, and the People of God*, 338.
14. Fee, *Paul, the Spirit, and the People of God*, 689.
15. Michaels, *1 Peter*, 100.
16. Pitre, *Jesus and the Last Supper*, 146.

encounter with God's personal presence. It is one way God is present to us. Notably, "the key difference, of course, is that in Jewish Scripture, the so-called showbread signified the presence of God, whereas the bread of the Last Supper signifies the presence of Jesus."[17] To recapitulate Pitre's argument: What was once intended only for the sons of Aaron is now made available to all who are in Christ. This new priesthood is meant to experience God's presence, as the presence of Jesus Christ, through the Spirit. Just as the bread of the Presence in the tabernacle was a symbol of God's desire to be in fellowship with Israel, even to the point of their eating a common meal in God's presence, so Jesus associates his very body with this simple element at the Last Supper.[18]

Regarding the bread from heaven, Jesus is also the one through whom new covenant believers know God and receive the life of God. Macaskill again offers insight on this metaphor:

> The key point of note is that the true bread in John's gospel is identified with the revelation constituted by the personal presence of Jesus: "For the bread of God is the one who comes down (ὁ καταβαίνων [ho katabainōn]) from heaven and gives life to the world" (6:33).
> His presence in the world, emphasized by the participle of descent, is therefore key.[19]

Jesus is the true bread of heaven required for life and sustenance. As recipients of this supernatural bread, new covenant believers are meant to find their spiritual nourishment from this Bread of Life.

Life-Giving Water

Just as Jesus renews our understanding of the bread of life, he also renews our understanding of water as the vitalizing presence of God. Consequently, the significance of baptism connects water, Christ, and the Spirit. In Romans 6, those now in Christ are joined to Jesus in his death and resurrection through the symbol of baptism. This baptism is a sign of their adoption, through the Spirit, a baptism through which they become members of the corporate body of Christ as they pass through these life-giving waters.[20]

The Johannine literature contains the most significant New Testament texts regarding this metaphor, especially John 4:13–14 and 7:37–49. Um argues

---

17. Pitre, *Jesus and the Last Supper*, 146.
18. Beale and Kim, *God Dwells among Us*, 55.
19. Macaskill, *Union with Christ*, 259–60. See also R. Hays, *Reading Backwards*, 93–110. Dewick goes further, to associate this with divine indwelling, specifically. *Indwelling God*, 109.
20. For a much more in-depth look at this practice, see Cuneo, *Ritualized Faith*.

convincingly that the water represents the eschatological Spirit, who is also the new creational life.[21] According to his argument, John 3:5; 4:10–14, 23–24; and 7:38–39 express "that the water-Spirit source is summed up in the person of Jesus Christ, who is the end-time dwelling of God's presence and the giver of eternal life."[22] Consequently, not only does water convey this message, but the person of Jesus Christ, the true temple, is the sole giver of this new life via the Spirit. Thus, Um can say that the new covenant believer's fellowship becomes "more intimate than their former ceremonial Temple worship," since they have God's Spirit dwelling within them.[23]

Morales supports Um's conclusions, recognizing that the "Levitical cult was promissory and prophetic, given to foster a holy thirst for living water and an earnest expectation for the dawning of the day—thirst/water and darkness/light being two of the chief symbols in the Fourth Gospel."[24] He goes on to argue the significant interrelation of the water imagery and the temple language.[25] Since John's first two chapters recognize Jesus "as the reality of the temple, who will pour out the living water, John 3 begins to address the dire need for the Spirit."[26] This point cannot be overstated, given the progression of the interiority of the divine presence seen thus far. For this reason, Morales can claim that the "theology of John's Gospel revolves entirely around this point: Jesus will ascend in order to pour out the Spirit—he is the giver of the Spirit; and he is so *because the Spirit is the essence of life with God*."[27]

Macaskill notes the significance of the "I am" statements in John and observes how John emphasizes that Jesus is unique because he alone has

---

21. Um, *Theme of Temple Christology*, 190.

22. Further, "The outpouring of God's Spirit (Joel 2.28) which was closely associated with water that would be provided (Isa. 44.3; Ezek. 47.1–12; Zech. 14.8) signaled the arrival of the messianic age." Um, *Theme of Temple Christology*, 180. Cf. R. Brown, *The Gospel according to John I–XII*, 140, who says, "If natural life is attributable to God's giving spirit to men, so eternal life begins when God gives his Holy Spirit to men."

23. Um, *Theme of Temple Christology*, 190.

24. Morales, *Who Shall Ascend*, 287.

25. "Thus understood, Ezekiel's depiction is not unlike the Eden mount, with a river flowing from the summit to water the earth (Gen. 2:10–14). The summit being the place of God's Presence, the river itself serves to symbolize his blessing: that all life on earth derives from God as the source of life. Secondly, as elsewhere in Ezekiel (36:25–27), water symbolizes, more particularly, the cleaning and restorative work of the Spirit. The water that flows from the sanctuary describes, then, the pouring out of the life-giving Spirit. Returning to John's Gospel, Jesus's role as baptizer with the Spirit may now be seen to accord fully with his identity as temple." Morales, *Who Shall Ascend*, 286–87.

26. Morales, *Who Shall Ascend*, 287.

27. Morales, *Who Shall Ascend*, 287 (emphasis original). He goes on regarding John 4: "The narrative therefore brings together (1) the Spirit as the gift of God, (2) Jesus as the giver of this gift, and (3) the Spirit's role in the new worship, which is nothing less than real heavenly access to and fellowship with the Father" (289).

"life in himself" (5:26). With Jesus being unique in this way, "[the] reality mediated by [him] is predicated on his own divinity . . . and not as a derived property."[28] Moreover, concluding the canon, the final chapters of Revelation are saturated with Edenic and temple language, while also containing a twist. The focus of Revelation 22:1–2 "is on the life-giving presence of God. Life flows as water from the throne of God and of the Lamb. . . . The life that is enjoyed by the occupants of the New Jerusalem is, then, constituted by the presence of God."[29] Yet Bartholomew also notes that the "most unusual feature of the city is the absence of a temple (21:22). This is because the whole city is filled with the glory of God—it has become a temple. This is confirmed by its cubic shape (21:16), the same as the Holy of Holies."[30] Perhaps temple language becomes unnecessary at this time, since all is now temple. That is to say, all space is sacred space as God's presence finally has its intended way.

Furthermore, before warnings and a blessing, the final words of the book are an invitation to drink of this life-giving water. This invitation comes from the Spirit and the bride: "The Spirit and the bride say, 'Come.' And let everyone who hears say, 'Come.' And let everyone who is thirsty come. Let anyone who wishes take the water of life as a gift" (Rev. 22:17). Thus, the water metaphor remains consistently associated with the presence of God, to which access is now granted by the Lamb, Jesus Christ.

Adopted by Grace

The significance of the divine presence is further strengthened by the concept of adoption. Notably, adoption is an external relation, even if the need for adoption is intrinsic to the adoptee. The adopter is the one moving toward the adoptee to bring her into a dependence relation. Thus, in regard to God's adoption of new covenant believers, Heim appropriately concludes that "adoption is a symbol of humanity's creaturely dependence

---

28. Macaskill, *Union with Christ*, 263. He continues: "The salvation envisaged, then, is fundamentally participatory in character: the life of the Father, shared in the Son, communicated by the Holy Spirit, and embodied in relationship. Such rich conceptual theology can hardly be stripped down to a matter of social inclusion, but neither can it be seen as a matter of Platonic participation. It is presence, covenanted."

29. Macaskill, *Union with Christ*, 188–89; cf. Bauckham, *Theology of the Book of Revelation*, 126–43.

30. Bartholomew, *Where Mortals Dwell*, 162. This point is also raised in Robert A. Briggs, *Jewish Temple Imagery*, 221–23; Koester, *Revelation*, 815–16. Koester also recognizes the immensity of the new Jerusalem's size, even while the numbers in Revelation are not meant to be taken literally.

upon God."[31] She goes on to argue for this dependence within its New Testament context: "Unlike Roman practices of adoption, the act of adoption in Ephesians 1 is not mutually advantageous for the Father and the children, but rather the children are depicted as wholly dependent on, and wholly incommensurate with the Godhead. Furthermore, in Ephesians 1, the adoption of children is not only carried out by all three members of the Godhead, but adoption actually holds together in the Godhead. Adoption occurs 'through Christ' as a result of being chosen 'in Christ' who in the fullness of time will gather all things in himself (v. 10)."[32] In other words, the Father adopts human children by the Spirit, through the Son who is the Son by nature.

The unconditional nature of this adoption also seems apparent in the fact that this has been the divine plan even before the foundation of the world (Eph. 1:4). This is bound to the *telos* intended for humanity even before there was a physical world.[33] At the same time, the "adoption of the saints" did not begin at the punctiliar event of the incarnation but develops throughout Israel's history. As discussed above, Israel had already been set apart, by grace, as God's children. Therefore, "Jesus' election is not an election next to or in competition with the election of Israel, but an election in the heart of Israel's space, displaying the trajectory of the Holy One toward communion with the elect."[34] According to Galatians, prior to Christ, the context was preparatory, requiring the law as a guardian until the "fullness of time" had come and this adoption was secured at the coming of Christ.[35]

Another definitive text for understanding New Testament configurations of adoption is Romans 8. Heim insightfully comments that, especially in Romans 8:29, "dependence is teleological."[36] Such a dependence is intended for all humanity to experience as its goal, even though not all will share this. Heim explains: "Although Romans 8 is quite clear that it is only *believers* in Christ who will progress toward humanity's *telos*, this *telos* is still the end goal for *all* people since Christ's image is determinative of what constitutes a restored humanity. Put simply, humanity was created to be conformed to the *Imago Christi* and to participate in the *Familia Dei* as children of God."[37] Given the centrality of the human need for God's personal presence, the

---

31. Heim, "In Him and through Him," 143. See also Levison, *Filled with the Spirit*, 272–79.
32. Heim, "In Him and through Him," 138.
33. Heim, "In Him and through Him," 143.
34. Jennings, *Christian Imagination*, 259.
35. Macaskill, *Union with Christ*, 222.
36. Heim, "In Him and through Him," 144.
37. Heim, "In Him and through Him," 144 (emphasis original).

question of how this is the intended end for all humanity—if only some can access it—will be raised in the next chapter. Minimally, however, it seems that this divinely intended *telos* of adoption must be foundational for any theological anthropology.

At the same time, humanity's need for God's personal presence to become like Jesus relates to distinctively different sonship from that of the Son. Following her examination of Romans 8, Galatians 4, and Ephesians 1, Heim affirms the conclusion I have already drawn in chapter 2—specifically, that Jesus Christ is the true image and that humans are meant to become like him insofar as merely human creatures may be conformed to this image.[38]

As a consequence of this adoption, new covenant followers of Jesus Christ have access to foreign qualities: glory and holiness. With reliance on the divine presence now operating as an ongoing inner reality, holiness and glory can be imparted onto the child of God. This kind of glory, Macaskill notes of 1 Peter, was visited on the temple and is itself the "inheritance" of the children of God. This is not an original glory restored to humanity, but a gift graciously bestowed to God's children.[39] Closely related is the impartation of holiness, which also appears in 1 Peter. Macaskill argues, "Most scholars would agree that the significance of ἐν ἁγιασμῷ πνεύματος [*en agiasmō pneumatos*] is not in describing the holiness of the Spirit in himself (though this is hardly irrelevant) but rather, given the dative construction with ἐν [*en*], as a description of his sanctifying role, his capacity to impart holiness to others."[40] The adoption of outsiders to Abraham's lineage is by the ongoing grace of God through the shared sonship of Jesus Christ, mediated and sealed by the *Holy* Spirit. Believers are adopted not only so that, as disciples of Jesus, they can be in the divine presence, but also so they can also be indwelt by this holy divine presence. Through "Jesus, and his gift of the Spirit, humanity becomes God's household, participating in the Godhead, enjoying the *koinōnia*—the fellowship that is a communion of both love and friendship—of the Father, Son and Holy Spirit."[41] Such an intimate, personal union was always God's intention for humanity.

---

38. To use Heim's words regarding the extent of conformity to the true image, "Indeed, the use of an adoption metaphor specifically points to the qualitative difference between Christ and his brothers and sisters. Moreover, 'adoption' communicates that the *telos* of humanity, which is ultimately conformation to the image of the Son, *maintains this qualitative* difference." "In Him and through Him," 145 (emphasis original).

39. Macaskill, *Union with Christ*, 161, 147. He notes the parallel of Exod. 24, as well as the communal nature of this indwelling divine glory in Ephesians.

40. Macaskill, *Union with Christ*, 161.

41. Morales, *Who Shall Ascend*, 291.

─────────────────── CONCLUSION ───────────────────

The story of God's intentions for humanity to dwell in God's own presence spans the entire biblical narrative.[42] Morales helpfully summarizes the grand scriptural narrative, bringing together several of the themes we have seen so far in this study: "In retrospect, we may say that all doctrinal roads lead to union with Christ: the temple theme, the Levitical cultus, its clean/unclean legislation all point to this most profound reality of union with the incarnate Logos, through which adoption into the household of God is realized."[43] The continuity across the canon points to the centrality of the divine presence for Israel and the church. The physical reality of the tabernacle and temple, constructed and maintained according to the covenant, communicates the centrality of relating to God's personal presence. Further, the metaphors of bread, water, and adoption are vital to Israel, are fulfilled in Jesus, and then expand to include children of God who are both Jew and gentile. The significance of these realities and metaphors stresses the need of all humanity to be in a second-personal relation with the divine presence. From Eden to the garden in Revelation, God's presence is the centerpiece of the biblical narrative, and human beings are meant to be in special relation to that presence. This special relation is one of dependence, especially in light of the metaphors used to describe how humans interact with this presence and how central it is to our flourishing. However, for God's personal presence to pervade all these eras of salvation history required the coming of the one who embodied this personal divine presence. Yet, as the divine presence, Jesus does more than simply depend on himself. Consistently, as noted in Strauss's view of Jesus's relation to the Spirit and Malatesta's recognition of the increased interiority in John's writings, Jesus truly does depend on the Spirit to commune with the Father and offers that communion to the rest of humanity. Today, that relation of dependence is commonly called "indwelling." We are now ready to examine the concept of fundamental human need theologically—as it relates to Jesus and then to the rest of humanity.

42. Beale and Kim, *God Dwells among Us*, 16. Beale summarizes this story by looking retrospectively from Revelation with a perspective that matches largely with the reading of this chapter.

43. Morales, *Who Shall Ascend*, 267–68.

PART 4

Divine Presence and Needs-Based Anthropology

EIGHT

Pneumatic Christology and Pneumatic Anthropology

A central claim of the Christian faith is that Jesus is not only fully human and fully God but that he reveals how humans are meant to be. As we have seen so far in this book, such a Christocentric anthropology is well founded. However, this Christocentricity requires that all of our Christian anthropologies, in some way, ground themselves in *Christology*, providing a "christological anthropology." Consequently, any christological anthropology requires some formulation of Christology proper. In light of this, the main contention of the present chapter is that one cannot adequately formulate a christological *anthropology* without including a *pneumatic*, or Spirit-emphasized, Christology. I will justify this pneumatic inclusion by returning to the concept of fundamental need.[1]

1. This chapter has been adapted from McKirland, "Did Jesus Need the Spirit?" Reprinted with permission. Since writing that article, I have come to appreciate a richer historical story than the gloss presented in that original article. As my claims for the necessity of a pneumatic Christology do not rest on the genealogy endorsed there, I will focus this chapter on the constructive claims connecting the humanity of Christ with our own. For an excellent summary piece that helped nuance my thinking, see Holmes, *Holy Spirit*, 123–30. Also, I am thankful to Andrew Picard for suggesting this resource.

Presuppositions and Clarifications

The incarnate Logos, Jesus of Nazareth, fundamentally needed the Spirit in the same way that all human persons, after Christ's ascension, fundamentally need the Spirit. Yet "fundamentally needing the Spirit" is a thicker description of Jesus's relationship with God than "a need for a second-personal relation to the divine presence" advocated thus far in this book (even though that thinner description remains true). This thicker description is possible because Jesus's very existence and ministry enables the possibility of such a persisting second-personal relationship with the indwelling Spirit.[2] So, while Jesus shared with all humanity before him a need for the second-personal presence of God, Jesus opens up a new way to meet this need through the Spirit, since he remains fully God while also being fully human.

How to describe Jesus's humanity and divinity in a coherent way has puzzled theologians for centuries, and using models has been one way to approach this puzzle. Although any model of the incarnation will fall short of exhaustive clarity, some models of the incarnation work better than others regarding compatibility with the proposed human need of this book. For instance, Gerald Hawthorne, Oliver Crisp, and Andrew Loke each endorse a weak kenotic Christology, sometimes called "kryptic" Christology. Such a model is helpful for making sense of the work of the Spirit while also recognizing Jesus's actual humanity and ever-active divinity.[3] As Hawthorne proposes, "By a preincarnate deliberate decision the eternal Son of God chose that all intrinsic power, all his attributes, would remain latent within him during the days of his flesh and that he would become truly human and limit himself to the abilities and powers common to all other human beings. Therefore he depended on the Holy Spirit for wisdom and knowledge and for power to perform the signs and wonders that marked the days of his years."[4] While neither Loke nor Crisp explicitly emphasizes the role of the Spirit and Jesus's Spirit-dependence in their own kryptic incarnational models, the Spirit's work in Jesus's life is nevertheless compatible with their views.[5] Held in common

2. See chap. 6 for a fuller defense of this claim.
3. Such a model of the incarnation still leaves some tensions unresolved—for instance, whether or not Jesus had a fallen human nature. Since this is a complex and ongoing debate, bringing in the apparatus of fundamental human need may be helpful here as well. Since this project has argued that Jesus, as a human, needs to depend on the divine presence, such a need remains constant regardless of whether or not Jesus had a fallen human nature.
4. Hawthorne, *Presence and the Power*, 218.
5. According to Strauss, "What is new about Hawthorne's thesis is not his emphasis on the functionality of the humanity of Christ, which is common to kenotic theory, but his emphasis that the Spirit mediated divine knowledge and authority to Jesus." "Jesus and the Spirit," 275. Crisp does not deny this possibility but acknowledges that Spirit-dependence is not the

across their views is that kryptic Christology is largely motivated by the desire to maintain the full humanity of Jesus Christ in such a way that it is an accessible ideal. If Jesus simply relied on his divinity to avoid every creaturely discomfort or limitation, this has a nullifying effect on his human mediation and his experience of relying on the Spirit. Consequently, these kryptic models maintain the activity of the Logos even as the Logos is hypostasized to the human nature of Jesus. The doctrine of inseparable operations remains in full effect even as the distinct temporal missions reveal the one true and triune God.[6] Jesus can need the Spirit without undermining his human perfection. This is the case for Jesus's humanity because one can need what one does not lack. Recall that I still need water even as I am drinking it.

However, Jesus's human need for the Holy Spirit does not collapse the "who" of the incarnation into the many "whos" of humanity, since the incarnate Logos always possessed this Spirit as his own Spirit of Sonship instead of possessing sonship in the way that other human persons, who are not divinely hypostasized, possess it—that is, after receiving it by adoption. Thus, according to the pneumatic Christology endorsed here, Jesus receives and gives the Spirit, embodying the eternal reciprocity of the Logos and Spirit, which is also shared with the Father.

Due to Jesus's unique personhood, Jesus had unique access to the Spirit compared to other humans. Yet this does not necessarily negate the fundamentality of his need for the Spirit. Furthermore, as Jesus was the original after whom all humanity is patterned, his intended need for the Spirit entails humanity's need for the Spirit. Moving forward, I assume that Jesus is indwelt by the Spirit without measure and typifies what it means to be a flourishing human, strengthening existent christological anthropologies. Since Jesus reveals the most flourishing expression of what it means to be human, his human need for the Holy Spirit must be actual. Importantly, Jesus is the fully flourishing example of humanity, not the only true human. Being human is bound to being made in God's image, is unimpeachable, and is non-degreed. Instead, what is degreed is the extent of our flourishing, and Jesus models the fullest human flourishing possible on this side of the eschaton.

To argue that Jesus truly needed the Spirit, I proceed in three parts. First, I define the pneumatic Christology advocated here. Second, by attending to the difference between incarnation and indwelling, I will explore the continuity and discontinuity between Jesus's Spirit of Sonship and the invitation

---

"conventional" view. Crisp, *Divinity and Humanity*, 25. See also Loke, *Kryptic Model of the Incarnation*.

6. For an excellent discussion of the distinction between the operations and missions of God, see Vidu, "*Filioque* and the Order of the Divine Missions," 21–35.

for humanity to become adopted into the family of which he is "firstborn." I understand indwelling as the most intimate divine-human relation that humans can experience on this side of the eschaton. Ultimately, union with God is the most fundamental end of human beings. Whether this union requires indwelling in the eschaton is entirely speculative, though whatever second-personal relation we have with God would surely be no less intimate than indwelling. Third, we will finally turn, in detail, to the concept of fundamental need. Since the indwelling relation is epitomized in Jesus and reveals the meeting of the fundamental need proposed throughout this book, this turn is not only appropriate but necessary. I will use this kind of need to make sense of the continuity between Jesus's Spirit reliance and our own, since Jesus himself needs the same Spirit that we do.

Pneumatic Christology: Distinction and Definition

Since "Spirit Christology" has been used in theology in a variety of ways, I will use the phrase "pneumatic Christology" for my position. Typically, Spirit Christology comes in three broad varieties. In its most extreme form, it supposes the divine element within the incarnate Son to be the Spirit him/her/itself and to be a replacement of the Logos with the Spirit.[7] The divine element is accidental to Jesus of Nazareth, not essential to him. This view denies the Trinity, since there is only the Father and Son/Spirit. However, in its less extreme and conciliar form, it means the "reciprocal relationship between the Spirit and Jesus."[8] The Trinity is maintained, as well as the full divinity and humanity of Jesus Christ. This conciliar understanding is the view advocated in this chapter: pneumatic Christology. Finally, in its weakest form, Spirit Christology views Jesus as merely human, but so exemplary that the Father anointed him with the Spirit and adopted him as his Son.[9] He was not always divine but became so at some point after his birth. This form of Spirit Christology denies the Trinity and Jesus's eternal divinity. Thus, we see *replacement* Spirit Christology, *pneumatic* Christology, and *adoptionist* Spirit Christology as possible understandings of the role of the Spirit in Jesus's life.

Historically, there has been a strong and needed focus on the Logos's true divinity. As a gloss, this focus has been labeled "Logos Christology."[10] In

---

7. As with the rest of the Godhead, there is no biological sex associated with the Spirit, as God does not have a body (except in the case of Jesus).

8. Habets, *Anointed Son*, 4. When I say "conciliar," I am referring to the Roman councils, especially from Nicaea (325) to Chalcedon (451).

9. Habets, *Anointed Son*, 57.

10. Habets, *Anointed Son*, 30.

contrast, the adoptionist Christology of a Jewish sect known as the Ebionites (as best can be determined based on reconstructing their theology) held that due to Jesus's obedience to the law, God anointed him to become the Messiah by the Spirit. Thus, at his baptism, he was adopted as God's Son.[11] Such a view elevated Jesus's humanity while denying his eternal divinity.

In the gentile world, this adoptionist Christology also surfaced in the writings of Theodotus and Paul of Samosata. Theodotus was active in Rome around 190, and Paul, bishop of Samosata, was active from around 260 to 268.[12] Both of these thinkers were concerned that the dominant Logos Christology "left insufficient room for the biblical theme of the messianic anointing of Christ." Also, the idea that God would become incarnate was reprehensible, since it impugned divine transcendence.[13] The thought that God might influence a human being through the Spirit was far more palatable to Greek sensibilities than the radical view of an incarnation.[14] Like the Ebionites, this adoptionist view magnified Jesus's Spirit-anointed humanity but denied his divinity.

Later, under Nestorius, the role of the Spirit was magnified again to the point of leading to an adoptionist Christology, which the leaders at the Council of Ephesus condemned in 431.[15] "Nestorianism" became the term for the heresy that Christ was two persons, one human and one divine. Under this view, it was believed that Christ required the Spirit to fulfill his saving work. This requirement confused his incarnation as a divine person with his need for the Spirit's indwelling for his human operations. However, such reliance on the Spirit was not (and potentially, could not be) disentangled from the rest of Nestorius's views. One entanglement was a lack of recognition that incarnation and indwelling are two different things and can also happen to the *same* person.[16] Cyril of Alexandria's ninth anathema against Nestorius sought to affirm the incarnation but made this seemingly incompatible with indwelling.[17] This anathema appears to pose a challenge to those wanting to establish Jesus's actual reliance on the Spirit as a separate, though inseparable person from the incarnate Logos.

This anathema can be addressed, however (and will be addressed again below), by recognizing the coeternal existence and operation of the Logos

11. Badcock, *Light of Truth and Fire of Love*, 39; cf. McGrath, *Christian Theology*, 233.
12. Badcock, *Light of Truth and Fire of Love*, 40.
13. Badcock, *Light of Truth and Fire of Love*, 40.
14. Badcock, *Light of Truth and Fire of Love*, 40.
15. Habets, *Anointed Son*, 77; cf. Crittenden, "David Coffey," 319–20.
16. Leidenhag and Mullins, "Flourishing in the Spirit," 196.
17. K. Tanner, *Jesus, Humanity and the Trinity*, 60.

and the Spirit in the immanent Trinity and recognizing their complementary missions in the economic Trinity. Consequently, a pneumatic Christology best complements a Logos Christology.[18] Pneumatic Christology is better able to account for the continuity between Jesus's need for the Spirit and common human persons' need for the Spirit, while Logos Christology helps determine Jesus's metaphysical discontinuity from the common human person.[19] Thus, the pneumatic Christology endorsed here cannot stand apart from Logos Christology, as the view itself requires an explicit recognition of the reciprocal relation of the Son and the Spirit.

Jesus and the Spirit: Continuity and Discontinuity

The continuity and discontinuity between Jesus and common humanity open the way to connect Christology and anthropology while also constraining their relation to each other. At this juncture, Ian McFarland's work on Christology and anthropology is especially helpful. He argues that the christological statement produced by the Council of Chalcedon (451) has been misunderstood by interpreters failing to understand the difference between nature and *hypostasis*. The nature is the thing, or "whatness," whereas the *hypostasis* is the person, or who. On this account, "the one *whom* we see in Jesus is none other than the Son of God, [and] *what* we see in Jesus is simply and exhaustively human flesh and blood."[20] *What* we see hungers, thirsts, tires, and needs to depend on the Holy Spirit even as the one *whom* we see has preexisted in aseity for all eternity. Yet because this divine *who* assumed this human *what*, the divine-human *who* also hungers, thirsts, tires, and needs to depend on the Holy Spirit. For Jesus, nature and *hypostasis* are distinct in such a way that the divine-human person experienced these things through his human nature but not his divine nature. He is one person with two natures. As for the rest of humanity, by contrast, we are our human natures—nature and *hypostasis* are inseparable. Human nature is shared between Jesus and humanity in such a way that Jesus is fully human—though, unlike humanity, Jesus is never *merely* human.

18. For scholars supportive of this complement, see Badcock, *Light of Truth and Fire of Love*, 45; Weinandy, *Father's Spirit of Sonship*, 26; M. Turner, "'Trinitarian' Pneumatology in the New Testament?"; Habets, *The Anointed Son*, 12, 50, 73, 82.

19. In consonance with the pneumatic Christology advocated here, Ian McFarland's concern over replacement Spirit Christologies motivates his proposal for a "pneumatic Chalcedonianism," which he sees as maintaining the role of the Spirit in understanding Jesus's humanity holistically. "Spirit and Incarnation," 144.

20. McFarland, *Word Made Flesh*, 8.

By contrast, mere human beings exist as human persons with human natures without being hypostasized to the divine nature of the eternal Word. In the case of Jesus, however, his divine personhood is united with his human nature. As Joanna Leidenhag and R. T. Mullins, interpreting the Council of Constantinople (553 CE), summarize, "The human nature is not, nor could have been, a person independent of the Son's assumption."[21] The incarnation is its own special divine-human relation, one not shared in common with other human beings. How this human nature is assumed is a trinitarian operation: the Father wills the *hypostasis* of the Son; the Son wills to be hypostasized; and the Spirit hypostasizes the Son to the created human nature. This act of union by the Spirit is how Jesus of Nazareth comes to exist (Matt. 1:18–20; Luke 1:35). Such a union is unique to Jesus as God incarnate.

In contrast to incarnation, Leidenhag and Mullins can go on to claim, "the relation of indwelling is a matter of human flourishing, not a matter of human existence."[22] Jesus required this direct act of the Spirit to exist. Common human persons still require the gift of God to exist, since all of material reality exists because God graciously wills this to be so, but this is quite different from being hypostasized to the material reality as an eternal person. By grace, God creates the world and causes all things to exist. However, the circumstances of history that God provides entail that human persons will also need to relate to God second-personally (which we see in human history as the relation of indwelling) to flourish maximally on this side of the eschaton.

Having established the distinction between incarnation and indwelling, we can now return to the ninth anathema from the Council of Ephesus, since this distinction between incarnation and indwelling is unclear in that text: "If anyone says that the one Lord Jesus Christ was glorified by the Spirit, as making use of an alien power that worked through him and as having received from him the power to master unclean spirits and to work divine wonders among people, and does not rather say that it was his own proper Spirit through whom he worked the divine wonders, let him be anathema."[23] Since Jesus is the Logos incarnate, the full Godhead is present in him. Therefore, the Spirit is Jesus's own proper Spirit. Jesus's divinity is what the ninth anathema aims to safeguard. However, while this helps protect one kind of divine-human relation (incarnation), it makes it difficult to discern another kind of divine-human relation (indwelling). This difficulty is a good example of where pneumatic Christology can helpfully complement Logos Christology by affirming

---

21. Leidenhag and Mullins, "Flourishing in the Spirit," 194; cf. Crisp, "Desiderata for Models of the Hypostatic Union," 40.

22. Leidenhag and Mullins, "Flourishing in the Spirit," 196.

23. Quoted in N. Tanner, *Councils of the Church*, 60.

both relations of incarnation and indwelling. The Spirit is uniquely Jesus's own because Jesus is fully divine. In no way was this Spirit alien to him. However, Jesus also relied on this Spirit, because he had a complete human nature. Such a claim does not weaken Jesus's divinity, but it does allow for a tension between Jesus's supreme uniqueness as God and his being fully human just as we are. Jesus's being human just as we are establishes why the relation of indwelling is so important. This indwelling relation is accessible to human persons, thereby opening a way to talk about anthropology in its relation to Christology.

McFarland further articulates this relation. He utilizes Aquinas's thought to extend his insights, arguing that the "grace of union" establishes Jesus's sui generis identity as the Son of God, since only he has the hypostatic union. While McFarland does not state whether this grace of union is the work of the Spirit (as Aquinas says), this particular grace is unique to Christ and precedes habitual grace, which God's indwelling Spirit gives.[24] While one need not follow Aquinas's whole theological system, this distinction of the experience of grace seems to map onto the difference between incarnation and indwelling. Aquinas is concerned with maintaining Jesus's supreme uniqueness while also grappling with scriptural statements about Jesus's likeness to humanity. Such grappling is a critical feature of Jesus's mediation and concerns one central theologian for pneumatic Christology—John Owen. According to Lucy Peppiatt, an Owen specialist, "Owen draws and builds on Thomist thought, where we find an insistence on the need for habitual grace in Christ, designated as a work of the Spirit."[25] The real human experience of reliance on grace, which for Aquinas and Owen is synonymous with the Spirit, is critical for Jesus's mediatorial role to be effective. Owen seeks to demonstrate Jesus's real reliance on the Spirit to account for the scriptural support for his learning and growth and likeness to our humanity. While Owen may go further than some theologians are comfortable with regarding the causative agency of the Spirit in Jesus's life, the fact remains that the scriptural picture of Jesus is of a fully human individual who grows and learns.

McFarland, whose pneumatology seems more constrained than Owen's, is still supportive of Jesus's reliance on the Spirit, recognizing that Jesus required the Spirit to be sanctified and thereby live by the will of the Father.[26] He believes this reliance of Jesus on the Spirit is consonant with Chalcedon, which is why he calls his view a "pneumatic Chalcedonianism." He explains,

---

24. Aquinas, *Summa Theologiae* III.7.13.
25. Peppiatt, "Life in the Spirit," 171, 173.
26. McFarland, "Spirit and Incarnation," 154.

"For it is only in and through the gift of the Spirit that any human being, whether Jesus or Mary or Chloe or Paul, may live as a child of God."[27] Radically, McFarland's pneumatic Chalcedonian reading advocates "that *the Spirit is not what makes Christ divine but rather what makes him human*, in that Jesus fulfils his specifically human vocation from conception to glory through the power of the Spirit."[28] Here we see another distinction, which may be deemed a difference in degree. Unlike the incarnation, which is a unique *kind* of relation between the Spirit and Logos, indwelling for Jesus and common humanity would be different by way of *degree*. Jesus experienced the indwelling of the Spirit from his conception onward and without measure. Human beings experience the indwelling Spirit only in part, not in fullness.[29]

For Jesus, and Jesus alone, the Holy Spirit is also his Spirit.[30] As Kathryn Tanner asserts, the "hypostatic unity is what makes the Spirit the sure possession of the humanity of Christ: the humanity of Jesus cannot lose the Spirit because he is the Word. One with the Word, the humanity of Christ receives the Word's very own—the Word's own Spirit."[31] Because of the eternal relation of the Son and the Spirit, when the Son assumes the human nature of Jesus, the Spirit establishes the union (grace of union) of the divine and human natures as well as indwelling Jesus. In the case of Jesus and Jesus alone, these two realities are contemporaneous. In the words of McFarland, "The grace of union establishes Jesus' unique identity as the Son of God, but it is by the Spirit's gift of grace that Jesus is sanctified so as to be able to live a life of faithfulness and love."[32] Even though Jesus is a divine-human person and therefore has a different instantiating relation to the Spirit than any other human being, this does not undermine his having the same indwelling relation to the Spirit made possible for other merely human persons. Logos Christology is adept at defending the former, and pneumatic Christology the latter, so holding them together provides a more robust Christology than when these stand alone. If this is the case christologically, then Jesus cannot be understood apart from the Spirit, nor can anthropology be understood apart from humanity's being adopted by this same Spirit. And such seems to be the case. By the Spirit, Jesus is hypostasized, empowered, anointed, led, and raised from the dead. Such

27. McFarland, "Spirit and Incarnation," 154.
28. McFarland, "Spirit and Incarnation," 158 (emphasis original); cf. Badcock, *Light of Truth and Fire of Love*, 264; Spence, "Christ's Humanity and Ours."
29. Giving of the Spirit in degrees has precedent even before Jesus in 2 Kings 2:9, as well as with reference to the Spirit being "poured out" in a new way and to a different degree in Isa. 44:3; Joel 2:28; Acts 2:17.
30. McFarland, "Spirit and Incarnation," 158.
31. K. Tanner, *Christ the Key*, 71.
32. McFarland, "Spirit and Incarnation," 154.

an intimate relationship between the Spirit and Jesus further reveals a benefit of pairing Logos Christology and pneumatic Christology—the practical significance of two doctrines: the doctrine of appropriation and inseparable operations. McFarland states clearly the inextricable relation of the Son and the Spirit: "Even apart from the incarnation, the Son is not the Son without or apart from the Spirit, so it is entirely consistent with the eternal identity of the Second Person that in his earthly ministry he should at every point be accompanied and empowered by the Spirit. And in the same way that it is only in and through the Spirit that Jesus is the Son, so it is only through the same Spirit that we, too, become sons and daughters of God."[33] The Spirit who empowers Jesus is the same Spirit that Jesus then gives to make humans God's children. Thus, one of the clearest and richest biblical categories for relating Christology and anthropology is the language of adoption.

As we have seen in prior chapters, in order to adopt humans into the divine family, God saw it as most fitting to send the person who is the Son by nature, through the Spirit, to extend God's family by this same Spirit. Only a Son by nature could accomplish such a feat. Heim makes a compelling exegetical case that adoption is the "telos of human existence." She provides a biblical category for what the Eastern and Western traditions have labeled *theosis* and "beatific vision," respectively.[34] Jesus, as the Son by nature, is the *locus* of adoption.[35] However, the Spirit appropriates this adoption, adopting human persons and allowing them to cry out, "Abba, Father," just as Jesus does.[36] Again, the difference between Jesus's sonship and our own is made clear in Romans 8 and Colossians 1:15. In these texts, Jesus is fastidiously ascribed the title "firstborn," such that "although those who live by the Spirit have received the Spirit of adoption, Christ is 'firstborn' among the many adopted brothers and sisters (8:29)."[37] This rich adoption language also appears in Romans 9:4; Galatians 4:5; and Ephesians 1:5, and thus "is a symbol of humanity's creaturely dependence upon God."[38] The New Testament language of adoption helps to highlight the continuity and discontinuity between Jesus and other human persons. The human nature of Jesus relating to the eternal Word by the Spirit must be different from an ordinary believer's relationship with the Spirit, because Jesus's relation to the Son by the Spirit "provides salvation,

---

33. McFarland, "Spirit and Incarnation," 158.
34. Heim, "In Him and through Him," 130.
35. Heim, "In Him and through Him," 130.
36. Heim, "In Him and through Him," 130; Mark 14:36; Rom. 8:15; Gal. 4:6; cf. McFarland, *Word Made Flesh*, 120.
37. Heim, "In Him and through Him," 134; cf. Habets, *Anointed Son*, 269.
38. Heim, "In Him and through Him," 143.

whereas our relationship to the Spirit allows us to receive salvation."[39] In other words, Jesus, as the Son by nature, not only depends on this same Spirit as his own but also gives this Spirit to those who become children of God (Matt. 3:11; cf. Mark 1:8; Luke 3:16; John 1:33; 6:63; 7:39; 15:26; 16:7; 20:22; Acts 2:33; Gal. 3:14).

As we have seen above, the Bible's lack of clarity regarding the difference between incarnation and indwelling can obscure how we interpret Jesus's actual reliance on the Spirit. But pairing pneumatic Christology with Logos Christology can maintain Jesus's absolute uniqueness without compromising his correspondence with the rest of humanity. Consequently, pairing pneumatic Christology with Logos Christology better accounts for how Jesus lived a truly human life. Since I have proposed that Jesus's reliance on the Spirit is different by way of degree and not kind (though *how* he has the Spirit is different in kind and not simply degree) from the way the rest of humanity relies on the Spirit, the question for the remainder of this chapter is how his need for the Spirit shares continuity with our need for the Spirit. Here, Garrett Thomson's analytic formulation of fundamental need provides one way to address the puzzle of how to connect Christology and anthropology.

Fundamental Need: Continuity with Jesus

We now move to a primary concern that pneumatic Christology seeks to address: that Jesus assumed a true humanity, a humanity that needed to rely on the personal divine presence (i.e., the Holy Spirit) and did not just appear to need the Spirit for our benefit. While not denying that everything Jesus did was ultimately for our benefit, I hold that the incarnation does not invalidate the actuality of him truly entering into the human condition and needing the Spirit.

The need for relying on God's personal presence (seen here as indwelling), as we have seen, is separate from the gift of existence. Existence is a precondition for flourishing, and how existence is instantiated does not undermine the conditions for flourishing. For this reason, I will qualify Thomson's rubric for fundamental need by stating that all "fundamental needs" are relative, given that God could have created the world differently than it is. However, as it stands, God deigned to make the world in such a way that to be human would be to have certain needs.[40] Ultimately, all is a gift.

---

39. Leidenhag and Mullins, "Flourishing in the Spirit," 198–99.

40. This language of creation is intentionally minimalistic and would include any account of how things are now the way they are whether on an evolutionary account or on an instantaneous-creation account. Either way, God is the source of all of the created order and created *ex nihilo*.

Assuming the gift of existence, we can move to fundamental needs while recognizing that they are ultimately relative. A fundamental need is that which is necessary for the flourishing of a certain entity and cannot be separated from the constitution of that entity. Thus, the concept of fundamental need helps provide a bridge between Jesus and the rest of humanity. This reasoning flows in two directions: from Jesus to common humanity and from common humanity to Jesus. In the first case, if Jesus is the perfect human being, he presumably models what human flourishing is meant to be in a fallen world (and then briefly, in a glorified state). Whether or not Jesus had a fallen human nature, understood as inheriting original sin, becomes secondary because the need persists regardless of the condition of this human nature.

Further, those who argue for and against Jesus having a fallen human nature still agree that his human nature was affected by living in a fallen world.[41] He hungered, grew tired, was tempted, and could die. None of these realities undermine fundamental need. Regarding the second flow of reasoning, from common humanity to Jesus, a strong scriptural case can be made that God's presence is central to a true understanding of humankind's identity and function. From what we see for *human* creatures, to be the kind of creature they are, anyone claiming to be human would require this need. As creatures made in God's image, humans have a unique relation to Godself and a unique royal-priestly function to carry out in light of this relation. God desires to dwell with humankind, and humankind flourishes when it is receptive to this dwelling. Progressively, this dwelling *with* becomes a dwelling *in* as the degree of flourishing deepens and is epitomized in Jesus, bringing us back to the first flow of reasoning.

However, both flows of reasoning face objections. First, one may doubt whether Jesus's relation to the Spirit can be prototypical and a possible human *telos*, since it is so unique. Second, there is the question of whether one can reason from mere humans to Jesus's human nature.[42] While these are both valid concerns, and likely only two of many, fundamental need remains a helpful concept. It can take into account Jesus's supreme uniqueness, since he reveals this fundamental need being met to its greatest extent. Further, as we have seen in the second part of this book, humankind is created in the image of Christ. While he is the true image, our imaging is derivative of his being the image. Since he is the true image as one fully empowered by the Spirit and perfectly expanding God's presence in the world, so too are we intended to

41. Crisp, "Did Christ Have a Fallen Human Nature?," 287.
42. Cole, *He Who Gives Life*, 175.

be fully empowered by the Spirit and expanding God's presence in the world (however imperfectly that may be).[43]

To the second objection, my response is one of plausibility. According to the scriptural witness, especially of the Gospels, we see Jesus hungering, tiring, thirsting, and dying—entering into the common experiences of human life. We do not have explicit statements about Jesus getting cold or hot, needing to use the toilet, and so on. However, we assume that he had these experiences based on common human experiences. Similarly, we see second-personally relating to God's presence as central to God's intention for humanity. This intention pertains to human persons in all stages of salvation history—from before sin, after sin, after Jesus, and in the eschaton. It is, therefore, reasonable that to be human is to be intended to relate to God second-personally— indeed, to be intended for union with God via the indwelling of the Holy Spirit. Given all that has been said about Jesus thus far, such a union with God finds its height of expression in Jesus, not only hypostatically but also in a dispositionally human way.

Returning to the positive case for fundamental need, one primary feature of this concept that has theological purchase is that this kind of need "indicates a disposition and does not imply a lack."[44] Illustratively, a human person continues to need food even while she is eating. If the need cannot be met, then a person lacks what she needs; however, fundamental need is not *necessarily* constituted by lack. By assuming a real human nature, Jesus assumed real human needs, not simply for nutrients, hydration, and rest but also for a deep and abiding relationship with the Father through the Spirit. For the first time in human history, the second-personal relationship with God was experienced as an ongoing and permanent indwelling of the Holy Spirit. However, Jesus's need for the Spirit does not imply that he lacked anything, but that he willingly entered into the human condition of receiving and relying on the Spirit. This reliance had many effects: knowing the mind of God, performing signs and wonders, having supernatural knowledge, and so forth. Furthermore, even though the Spirit was indissolubly bound to Jesus, this does not negate the actuality of the need, nor does having a need undermine perfection.[45] Jesus has a human nature even though he is also a divine-human person. Human beings who are not divinely hypostasized share this same human nature. Because Jesus and other human beings share a human nature, Jesus, as a

---

43. Recall from chap. 2 that this expansion of God's presence will be characterized by love of God and love of neighbor.

44. G. Thomson, "Fundamental Needs," 175.

45. Recall that the reason this is true is that having a need does not necessarily entail having a lack.

person who subsists in a human nature, shares with other humans the need for the Spirit. This continuity of human nature provides sufficient warrant for connecting Christology and anthropology even while the distinctiveness of Jesus's personhood is maintained.

In contrast to incarnation, indwelling is the divine-human relation well suited to the category of fundamental needs. Indwelling brings us back to the technical definition of fundamental need, since this is the maximum second-personal relation to God on this side of the eschaton. Recall that for a need to be fundamental, it must meet certain criteria that ensure that this need is bound to the entity's nature. Additionally, a fundamental human need is one whose satisfaction is necessary for the well-being of a certain entity.[46] The need must not have any other needs beneath it (must be nonderivative); it cannot change based on the external conditions of the being (must be noncircumstantial); and it must be bound to the constitution of the being (inescapable). We will move through Thomson's criteria in more detail by applying them to Jesus's need for God's Spirit.

First, for a need to be nonderivative, according to Thomson, its satisfaction must be necessary in and of itself. Since the biblical and theological traditions converge in showing that the ultimate end of flourishing humanity consists in a second-personal relation with God that looks like union, and given that the Spirit provides this union, the need for a second-personal relation to God is a fundamental human need.

The second criterion is that of being noncircumstantial. The need for a second-personal relation to God is reasonably applicable regardless of the human condition: prelapsarian, postlapsarian, redeemed, Jesus's humanity, and glorified humanity. Through the biblical witness, we see Jesus uniquely conceived by the Spirit (the reference to the Spirit here expressing a second-personal relation to God), then led by the Spirit during his earthly ministry, and raised by this same Spirit at his resurrection. Although he would have initially received the Spirit differently from other human beings, his dispositional need for a second-personal relation to God is shared in common with other human beings. Again, while God could have created the circumstances to be different than they are, the world, as gratuitously given, entails that humans will be the kind of creatures who need a second-personal relation to God for their full flourishing.

A need is inescapable if there is nothing a human being can do to avoid having this fundamental need. In other words, God has created the world in such a way that only by union with Godself can one experience ultimate well-being,

---

46. G. Thomson, *Needs*, 88–89; Thomson, "Fundamental Needs."

and the fundamental need for a second-personal relationship with God is the prerequisite disposition awaiting fulfillment. So, whereas fundamental need is noncircumstantial regarding external contexts of the person, it is inescapable internally in that no matter what the subject does or does not do, having this need is required due to her nature. In other words, the thing that is needed cannot be substituted by anything else, which means that if the subject does not have what she needs, she is harmed.

Returning to Thomson's two questions by which to analyze harm: What does harm deprive humans of? And why is that thing good?[47] This "good" can even be something that the human person has never experienced, such that her quality of life is affected without her knowing it. So, what does harm deprive humans of? Union with God's very self. Why is that thing good? It is the end for which humans were created.

Recalling pneumatic Christology as previously articulated, in the same way that human persons have been intended for union with the divine life by becoming children of God, so Jesus of Nazareth embodies that filial relationship with the Father through the Spirit. He reveals what human nature is supposed to look like, even though his is assumed by the eternal Logos. Here, Logos Christology is again critical and opens one more avenue by which fundamental need might be theologically useful; that is, the divine life of the Godhead, as relationally constituted, epitomizes need without lack. Each person needs the other to be who they are, yet this is a need unlike any need in the contingent order—one might call it the "Supreme Fundamental Need." Need is not an external constraint on God, as God has no need for anything outside of Godself. However, this does not mean God does not need something within Godself. As McFarland states, "The three divine persons are not in any respect threatened by one another; each one lives entirely in and by the other two, such that at no point does the flourishing of one come at another's expense; quite the contrary, it is the nature of divinity that the 'expense' of giving whereby the divine life is sustained does not diminish any person but rather constitutes the persons as the one God."[48] Perhaps the need that grounds all others is found in the Godhead itself, where again the need to exist and the need to flourish run in eternal parallel. To be who they are, the Father needs the Son and the Spirit, the Son needs the Spirit and the Father, and the Spirit needs the Father and the Son. The Son lives in this eternal union, and when the Son assumes a human nature, he then expresses the maximum creaturely

47. G. Thomson, *Needs*, 44.
48. McFarland, *Word Made Flesh*, 59.

dependence on the divine life in the fallen contingent order as the divine-human person of Jesus.

In summary, a fundamental need is nonderivative, noncircumstantial, and inescapable, so that the entity experiences serious harm if this need is not met. However, even in the "meeting" of this need, since this need is bound to the disposition of that entity, to *be* that being is to *have* that need. Yet the entity does not have to be aware of the need or the harm she is experiencing by its being unmet for the need to be real. Insofar as that need *is* met, the entity experiences flourishing instead of harm, but the need itself is constitutional. The fundamental human need is relating second-personally with God, so that one is not human without this need. Jesus experienced this need in a real human way because he was fully human. He reveals what a fully flourishing human being can look like in a context constrained by the effects of sin. However, while he truly needed the Spirit, as God by nature, he could not *not* have the Spirit at all times. Though the nature of his Spirit reception is different from mere human Spirit reception, this does not negate the actuality of his fundamental need.

CONCLUSION

Given the essential role of the Spirit in the life of both the eternal and incarnate Son, a pneumatic Christology that is complementary to Logos Christology enriches how we think of Christ. A further consequence of this thinking will be that our christological anthropologies will become more pneumatic as we take this need seriously. Such an understanding of Christology comports with the biblical picture of the relationship between Jesus and the Spirit. It also provides a pivotal thread of continuity between Christ's humanity and our own—a fundamental need for a second-personal relationship with God that is now experienced as God's indwelling presence.

NINE

Christ the Key to Need

So far, we have seen that Jesus is the teleological prototype for what it means to be human and that relating to God's personal presence was essential to humanity's identity and function before sin. God's intention for humanity to depend on God's presence persisted after sin, and God provided a way for humanity to dwell with him by instituting the tabernacle and temple. However, Christ enabled humanity to more fully attain its *telos* under the new covenant by depending on God's Spirit through a permanent union.[1] Thus, Christ and the Spirit are both the means and the end of human existence.[2] In other words, only by Christ and through the Spirit are humans able to become like Christ and intimately relate to the Spirit—to the glory of the Father. Having examined Jesus's need for a second-personal relation to God, I will examine the beginnings of the continuities between Jesus's need and our own through Kathryn Tanner's theological work.[3]

1. Cortez's observations about John's Gospel recognize this need as well: "Throughout the gospel, we see further indications that the outpouring of the Spirit in the new creation transcends that which was originally available. . . . The permanence of the Spirit in this new creation stands in sharp contrast to the Spirit's presence in creation in the beginning. Although we must affirm that the Spirit was essential to God's creational purposes, only with the new creation do we have assurance of the Spirit's permanent presence with God's people in his creation forever." *ReSourcing Theological Anthropology*, 49; cf. Morales, *Who Shall Ascend*, 286.

2. By "end" I do not mean that what Christ accomplished has finished God's project of restoration, but instead that the Spirit is given as a "deposit" guaranteeing that the restoration will one day be complete.

3. While sociologists, psychologists, and anthropologists have long discussed "need" as a basis for understanding people and societies, only more recently has this been discussed by philosophers, especially within political discourse. This book will not be able to engage with

As with this book, Tanner centralizes Christ to understand the cosmos and humanity's place within it. She also fruitfully emphasizes creaturely dependence and is an excellent dialogue partner for this chapter, as her account opens new horizons for engagement while also helpfully corroborating the ideas of this project. We will begin with the key themes of Tanner's work, turn to the category of fundamental need, and finally integrate her theology and this concept.

Tanner's overarching vision of Christianity, which she articulates in *Jesus, Humanity and the Trinity* and then expands on in *Christ the Key*, is that "in all God's dealings with the world, God is trying to give creatures the good of God's own life by way of increasingly intimate relationships with them that culminate in Christ."[4] Most simply, God's personal presence is a gift. This gift is God's own life and constitutes grace. Such a vision drives her theological anthropology, though this chapter will focus on her understanding of human nature and its relation to grace. Specifically, in *Christ the Key*, Tanner argues for human dependence on the divine life for both existence and flourishing. Humans intrinsically need what they cannot provide for themselves. Instead of a liability, this is the greatest possible creaturely dignity—that humans are intended to participate in the triune God. Fortunately, unlike rocks and trees, humans have uniquely plastic, open-ended natures that ideally suit them for this kind of participation.[5]

Human Nature in *Christ the Key*

Human beings have been intended for an intimate relationship with God from the beginning of human existence, culminating in Christ. However, even though this is the case, Tanner does not put humans at the center of the theological story. Instead, her prior development of the dual principles of radical transcendence and noncompetitiveness between God and creation continues to structure her theological program. God is completely other to the created order (radically transcendent) without having conflicting agencies

---

all of this literature but will pull from the rubrics developed within analytic philosophy, since they provide the clearest criteria by which to judge the fundamentality of a given need.

4. Soskice, Koster, McFarland, Lösel, McDougall, and Tanner, "*Christ the Key* Book Forum," 342.

5. Some might be concerned that Tanner's view of human nature is too undetermined, given how open-ended it is. The beauty of a needs-based anthropology is that it can work with very thin descriptions of human nature all the way through to thick descriptions. If Tanner's account is indeed thin, what is most important is that even given that, the need for God's presence (termed grace, for Tanner) remains.

(noncompetitive). *Christ the Key* provides a robust theological anthropology that remains consistent with these principles.[6]

Tanner understands human nature by looking at Jesus Christ, the one in whom the image of God subsists. By beginning in the initial creation accounts, we see that humanity is explicitly made "in the image of God" (Gen. 1:26–28), and from here, Tanner takes a prospective, trinitarian reading of this text. The Father, Word, and Spirit were present at creation as the Spirit hovered over the waters and the Word of the Father was spoken to bring all things into existence.[7] While recognizing that this is exegetically unlikely, given the anachronism of trinitarian thought, she appeals to a theological reading of these early accounts, which has a rich tradition in the early church.[8] On this reading, humanity is initially created with the gift of God's presence all around them, and even possibly in them (26). Even so, humans are not themselves the image of God but made "according to" or "in" the image and likeness of the divine image—the Word. Nevertheless, they are meant to be attached to this Word by the Spirit.

Tanner introduces weak and strong imaging categories as they relate to weak and strong participation, respectively. To participate weakly "means nothing more than being a creature of God" (8, 37). However, while any creature may weakly participate in God, humans have unique natures that allow them to move beyond weak imaging to strong imaging (23). Humans, even at creation, were "images of the strong sort in virtue of our attachment to the divine image itself, a divine image that in imprinting itself upon our minds and thereby making us wise produced in us a very strong image of the weak sort, human life made over according to the Word's own wisdom in imitation of it" (23). Humans are strong images of a weak sort at creation, but in Christ will have access to strong imaging of the strong sort.

Humans have uniquely plastic natures that are open to shaping. These natures provide "the opening for the divine image itself to become their own, present within them, in a way that reforms their humanity according to and in strong imitation of itself" (37). In other words, from the very beginning, humans have always been intended to unite with the divine life, and this was enabled through the Second Person of the Trinity being the divine image and

---

6. K. Tanner, *God and Creation in Christian Theology*; Tanner, *Jesus, Humanity and the Trinity*, 1–2; Tanner, *Christ the Key*, 79.

7. K. Tanner, *Christ the Key*, 26. The next several citations of this work are in the text.

8. Granted, a trinitarian reading could not have been conceived by the human authors of the Genesis accounts; however, she is on firmer exegetical ground than she acknowledges regarding humankind being derivative images and regarding the role of the inbreathing of the Spirit. See chap. 4. Cf. McDowell, *Image of God*, 119, 169, 204.

through humans having uniquely plastic natures that would allow them to be taken into the life of that person.[9] And yet such attachment to the divine image also required a bridge, which is why the incarnation remains necessary even apart from sin. Before sin, the Spirit and Word could be "in" a person, in a sense, but not permanently, since the divine presence was still entirely foreign to them.[10]

According to Tanner's theological reading of Genesis, humankind is uniquely invited into and suited for a relationship with the divine, even as the divine life remains radically other to the human. However, this claim is even stronger than mere invitation and suitability. Tanner's work expounds on the actual *necessity* of strong participation in the divine life for humans to be the kind of creatures they are: "The strong form of participation—participation by having the divine image for one's own—is what allows the still weak way that humans image God by participating in God as creatures to be strengthened as much as possible. By having the one whom they are not, the Word, for their own in Christ, they should one day be able to lead human lives that imitate God in the most perfect way possible for mere humans" (17). The closer they draw near to the true image, the more they become who they were meant to be while also not undermining the integrity of their own natures.

However, the fact that humans have natures that enable strong imaging of the true image does not mean they become the divine image themselves or can strongly participate in the divine image on their own (17). Instead, from the beginning, they are intended to strongly participate in the divine life as creatures made in the very image of God and existing in God's own presence. And yet for this participation to be maximal, the incarnation was still required: "Such strong imaging is impossible for humans unless they are given something beyond their created nature, that is, the divine image itself; imaging of that sort requires a gift of grace, in short. Why suppose such a gift is theirs before the actual incarnation of the Word?" (19). So, despite being in the presence of the triune God and intended for strong participation, humans did not have the means necessary for strong imaging at creation. Before the incarnation and before sin, humans were able to move beyond the weakest sort of imaging by relating to the divine life of Word and Spirit, while not

---

9. Strong imaging versus perfect imaging is thus a critical distinction for Tanner, and she finds support for this especially from Athanasius and Gregory of Nyssa. *Christ the Key*, 6.

10. Again, while vocation is not the focus of this work, it is critical to mention that the vocational consequence of this anthropology is service to the world. Indeed, if the truest human expression of the image of God is Jesus Christ—the one who always cared for the weak and marginalized and who ultimately laid down his life for the world—such an anthropology is intrinsically ethical, communal, and ecclesiological.

yet being the strongest strong images of God (20). Before the incarnation, humans could still relate to God second-personally and needed to do so. However, the extent of that second-personal relational intimacy increased with the coming of Christ.

Humans were and are meant to participate in God's life beyond the weak participation of all creation. Yet as creatures made in God's image, humans are meant to become like the true image, which is only fully possible once the divine image takes on human form. Hence, the incarnation becomes the most fitting way to enable strong participation in the triune life. Echoing arguments from Cyril of Alexandria and Athanasius, Tanner explains that "God must attach us, in all our frailty and finitude, to God" (viii). Again, operative here are her dual principles of radical transcendence and noncompetitiveness. God is radically other to humankind, which is why this kind of mediation is necessary. However, such inclusion of the human into the triune life does not change what humans are by nature, nor what God is by nature. God remains fully what God is, by necessity. Humans become more fully who they are meant to be by grace.

So, while nothing in the created order can exist apart from God, humans require God both to exist and to flourish. While this may seem like a liability, it is instead the greatest possible created dignity. Tanner frames this in terms of a nobility distinct from the nobility of nonhuman creatures: "a nobility that comes from not being, as others are, the sort of creature that can properly exist without the grace of God's very presence to them" (138). This incapacity persists even when humans are united to God's presence before or after sin. Such is the case because even after sin does enter the human story, human nature itself does not change, as it remains fundamentally open to strongly imaging God, even if it has become hardened to divine inputs. Instead, Tanner focuses on what does change: the surrounding environment. Such an understanding of sin does not diminish sin's weightiness, since humans are creatures conditioned by their environments: "Because it is our nature to be bound up with our environments, what we become through sin forms a kind of second nature. What we become is knit into us in a way we cannot remove. Taking within us what is not good for us as our constant diet, we have so incorporated this material over time as to become inseparable from it" (69). Due to sin, God's personal presence is no longer immediately accessible. Humankind no longer actively relates to Word and Spirit, even though they are still active: "Lost through sin, the gifts of Word and Spirit that made humans the image of God at their creation would need to be restored to humanity by Christ in some new way that improves upon the original situation that permitted their loss" (32; cf. 69–70). Here again, Christ becomes the key, since he is the perfect human image, able to restore what was lost while also providing the permanence of strong participation in and through himself (35). Due to the incarnation, humankind would become like the perfect human image of God, though still imperfectly before glorification.

Also, due to sin, the incarnation must involve atonement to address the sinful environment in which we all now live and to disarticulate the human person's true nature from what it has become (69). Tanner conveys this disarticulation and rearticulation elsewhere, stating that the "clothing of the Spirit that we had at our creation and lost through sin is returned to us as more than the mere exterior garment it seemed to have been then; it is now knit into the fabric of our humanity by way of the incarnation in much the way the created inputs that do us harm have been" (72). So, because Jesus is the Son by nature and not by grace, we can become sons and daughters in the image of the divine image of the Father, through the Spirit (25). Jesus provides the way to this strong imaging, which would have been necessary with or without sin.

To conclude this summary of Tanner's understanding of human nature, a few objections should be briefly addressed. For those concerned that Tanner's reading of grace's necessity for the human life undermines God's gracious gratuity or the integrity of a human nature, she has thorough responses to both charges. First, God's graciousness remains gratuitous: "A single divine intent to give us the grace of God's own life underlies the whole of what happens to and for us, from our beginning to our end in salvation; this intent is entirely gracious in that it has its basis in nothing but God's free love for us" (115; cf. 109). In other words, God freely chose to create the cosmos and could have chosen otherwise. However, to create at all establishes certain entailments. For example, creatures require external inputs for their existence, since only God is *a se*, existing Godself without any prior cause. By freely creating, God freely chose to provide the ongoing sustenance of all that is including, for instance, God's provision of water, sunlight, and soil for plants to survive and flourish in the maximum way a plant can flourish. In the case of humans, they also require water, food, shelter, and so on to survive, but they need more than that to flourish. God freely chose to uniquely relate to creatures of the kind "human" beyond simply sustaining their existence but also to be their means and end of flourishing. However, in the same way that God's decision to sustain all creation and provide environments for creaturely flourishing does not undermine God's freedom or the gratuity of God's grace, neither does God's provision of open-ended human natures, for which God intends union with the triune life, undermine God's freedom or grace's gratuity. Instead, God's grace structures everything—not only at creation but in choosing to create in this way. If anything, this underscores the depth of God's graciousness.

Second, natures maintain their integrity since they remain open-ended—capable of receiving grace—whether or not they ever do. Humans are made to be "beneficiaries of God's own life," whether or not they ever experience those benefits (115). Human nature's plasticity and fundamental openness remain the same, even if they are hampered by taking in lesser goods (i.e., the issues that sin raises). Just as a flower remains a flower with or without sunlight, human nature remains a human nature with or without strongly participating in the triune life. While the extent to which human nature can flourish without participating in its ultimate end can be debated, this does not undermine the integrity of that nature.

All creation weakly images God by way of sheer existence. However, even in their weak imaging, humans, as creatures made in the image of God, have uniquely open-ended natures that are postured to relate to God's very presence intimately, thereby strongly imaging God. In this way, humans receive grace upon grace upon grace—receiving, first, the grace of existence; second, the grace of existing in this open-ended way; and third, the grace of God's self-giving, not only through Word and Spirit but also through the incarnate Word by the Spirit. Humans are creatures who need grace, but instead of a liability, this is their greatest beauty.

Fundamental Need

For Tanner, grace is the giving of God's very self. In the previous chapters of this book, we have seen this as God's personal presence, and thus, humans fundamentally need this grace. Weak participation in God, which is already a gift of grace, is required for the contingent order to exist. Yet, in keeping with this distinction between weak and strong participation, the focus here will be on the human need for a second-personal relation to God. The meeting of this need looks like strong participation in God's life. In other words, humans uniquely need to strongly participate in the divine life beyond weak imaging to flourish as the kinds of creatures they are. Consequently, humans need a second-personal relation to God, which is then satisfied in an ongoing way through participation in the triune life.[11]

Such a way of framing fundamental need differs from what has been argued so far in this book, as Tanner's emphasis is on God's presence to the creature, whereas the focus of this book has been on the creature's need for God's personal presence. However, on Tanner's account, not every human person

---

11. This participation language (especially of a strong sort) is synonymous with the union language we have seen before.

is aware of this presence, even if God has made this available to everyone.[12] Regardless of whether we begin with God's presence to us or with our need for God's presence, the need remains.[13]

Having focused specifically on Jesus in the last chapter, we will now integrate Thomson's criteria with Tanner's understanding of grace to offer insights into grace as something for which humans have a fundamental need, applied universally. First, since the God-to-human relationship constitutes grace, grace meets the nonderivativeness criterion. That this is the case finds support most significantly in the Creator/creature distinction. For an infinite God to create and sustain finite creatures can only be understood as gracious on God's behalf. However, as stated in the discussion of weak participation above, humans are meant for more than existing and persisting.[14] Weak participation is technically a precondition for the fundamental need described here, since a creature must exist before it can have a need. However, this undermines discussion of any fundamental need, since, ultimately, existence undergirds all fundamental needs. Given this, we will not count the need for existence as scaffolding that would undermine the fundamentality of the need for strong participation in the divine life. Instead, strong participation (union) is the ultimate end for which humanity was made. Such participation requires grace, since humanity cannot strongly participate in what they are not without God's gracious intervention. Humankind's very nature is open-ended toward this *telos* wherein the divine-human image, Jesus, is the means and the end of eschatological consummation.[15] One might say that the incarnation is the greatest expression of God's grace to meet the human need for strong participation in God's life. Thus, the human need for grace fits the nonderivativeness criterion. The most fundamental need of a human person is to relate to God's personal presence—grace—and a person has this need met by strongly participating in the divine presence.

Second, the human need for grace does not change because of any external conditions. Thus it meets Thomson's criterion of noncircumstantiality. From Tanner's arguments above, the need for strong participation in God

12. For instance, she quotes Augustine: "Unless man turns towards the immutable Good, which is God, and stands firm in Him, he cannot be formed so as to be just and happy." *Literal Meaning of Genesis* 8.10.23, p. 49.

13. In fact, this supports the discussion of dispositions and their stimulus-response structure in the case of the glass's breaking in chap. 1. In terms of the disposition—which is only had on the part of the human—the primary stimulus is God's provision of the need; however, the human must also receive that provision in order to flourish.

14. K. Tanner, *Christ the Key*, 37.

15. This also supports an "incarnation anyway" situation, since the incarnation is the most fitting way to achieve divine-human union, regardless of sin.

applies to prelapsarian humanity, postlapsarian humanity, the humanity of Jesus, redeemed humanity, and glorified humanity. Such a need is "met" only through God's gracious condescension, whereby God makes Godself accessible to human persons. Such graciousness is compounded with the entrance of sin, since God still pursues this relationship of strong participation despite the effects of sin. However, God's loving condescension remains gratuitously gracious even apart from sinfulness.

Thus, we see that, regardless of circumstance, this need also persists across all theological stages of human being. In the Genesis narrative, the man and the woman could be in God's presence, and this capacity implicitly conditionalized their flourishing.[16] Their initial engagement with God second-personally may have matched their capacity for flourishing, given their stage of development. Therefore, they were not in a state of harm, since there was no sin, but they were intended to grow in this second-personal dependence relation. When sin entered the narrative, it protracted the plan for humans to experience deeper levels of intimacy with God. However, the need to relate to God second-personally persists even after sin, and God provisionally meets this need through the mediation of the Levitical priesthood and the tabernacle system. Recalling Tanner's category of "weak participation" above, we can say that such general access to God's presence persists. However, the "strong participation" came about either by God's unique empowering Spirit (such as the anointing of prophets and kings) or through the nation's corporate worship through the tabernacle rituals—though it was still not of the strongest sort of participation. With Jesus's birth and life, we see the strongest example of participation possible on this side of the eschaton. Yet this is not only because he is the Logos but because he, too, having taken on humanness and the need for a second-personal relation to God, chose to depend on the divine presence. Due to Jesus's inauguration of the new covenant and return to the innermost sanctum of the heavenly temple, he sent his personal presence—the Holy Spirit—to live within those who trusted in him. Under the new covenant, access to God's indwelling presence constitutes the identity and function of followers of Christ. In the eschatological domain, it would seem that humans maintain their need to be in a second-personal relation with the divine presence (John 14:16). The Edenic themes, with all their saturation of

16. Such a relation could have still been degreed in that the dependence would not exceed the creaturely capacity, and yet perhaps this capacity could grow. Thus, in Eden the man and woman could be in the divine presence, even if they were intended to be in ever deepening relation to the divine. Such a scenario seems possible given the process of discovery granted to the man in the creation of woman in order that he might learn the full value and partnership of the one like him. I am thankful to Dru Johnson for drawing my attention to this potential parallel.

God's presence, return in the closing of Revelation. However, now the throne of God is present, as the whole cosmos is the holy of holies (Rev. 21–22). The inhabitants of this renewed heaven and earth are also a kingdom of priests serving God and reigning on earth (5:10). Hence, the need to be in a relation of dependence on the divine presence is not bound to circumstance across any era of human existence.

The need for a relationship with God persists in the eschaton and is epitomized in the life of Christ. In his humanity, he needed the grace of God (the Spirit) to strongly participate in the triune life.[17] In light of the Word becoming flesh and relying on the Spirit, God's being is maximally present to the human person of Jesus in that Jesus strongly participates in the divine life. Jesus is the means and end of God's grace. Tanner makes this connection explicit when she notes, "In virtue of the humanity we share with him because the Word has made our humanity its own in him—we can have the Spirit that forms Christ's humanity according to the divine image as our own too, with the same sort of consequences."[18] Regardless of human nature's circumstances—sinless, sinful, redeemed, glorified, or hypostasized to the second person of the Trinity—the need to relate to God's second-personal presence does not change, even if it can be more deeply satisfied, spanning every instance of humanness.

The criterion of inescapability means our need for grace is unavoidable internally. To put this unavoidability more stringently, "The concept of a fundamental need restricts the viable courses of action down to only one."[19] God has created the world in such a way that only by strong participation in Godself can a human being fully flourish. More specifically, that viable course of action is only found through the incarnate Word by the power of the Spirit. So, whereas fundamental need is noncircumstantial regarding external contexts of the person, it is inescapable internally in that no matter what the subject does or does not do, having this need is required due to her nature. In other words, the need is unsubstitutable by anything else, which means that if the subject does not have what she needs, she is seriously harmed (though she may not realize it). Again, being noncircumstantial connects a need to its being inescapable. Whether or not sin is a factor, to be human is to need a second-personal relation to God—before sin, after sin, or in glory.

---

17. Recall that his need for grace is not utilizing a typical understanding of grace as "getting what he did not deserve" but of grace as a shorthand for the gift of Godself, especially as the Spirit. See chap. 8 for a defense of Jesus's need for grace on this account.

18. K. Tanner, *Christ the Key*, 36; cf. 17, 25.

19. G. Thomson, *Needs*, 27–28; cf. 126.

Further, the only way flourishing can occur regarding this aspect of human-ness is through a dependent relation to God's presence. Depending on this presence (i.e., meeting this need) has looked different across human history, but it has always been unavoidable and limited to one way of realization. For the man and the woman, the realization of this dependence required faithful-ness to the instruction of God, which maintained the holiness of the Edenic space so that God's presence could dwell among them. For Israel, depending on God's presence meant obeying the law of God, which included tabernacle rituals and corporate representation of Israel through the priesthood. Under the new covenant, Jesus is the permanent way to meet this need and to meet it in a deeper way than was yet possible.[20]

In the eschaton, meeting this need will again be externally unmediated. Humanity will be able to be in the actual presence of God and able to relate second-personally, however union in the eschaton occurs. How this relation currently works for Jesus as he is seated at the right hand in the heavenly places is a mystery. However, given that the doctrine of the ascension implies he has not forfeited his humanness in his glorified, exalted state, it seems he is both humanly dependent (still embodied) and divinely interdependent (still the Second Person of the Trinity) on God's presence.

Consequently, undergirding all these criteria is the notion of harm.[21] Thomson defines harm as a person's being "deprived of engaging in non-instrumentally valuable experiences and activities as well [as] of the possibility of appreciating them."[22] To clarify what we are deprived of and distinguish his theory of harm from desire-based theories of harm, we return to Thom-son's category of inescapable interests.[23] In the context of this chapter, an inescapable interest tells us what we are deprived of when we are not strongly participating in the divine life and what consequential desires *may* emerge from that experience. This understanding occurs because "the concept of an interest demonstrates in what sense our well-being consists in living in

---

20. Again, with the caveat that "meeting" the need does not mean it is no longer a need.

21. Recall from chap. 1 that Thomson seeks a theory of harm that is not dependent on desire satisfaction. To do this, he employs the concept of interests. Interests can motivate desires, and inescapable interests, in particular, are bound to human natures in that such interests are unal-terable. They "define what types of activity we are deprived of when we are harmed." *Needs*, 88. These interests reveal what is of primary value to us (77–78). Unlike Thomson, much of my work has been to argue what Christian Scripture and theology propose is of primary value to humankind.

22. G. Thomson, *Needs*, 178.

23. G. Thomson, "Fundamental Needs," 185. Cf. 88–89: "The value of needed things should be explained in relation to harm and, thus, interests. Interests define what harm consists of; needs are necessary to avoid that harm."

accordance with our nature, rather than consisting of getting what we desire."[24] So, regarding the relationship between harm, inescapable interests, and fundamental needs, we must note that an interest explains harm, and harm is necessary to understanding fundamental need.[25] Thus, inescapable interests "provide a certain starting-point for deliberation and a certain fixedness in what is to count as good or bad for a person."[26] So, the interest tells us what we are deprived of when we are harmed. The fact that we would be harmed without meeting that need is what makes it fundamental. We will apply these categories specifically in the framework below.

Supplementing Thomson's Work

In writing an unapologetically theological work, I must make some additions to Thomson's rubric before turning to my framework. First, in Thomson's works on need, he does not clearly define the constitution of flourishing.[27] On my account, flourishing is itself constituted by union with God. Union (strong participation) with God is the ultimate need satisfaction, even if this satisfaction is ongoing. This understanding of flourishing is entailed by the proposal that union with God, from what we have seen in Scripture and in light of the incarnation, is God's universally valuable end for humanity.[28] Such an end is grounded in the triune life itself, which Tanner relates to the kingdom of God: "I would venture that the kingdom is like the trinity in that both are supremely life-affirming of all their members, organized to bring about the utmost flourishing of all. Both are paradigmatic instances of what I have called elsewhere a community of mutual fulfillment in which the good of one becomes good for all. The trinity is coming to us to give us the sort of life-giving relations of mutual flourishing that the trinity itself enjoys."[29] She

24. G. Thomson, "Fundamental Needs," 185.

25. G. Thomson, "Fundamental Needs," 185.

26. G. Thomson, *Needs*, 38.

27. His most recent work, coauthored with Scherto Gill and Ivor Goodson, does attempt more of a definition of well-being/flourishing, but it does not require God for its constitution. See Thomson, Gill, and Goodson, *Happiness, Flourishing and the Good Life*, 138–68.

28. In the language of Schuppert, who engages with Thomson's work, that would make this a fundamental interest. Schuppert, "Distinguishing Basic Needs," 27. Thomson would arguably use the language of inescapable interest. However, I hesitate to use language of "inescapability" with God. There are other ways God could have acted; however, this is the end that God seems to have fixed as universally and unimpeachably good for all humankind.

29. K. Tanner, *Christ the Key*, 241. Consider also that God's potential reason for wanting this could be that God desired the closest possible creaturely analogue to the interrelations of the divine life. Barth's *analogia communionis* is a good parallel here. For more on this parallel, see A. Torrance, *Persons in Communion*, 308.

relates this to the incarnation, since the inner life of the Trinity is notoriously difficult to model human relationships after. In the incarnation, God "sets up a kinship, in this case between humanity and divinity, a community of now mutual fulfillment in that the human is to benefit from what the divine already enjoys."[30] Therefore, we can fill out the content of flourishing more robustly than Thomson does. The constitution of flourishing is union with God.[31] A second-personal relationship with God causally contributes to that flourishing.

To note Thomson's lack of engagement with divine-human union is not to criticize his work, since it is expressly philosophical and not theological. However, given this, the fact that he refers explicitly to "union with God" is quite surprising. In a footnote about interests and desires, he says, "Suppose, for instance, that many of our desires are motivated by religious interests pertaining to union with God. If this were so, then this would be true of atheists and agnostics as well as theists. But it would be false to say that atheists desired union with God."[32] In Thomson's hypothetical, he links union with God to what seems to be an inescapable interest. The implication is that union with God is bound up with flourishing, even on Thomson's account. While I would go further than saying this is a religious interest, since I think it encompasses the whole of life, Thomson's example tracks with the ideas proposed so far. Additionally, his example shows why a lack of desire does not undermine the reality of this need.

Second, and flowing from the first, recall that for Thomson, the constitution of the subject determines the kind of fundamental needs it has, so that "the need is innately rather than environmentally and socially determined."[33] Here we can see where theology may press back on Thomson's rubric, in that God may have determined that the need logically precede the constitution of humankind. God may have desired to share with creatures the maximal intimacy that creatures could experience and have decided that this need for a second-personal relation to God would condition the creature's constitution. So, instead of the creature's constitution determining the need, God may have determined the creature's constitution based on this fundamental need. Put another way, perhaps out of God's deep love for humanity, God conditioned humanness for the kind of intimate relationship God desired to

30. K. Tanner, *Christ the Key*, 241.

31. Which, as discussed in the introduction and in chap. 2, is itself a shorthand for whole-hearted orientation toward God, *shalom*, theosis, and the beatific vision. All these concepts have, at their core, a second-personal relation to God that is unitive.

32. G. Thomson, *Needs*, 133n4.

33. G. Thomson, *Needs*, 32.

have with all humankind. This intimate relation was always the end for which humanity was purposed. While shared in common with the true image and made possible through the true image, the need for a second-personal relation to God as the precondition of union with God may have determined the human constitution, and not the other way around. With these supplements in mind, we can now turn to a framework that fundamental need provides for thinking about humanness.

A Framework for Humanness Using Fundamental Need

Tanner's articulation of human nature can be integrated with Thomson's concept of fundamental need to conclude that Tanner's theological anthropology assumes humans fundamentally need a second-personal relation to God. The meeting of such a need looks like strong participation in God's own life, which is epitomized and enabled through Jesus Christ.[34] Let us turn to the rudiments of a framework for understanding humanness based on fundamental need.[35]

Since I am writing a *theologically* grounded anthropology, the best starting point for a framework is God. God is the source of meeting the need for existence of all things (weak participation). God is the source who created humans with a need for God's very self—a second-personal relation to God.[36] Further, God actively pursues the meeting of this need while desiring human response.[37] Regardless of a person's experiences of feeling this need, she has this need, because the fundamental need is a passive disposition. It is a necessary, though not sufficient, condition for humanness. Its existence reflects God's desire for a special kind of relationship with humankind, one that we have seen borne out in the scriptural accounts as a covenantal relationship.

For a human person, the meeting of this need for a second-personal relation to God causally contributes to flourishing. The nonmeeting of this need causally contributes to harm. One of the ways Thomson defines harm is that

---

34. The explicit conceptual overlap of need within Tanner's work is striking: "Rather than leading self-sufficient lives, all living creatures become themselves, moreover, by actually taking in things from outside themselves. Their natural processes of growth require nourishment from without. Seeds, for example, will not germinate without water. All living things, in other words, are dependent on their environments in requiring external inputs for the achievement of their proper functioning. And humans would be no exception. What is exceptional in the human case is the nature of the inputs. Because they are made to be in the image of God, humans require God for their nourishment." *Christ the Key*, 41–42; cf. 10.

35. The next chapter will more fully develop this.

36. Both existence and existing with the kinds of needs that we have are gracious gifts.

37. We will return to this in the next chapter.

"a person is harmed whenever this level of well-being is below a certain level or norm, even if it has not actually fallen."[38] Harm consists of deprivation of the things that she has an inescapable interest in having. So, in this context, the inescapable interest is flourishing, which, we have seen, is the same as union with (i.e., strong participation in) God. Such flourishing involves a mental state (again, we are distinguishing an inescapable interest from a fundamental need). The inescapable interest is universally valuable. Desires for full flourishing are motivated by this inescapable interest to pursue other means of fulfillment. Still, they may or may not indicate the true inescapable interest at their motivational root. Hence, sin (be it personal, interpersonal, systemic, or otherwise) can inhibit the meeting of this need, and thus sin is harmful. However, central to the Christian message is the affirmation that this harm has been overcome, and access to life, and life in the full, has been provided in Jesus Christ.

Let us return to Thomson's two questions by which he analyzes harm: What does harm deprive humans of? And why is that thing good?[39] In light of Tanner's Christocentric anthropology, these questions have clear answers: What does harm deprive humans of? Strong participation in God. Why is that thing good? Strong participation in God constitutes flourishing, and this is the end for which we were created. Most simply, if God is good and intends the good for creatures, then the path of maximum flourishing will follow from these divine intentions. Add to this the fact that the divine intention for humanity is to look like the humanity (which is created) of the Second Person of the Trinity, who embodies the most intimate kind of union a creature can have with the Creator. Strong participation in the divine presence, as embodied in Christ, yields becoming more like the one who is most intimately dependent on the divine presence in his very being.[40] God, who has been flourishing self-sufficiently for all time, now extends that possibility of flourishing to human creatures to the extent that this second-personal relation matches their creaturely capacities.[41]

Consequently, I propose the following framework for theologically describing humanness: (1) humans fundamentally need a second-personal relationship

---

38. G. Thomson, *Needs*, 93.

39. G. Thomson, *Needs*, 44.

40. Such a relation leads to worship and adoration of the Creator as God's glory is expanded all the more into the creaturely realm. God's glory and humanity's flourishing are not at odds but interrelated. As Pennington notes, that these are dichotomized is unfortunate, since the "Bible's telos is simultaneously God centered and human focused." *Sermon on the Mount*, 293.

41. There is a whole raft of issues relating to how far humans depend on God to bring them to the point of making that choice, but this is beyond the scope of this work. *That* humans are the kinds of creatures who are intended to enter this kind of unitive relation is the focus of this book.

with God; (2) whatever a human nature is, it has this property; (3) the meeting of this need causally contributes to human flourishing; (4) human flourishing is union with and strong participation in God; (5) harm is the not-meeting of this need; (6) Jesus needs a second-personal relationship with God; (7) Jesus has this need perpetually met and is thus fully flourishing; (8) Jesus is also himself the second-personal presence of God; (9) Jesus enables access to the permanent second-personal presence of God (the Spirit); (10) even as this need is being met, it persists, and thus there can be need without lack.

CONCLUSION

According to the Christian story, the standard for human flourishing is the person of Jesus Christ. He is the norm. Consequently, a person is experiencing harm if she experiences inhibition to a relation of dependence on the personal divine presence that Jesus had (and has) in his humanity. Given that this fundamental human need is relational and dynamic, flourishing is degreed based on the capacity to grow in this dependence relation. Thus, the need remains constant across all expressions of humanness, even eschatologically, but *how* it is met can evolve and grow over time. We will now turn to one possible theological anthropology that builds on this framework: a pneuma-christocentric anthropology.

TEN

A Constructive Proposal

Pneumachristocentric Anthropology

Having established second-personal relationship with God as a fundamental need, we are now ready for a constructive turn. While fundamental need provides a helpful supplement to any Christian theological anthropology, I would like to propose a stronger form of this needs-based approach, one that makes the best sense of all the content thus far. If the content from earlier chapters and the framework from the last chapter are the skeleton of this project, a pneumachristocentric anthropology puts flesh on those bones.

Pneumachristocentric Anthropology

To remind us of those bones, we began in chapter 1 with clarifying what is meant by "fundamental need." Since this need is bound up with what kind of entity something is, we turned to the biblical narrative to establish that humankind is the kind of entity that needs a second-personal relation to God in chapters 2–4. Such a need is instrumental for full human flourishing, which is itself union with God. Humankind is, therefore, intended for a unique relationship to the divine presence, which we saw as we looked at the image of God and the role of temples for Israel's theology. Further, while humankind is created in God's image, Jesus himself is the image and the temple.

After establishing how significant depending on the divine presence is for what it means to be human, we turned to the importance of that presence for understanding flourishing, especially through the language of bread, water, and filial relation in chapters 5–7. These metaphors show how central God's personal presence is for human flourishing, while also reiterating the centrality of Christ as both the embodied answer to human need (as the personal divine presence) and as a human being who needed God's personal presence, himself. Hence, Jesus brings everything together in himself. He is the true image, the bread, the water, the Son by nature, and the fullest expression of human flourishing.

Jesus perfectly depends on the Spirit (like us) while perfectly being the presence of God (not like us). We cannot understand a theological anthropology without understanding the relationship between Jesus and the Spirit while also recognizing that we are distinct from Jesus and this was the focus of chapter 8. In chapter 8 and 9 fundamental need returned to our conversation to provide a helpful framework for maintaining these continuities and discontinuities.

Recall that a fundamental need can be nonderivative while still being instrumental "for achieving the universally valuable ends of persons."[1] The universally valuable end is union with God—the constitution of human flourishing. The fundamental need is a second-personal relation to God. In this way, we see the cyclical nature of this need: humans fundamentally need God's personal presence to flourish, which is union with God, and this union requires the ongoing need for God's personal presence, though the need persists even as it is met. This need can continue to be met through time and still be a need because need is not necessarily constituted by lack. The fundamental need for a second-personal relation to God is a necessary feature of humanness.

So, in summary, God always intended to have a special relationship with human creatures whereby they would depend on God's own presence and become more like God's self as expressed in the incarnate Logos. At the incarnation, the Logos chose to enter into our same human needs and depend on the Spirit as a fundamental aspect of this humanness. The continuity of this fundamental need as a creaturely reality—from God's precreational intent to the incarnation and even to the Logos's glorification—is central to the true image. On such an account, the concept of the "image of God" functions as the mechanism connecting Christ's humanity to all humanity. Essential to this image, both prototypically and derivatively, is a need for God's personal presence. This need fits the criteria of a fundamental human need since it is nonderivative, noncircumstantial, and inescapable.

Turning to my constructive proposal using the language of need, let us turn to hunger to help us develop this theological anthropology. Think of a

---

1. Schuppert, "Distinguishing Basic Needs," 32.

meerkat.[2] One of its fundamental needs to flourish is nutrients.[3] Hence, the meerkat has an inescapable interest in finding food to flourish. The extent of flourishing for the meerkat would include experiences such as feeling full, being able to reproduce, not being eaten, and so on. A desire, such as the desire to eat, often indicates an inescapable interest.[4] Eating insects, lizards, and scorpions satisfies the inescapable interest and meets the meerkat's need, even as the need for food is ongoing. Satisfying its inescapable interest constitutes the meerkat's flourishing. The meerkat is harmed if it cannot find food. Its desires (or, more likely, its appetitive instincts in this case) are motivated by the inescapable interest to find food, whether the meerkat knows that it needs nutrients or not. However, even if it is starving and not getting this fundamental need met, it remains a meerkat.

Humans have fundamental needs as well. A human person fundamentally needs a second-personal relation to God to flourish. Hence, humans have an inescapable interest in flourishing, which is constituted by union with God's presence.[5] Relying on God's personal presence satisfies the inescapable interest and meets their need, even as the need for God's presence is ongoing. Satisfying their inescapable interest constitutes their flourishing. They are harmed if they cannot second-personally relate to God. Their desires are motivated by this inescapable interest. The object of this interest is not always discernible, but desires can indicate what is truly needed by the human person. Regardless of whether a human is having this need met (however that happens), she is still a human person.

Obvious differences between the meerkat and human emerge from this parallel—first, in the kinds of needs they have, and second, in their motivational

---

2. Both the human and the meerkat need God for their existence (weak participation). Further, humans share with the meerkat a fundamental need to survive. However, what contributes to flourishing would be distinctive. This is not to say that nonhuman creatures could not possibly be aware of God (e.g., Ps. 148:10–13); yet the kind of second-personal relation that would meet the need for union with God is not clear enough from Scripture or what has been observed thus far empirically to argue that nonhuman creatures have this fundamental need for a second-personal relation to God. In these ways (need to exist and survive), all creatures share some fundamental needs in common that can helpfully correct our tendency toward speciesism. For an argument that animals can experience some degree of communion with God in this life, see Pawl, "Exploring Theological Zoology."

3. Concerning the difference between survival and flourishing, I am assuming that the meerkat's readily accessible food is one aspect that would causally contribute to its flourishing. See chap. 1 for more on the inescapable interest in survival.

4. Though this is not necessarily the case. Especially for humans, one could have a desire to eat but it could be out of boredom, to find comfort, or based on other reasons.

5. Again, this is an ultimate end and not the only constitution of flourishing for humans but is the focus of a Christian theological anthropology (i.e., physical, psychological, social needs are all critically important, but these are addressed across a range of other disciplines).

structures, which may or may not sublimate certain desires in pursuit of other ends. Further, the reason for this need in humankind is humans' conformity to the image of God as seen in Jesus Christ. In light of the scriptural material we have examined in this book, only humans are covenant partners with God. However, this entails greater responsibility to rely on and steward the presence of God well, especially in the created world. Consequently, this proposal requires a strong theology of the Spirit.

As we have seen, the Spirit is the empowering personal presence of God, and Christ is the true image in human form, mediating the divine presence while also needing the divine presence himself. Thus, the conceptual mechanism connecting the humanity of Jesus with universal humanity is the image of God. Following from this line of argument, proposing a pneumachristocentric anthropology is justified. By this, I mean that Christ is the center of anthropology. Still, the Spirit cannot be separated from Christ—not only because of his divinity but *also* because of his humanity. Jesus lived a Spirit-directed life, which is why this is not a Christocentrically pneumatological anthropology. Giving the Spirit priority as the one enabling Jesus's existence, empowering his ministry, and being actively relied on by Jesus warrants first mention in this view. Further, this phrasing pushes against the tendency to put the Spirit after Christ as an addendum. Yet, like a combined last name, they go together.

Pneumachristocentric anthropology recognizes that God crafted humanness in such a way that humans must rely on God's Spirit to flourish fully. On this reasoning, the image of God is not possessed by a human person; it simply is the Logos—made incarnate as Jesus of Nazareth. However, the capacity to become like the true image requires being the sort of creature that can depend on God's personal presence as the meeting of that need for God's presence. For this reason, the image of God and what it means to be human are conjoined but not collapsed into one another.[6] This conjoining allows for all humanity to be understood as made in the image of God, intended toward becoming the image of God in a uniquely human way, and yet thwarted from realizing this reality due to human sinfulness.

At this juncture, a metaphor may help connect the ideas of being the image, being in the image of God, and the Trinity. Imagine an artistic masterpiece

---

6. Not collapsing them enables this theological anthropology to overlap with myriad substantival/structural theological anthropologies (Augustinian, hylomorphic, Thomistic, etc.). My main pushback on these is not that human natures may have a particular substance but that the image of God should not be defined by that understanding. However, that we need a certain kind of nature in order to be in union with God seems quite reasonable. I simply think that we can be more minimalistic in our assertions about what those natures must have. This particular need would be required in that minimum.

such as da Vinci's *Mona Lisa*. While there is only one original, millions of prints have been made of this piece. However, even if a single print is crumpled up, smeared with dirt, or torn into little pieces, the original painting remains perfect. The relation between the print and the masterpiece is that the print's value is fixed no matter what happens to it since its value is derived from the masterpiece. At the same time, the print is intended to "grow" into becoming like the masterpiece (and here, the metaphor breaks down since prints are inanimate objects). God, the divine artist, intends that the prints all become like the masterpiece, and this progression is only possible through a reliance on the presence of God the artist.[7] Such a progression requires the Holy Spirit (as God's gift of grace), Jesus (the masterpiece), and the Father (the artist).[8] Further, we have always been the prints, derivatives of the masterpiece, but intended to become more like the masterpiece. Such a view has an ancient pedigree. It was Athanasius who wrote, "You know what happens when a portrait that has been painted onto a panel becomes obliterated through external stains. The artist does not throw away the panel. Rather, the subject of the portrait has to come and sit for it again, so that his likeness can be drawn again on the same material. It was the same with the all-holy Son of God. He, the Image of the Father, came and dwelled in our midst, in order that he might renew humanity, which was made after Himself, and seek out his lost sheep."[9]

Such a progression indicates that the need for a second-personal relation to God was a creational reality oriented toward eschatological consummation—the ongoing meeting of this need. Thus, creation and eschatology are divinely paired. The critical linkage of this pairing transpires through pneumatology. In light of this, Cortez claims, "The outpouring of the Spirit also brings about a participation in the life of God and God's people that seems to transcend what we see in creation alone."[10] The flourishing that humans were meant to experience was always intended to be perfected in Christ. Colin Gunton affirms this understanding, claiming, "The distinctive work of the Spirit is, through Christ, to perfect the creation."[11] Again, such a view is not novel. Christopher Beeley gives a historical summary of this view: "In patristic theology human flourishing

---

7. A similar illustration can be found by Oliver Crisp, although using a sculpture. See "Christological Model of the *Imago Dei*," 223.

8. All trinitarian analogies tend toward one heresy or another. However, in seeking a model, we may find these metaphors helpful. Further, I have found Adonis Vidu's work on inseparable operations and distinctive missions incredibly insightful and clarifying. For example, see "Triune Agency, East and West."

9. Athanasius, *On the Incarnation of the Word* 3.14.

10. Cortez, *ReSourcing Theological Anthropology*, 49.

11. Gunton, *Christ and Creation*, 50.

is defined chiefly in terms of the divinization of human beings. Divinization or deification (*theôsis*, *theopoiêsis*, *deificatio*) means the transforming participation of human beings in the very being and life of God, with the result that they become divine or godlike as human beings. The divinization of humanity in Jesus Christ is the aim of our original creation, our deliverance from the fallen condition in which we currently exist, and our eschatological fulfillment. It is the rationale of the entire divine economy."[12] While the extent to which one becomes part of the very being of God is debated in these early thinkers, that humanity's trajectory was always intended to need the divine life is consistently affirmed. Yet this raises the question of whether humans will ever reach maximal flourishing and, if so, whether this process is consummated in their becoming divine. The conclusions from this book point in the negative, because God's cosmic intentionality seems to go to the greatest possible lengths to uniquely craft, embody, redeem, and glorify *humanity*.[13] Given that God goes to such great lengths for beings that are by nature "other" than God and whose otherness is their greatest creaturely dignity, it seems odd to say that they are to be absorbed into the divine life at some future time. Instead, this otherness appears to be "very good" (Gen. 1:31), so that doing away with humanness (or the created order) altogether would impugn God's provision of creational uniqueness to humanity. Therefore, I affirm a weak version of *theosis* so long as it can affirm some sort of transformation of humanness yet retaining its essential humanness.[14] While I do not know all that would be deemed "essential" to humanness, the property of needing a second-personal relationship with God would be necessary.

Cortez urges cautious speculation about eschatological humanity based on Jesus's postresurrection appearance, yet most agree that "some kind of transformation has taken place."[15] Given what Paul argues in 1 Corinthians 15, this is not entirely surprising, as "it seems reasonable to conclude that the ontological transformation of creational humanity was always part of God's plan."[16] At the same time, such a transformation has never been attainable by purely human means or effort but has always required the work of the Spirit and the incarnate Logos.

Additionally, while most current and historical understandings of the role of the Spirit are contingent on the need for redemption, the significance of sin does not mean that this is the *only* role of the Spirit. Instead, the Spirit is integral to

12. Beeley, "Christ and Human Flourishing," 136.
13. This is not to exclude the rest of the cosmos but to see its redemption as an extension of God's work with humanity.
14. This view finds resonance in classic Reformed anthropologies.
15. Cortez, *ReSourcing Theological Anthropology*, 251.
16. Cortez, *ReSourcing Theological Anthropology*, 251.

enabling humanity, as beings in the image of God, to move toward becoming like the one who alone is the true image of God. Grace has always been necessary for the purposes God intended for humanity, with this grace sourced in the Son and mediated through the Spirit.[17] Furthermore, even after sin and death are conquered through Christ, the progressive nature of the interiority of the divine presence continues to be reinforced after the giving of the Spirit by the Son. This indwelling presence is a foretaste of eschatological consummation, reflected in the language of the Spirit's being a "deposit" of what is to come.[18]

Even as a deposit, this Spirit is the one who enables children by grace, not by nature, to cry out "Abba, Father" (Mark 14:36).[19] Macaskill's interpretation of Galatians helps knit together the Spirit and Christ for the end of adopting humans into his family: "The combination of identification and individuation [of the Son and Spirit] means that the Spirit can meaningfully constitute the presence of the Son in his physical absence and can conform those in whom he dwells to the likeness of Christ."[20] However, if likeness to Christ, and his attendant dependence on the Spirit, is the precreational human *telos*, how this relates to soteriology is significant.

The Spirit's role is not only soteriological but also intentionally embedded in humanity's teleology. So, "whether we think 'all' are elect, that only some are chosen, or that our election is grounded in God's foreknowledge of our own belief, Scripture is clear that the proper *telos* of humanity is communion with God secured through adoption."[21] In light of the entrance of sin, however, a person's motivational reasons for being united with the divine presence are thoroughly impeded. The extent to which the intervention of the Spirit is necessary to provide the motivating reasons for choosing this unitive relation is a debate beyond the purview of this book. The central thesis of this

17. As has been argued in chap. 3, the divine presence in Israel's history becomes increasingly personal both in Israel and then, far more radically, in the New Testament. Cf. Lagrange, *Le judaïsme avant Jésus-Christ*, 446, cited in Congar, *Mystery of the Temple*, 18.

18. Cf. 2 Cor. 1:22; 5:5; Eph. 1:14. While the interpretation of "deposit" is the majority view, for a critique of this interpretation, see Kwon, "Αρραβων [*Arrabōn*] as Pledge in Second Corinthians." Both Malatesta and Macaskill note that this language indicates a pledge or down payment of what God promises. Malatesta, *Interiority and Covenant*, 213; Macaskill, *Union with Christ*, 248.

19. Since this book cannot develop a full theology of the Spirit, for a defense of the view that the Spirit operates in new ways in the New Testament I refer readers to Hamilton: "Baptisms in the Spirit, fillings with the Spirit, and indwelling by the Spirit are three distinct manifestations of the eschatological gift of the Spirit." Hamilton, *God's Indwelling Presence*, 99.

20. Macaskill, *Union with Christ*, 224–25.

21. Heim, "In Him and through Him," 145n45. Cortez concurs with this *telos* even though this does not mean that all humans will experience it. Cortez, *ReSourcing Theological Anthropology*, 177.

book is that God has intended all humanity to move toward union. However, how and in what ways human agency is involved will continue to be debated.

More can now be said about how this need sets humanity apart from the rest of the created world. This "setting apart" is rooted solely in God's divine intention and actions in human history. Therefore, human value, as distinct from the value of nonhuman creatures, proceeds exclusively from God's graciousness. Humanness is not degreed, since the need itself is not degreed. However, flourishing is degreed, since this is contingent on the meeting of the need. This view allows for a non-degreed understanding of humanness and value because God's determination to intend a unique relationship with humanity grounds human beings' identity. God wanted to form creatures who could be in an intimate relation of dependence on God's very presence, and it would seem that "human personhood is a logical consequence of God's determination to make humans in his image but that the *imago Dei* is logically prior to human personhood."[22] In other words, God could have determined what kind of relation was desired with these creatures and then decided what "conditions of possibility" would be required for this to occur.[23] Such an understanding guards against equating the image of God with human personhood. Instead, a fundamental feature of being human is the need to be in God's second-personal presence and to become like the true image of God, which is a person; such a *telos* requires humans also to be persons.[24] This approach makes personhood relationally determined, so that to pursue the satisfaction of that need, as a salient feature of humanness, one must also be a person.[25]

To be human—or at least possess one essential property of humanness—is to have the fundamental need argued herein. However, because this need is a part of humanness, like needing nutrients and hydration, value is not contingent on this need being met. In other words, the possibility that a human being may never consciously depend on the divine presence—whether because she lacks the mental awareness, never has the chance to discover this presence, actively rejects this kind of second-personal relation, or for some other reason—does not impugn her humanness or her value. Because this

---

22. Peterson, *Imago Dei as Human Identity*, 21n69.

23. Peterson, *Imago Dei as Human Identity*, 80.

24. "Human personhood should not be equated with the image of God. Rather, personhood is a condition of possibility for the realization of the image of God. In other words, humans could not live successfully as God's image without being persons." Peterson, *Imago Dei as Human Identity*, 80.

25. On Peterson's account the image of God is what constitutes human identity, and this account is consistent with my claims. For him, the identity is God determined and unimpeachable. On my reasoning, part of that identity is needing a second-personal relationship with God, which we see strongly associated with the image of God.

humanness is eschatologically grounded in the divine intentions of God, the value of human life cannot be compromised. Further, this pushes against any anthropology that degrees humanness based on an individual's reliance on the divine presence or on any other attribute. Instead, the degreed aspects of flourishing and harm are here salient. Those who are not in this second-personal relationship are experiencing harm and are consequently not flourishing in terms of this fundamental human need. This harm in one aspect of human life does not mean that other aspects of human flourishing are inaccessible. Even without meeting the need for a second-personal relation with God, needs for food, water, and human relationship may still be met. However, without this particular fundamental need being met, the potential for full human flourishing is impossible.[26]

Ultimately, a pneumachristocentric anthropology can assimilate the major features of substantival, functional, and relational anthropologies so long as the image of God and human nature remain distinct. For instance, being "in the image of God" is a noncontingent *relation* of the Spirit to humanity, a relation in which the Father chooses to pattern all humans after the true christological image. Such a relationship requires having some kind of *substance* with the dispositional property of a stimulus-response structure for needing a second-personal relation to God.[27] Given God's unique relationship to humanity, this entails the *functional* consequence of being intended to rightly represent God through Christ-like dominion on earth that is like Christ's dominion in heaven.[28] However, regardless of whether someone wants to embrace my whole theory of pneumachristocentric anthropology, there are further benefits to integrating fundamental need into our theological anthropologies if a pneumachristocentric anthropology is too robust. We will turn to these additional benefits and also address some of the concerns and objections to a needs-based anthropology that are likely to arise.

Benefits of a Needs-Based Anthropology

By now, the significance of "need" for any theological anthropology should be clear. However, to fill out the theological significance of need for a Christian

26. This raises important questions about whether there is a taxonomy of needs, but these questions must await research in my future work.

27. Using language of "substance" does not entail a substance dualism. Another benefit of this view worth brief mention is that such a needs-based anthropology can comport with several different views of human constitution. One does not need to have two distinct substances to have this need, though one could.

28. As mentioned in chap. 1 above, this will manifest as love of God and love of neighbor.

theological anthropology, we will look at several areas in which the category of fundamental need has explicit bearing. I hope that the theological purchase of such a category is compelling enough to provoke more engagement with this concept.

Human Ontology

One major benefit I believe a needs-based anthropology yields is a more minimalistic view of human nature. Given the debates theologically, philosophically, and scientifically on what a human nature is, recognizing the need to relate to God's second-personal presence as a necessary condition of humanness provides a way of discussing human uniqueness without setting humankind over against the rest of the created order. Since humans share the grace of weak participation with all other creation, we share a creaturely, contingent, and dependent ontology. Unlike God, who is *a se* and has no need for anything outside of Godself, humans (as with all creation) need what is external to themselves. And yet humankind remains unique because of their invitation to strongly participate in the divine life. Such a need is ontologically distinctive and determinative. However, humans could have this need with or without an immaterial substance.[29] This possibility does not undermine certain faculties like reason and will, but it does deemphasize the robustness of their expression. Moreover, the determination of God's second-personal presence as a fundamental need for all human beings opens theological horizons on, for instance, people with disabilities as those who can and do strongly participate in God.

At the same time, recognizing God's second-personal presence as a fundamental human need seems to provide the lowest common denominator across all expressions of humanness, so that the stages of salvation history about which we know least, especially the phases before sin and after glorification, are not pushed too far beyond their textual description. In other words, minimally, we seem able to say *something* about the significance of humanity's unique relation to the divine presence when sin was not and will not be a factor, and "need" both strengthens and constrains these assertions. For example, need supports claims about "what it means to be human." If a fundamental need can be identified and argued, it will then pertain to all

---

29. There is no shortage of debate on human ontology, which is one appeal of a needs-based anthropology, since it does not need to be dogmatic on whether or not there is an immaterial aspect, property, or substance to a human person. For a brief overview of these debates, see Cortez, *Theological Anthropology*, chap. 4. And see a range of other views from Green, "What Does It Mean to Be Human?"; Green, *Body, Soul, and Human Life*, 144–47; Farris and Taliaferro, *Ashgate Research Companion to Theological Anthropology*; Moreland and Rae, *Body & Soul*.

expressions of humanness. However, if a need is not necessary, thereby no longer being a need, then either it is not fundamental to humanness or the entity does not fit the category of being human.

The concept of fundamental need would bring a renewed valuation of creaturely need, which is not seen as imperfection or deficiency but as an invitation to have the need met—in this case—for union with God. Because this need is both dispositional and relational, it is a permanent feature while also being dynamic, as in any relationship, with the potential to expand and deepen. Such an understanding provides a way to talk about the Holy Spirit's work as the embodiment of the divine presence in the life of the new covenant believer. The Spirit enables humanity to participate in the Son's filial union with the Father—an ever-deepening relational dependence developing throughout the eschaton. Thomson, though not discussing need in a relational context, seems to have space for this kind of ongoing second-personal relation in his rubric, whereby need "indicates a disposition and does not imply a lack. I need food even when I am eating."[30] Thomson challenges the intuition that to need something is to lack something. Instead, a need is a passive disposition, which is why it is tied to a subject's ontology.[31] Therefore, such a rubric allows for an ongoing need to relate to God second-personally, growing in capacity to depend on this God's presence. Imagine that human nature is like a water balloon. It will still be a water balloon whether or not it is filled with water; however, it can be filled with varying amounts of water. Assuming there could be such a thing as an infinitely expandable water balloon, this could be what our natures are like in the eschaton. They are still water balloons, but they are filled more and more and more with the life-giving presence of God.

We see this dynamism throughout Tanner's work. She refers to Gregory of Nyssa's metaphor of an expanding container when referring to the plasticity of human nature and engagement with the divine life. There is "an expansive openness that allows for the presence of God within it." And thus, it "must be the sort of nature that has or makes room for the divine within its basic operations." Gregory describes human souls as "receptacles with free wills," with capacities "able to receive [God's] blessings and become continually larger with the inpouring of the stream."[32] Since need is not necessarily constituted

---

30. G. Thomson, "Fundamental Needs," 175.

31. Recall that needs are constitutional instead of actions. Thomson notes, "Needs are never mental acts, but are passive dispositions to suffer certain harms because of certain lacks. There is no act of needing water." *Needs*, 100.

32. K. Tanner, *Christ the Key*, 37, quoting Gregory of Nyssa's *On the Soul and Resurrection*. Cf. 38.

by lack, "unlimited openness" fits best with this concept.[33] Since a person can be eating while still needing food, she can be strongly participating in God and still need God. Jesus, even in perfectly experiencing a humanly strong participation, still needed God's Spirit even though nothing was lacking in his relationship with God. Recalling the distinction between desires and needs, however, we should add that Jesus could have had his desires for union with God fully satisfied even while continuing to need to strongly participate in the triune life dispositionally. This satisfaction of desire but persistence of need opens up further possibilities for describing human participation in the divine life, even in the eschaton. The dispositional need never goes away, and the need to receive the divine life ever remains. This account does not entail a state of perpetual frustration, given that desires can be satisfied. Still, it does entail an ongoing need for strong participation, since this remains a necessary input for the kinds of creatures humans are.

Value and Evaluation of Desire

The relationship between need and desire is, as we have noted in preceding chapters, ripe for further exploration.[34] First, the technical category of need stresses the creaturely necessity of strong participation, for which Tanner argues. As opposed to the language of desire, which may or may not determine creaturely flourishing, need is a metaphysically richer category for describing the human constitution and its ontological need for relation with God.[35] As Thomson puts it, "One can desire what one does not need and one can need what one does not desire."[36] Later, he says, "'Need' is more forceful than 'desire' because the concept of need is tied to the notion of serious harm and the concept of a desire is not."[37] If a human person does not have what she needs, she is seriously harmed. However, not having what she desires does not require this kind of logical entailment. In other words, on Thomson's account, needs and desires are separable.[38] So, whether one has

---

33. K. Tanner, *Christ the Key*, 39.

34. Consequently, this will raise questions about the relation of nature and grace that will be addressed below.

35. A renewed and focused theological interest in desire can be seen in several recent publications: Coakley, *New Asceticism*; Coakley, *God, Sexuality, and the Self*; Jensen, *God, Desire, and a Theology of Human Sexuality*; Kamitsuka, *Embrace of Eros*; Smith, *Desiring the Kingdom*; Houston, *Heart's Desire*; Graham, "Towards a Theology of Desire"; H. Walton, "Theology of Desire"; Moore, *Jesus the Liberator of Desire*.

36. G. Thomson, *Needs*, 99.

37. G. Thomson, *Needs*, 101.

38. G. Thomson, *Needs*, 66: "Cases where the reasons for desire (i.e., interests) do not coincide with the object of desire are quite commonplace."

a natural desire for God does not undermine the reality of the need. Again, this account accords with Tanner's understanding of theological anthropology as she recognizes the role of desire in human experience. We desire food, a sense of worth, friendship, and a multitude of other things, but what we make of these desires is distinct from the desires themselves. In other words, "One may have the natural desire to eat, for example, but one need not shape one's life around the importance of food."[39]

In fact, in light of human sinfulness, one's desires may or may not indicate God's intention for humankind. Thomson continues, "My need for X is independent of my beliefs about the desirability of X; it depends on the actual desirability of X."[40] So, while a "natural desire for God" is one way to account for the significance of grace (on Thomistic terms), need opens up the possibility of desires either beneficially indicating this need or indicating lesser goods.[41] This possibility becomes even more apparent with Thomson's understanding of inescapable interests that form the roots of desire. Desires can help reveal what we are being deprived of (harm) even if they are not the same as what we fundamentally need. Further, someone can be unaware of a fundamental need, though typically, she is aware of her desires.[42] If a fundamental need somehow incites an attendant desire, this may provide an inroad for discussing the value of some desires for indicating a fundamental need. Though this desire may take many forms, beginning to develop a taxonomy of desire seems to require some sort of preliminary criteria.[43] Fundamental need may provide just such standards. Thomson is helpful here as he connects harm, need, and desire: "The suffering of such harm is not merely a question of a person's not getting what he specifically wants or desires, but is more a question of his not getting what lies at the root of a whole range of wants."[44] Fundamental human need may help provide content to that which "lies at the root" of many human

---

39. K. Tanner, *Christ the Key*, 47.

40. G. Thomson, *Needs*, 100.

41. Tanner already seems to be moving in that direction within her own work; see *Christ the Key*, 110.

42. G. Thomson, *Needs*, 74.

43. The possibility for this inroad can be found throughout Thomson's work, but this excerpt is particularly promising: "We cannot truly say that a person ought to have different needs. This is because fundamental needs are inescapable. Consequently, when we justify an ideal or an aim by claiming that it answers certain fundamental needs, we cannot challenge this claim by arguing that the persons concerned ought to have different needs or ought to have different desires. It is pertinent to ask whether a person ought to have different desires. If he ought to, then the desires in question cannot be used as a clear and firm basis of evaluating other goals and ideals." *Needs*, 126.

44. G. Thomson, *Needs*, 127.

desires.[45] Consequently, it seems that desires that indicate this fundamental need are at least instrumentally valuable.

In relating this to desire, Tanner proposes that the gift of desiring God "is still being offered even as we turn away from it in sin. When we shut our eyes to the light of God, it is we who produce the barrier to the light without the light of God itself retiring or withdrawing from us. . . . It is only because of this ongoing influence of the presence of God on us despite our refusal that we retain any desire for God at all, some attraction to God as our good, even as we lead lives of sin."[46] A needs-based anthropology can account for the consequences of sin as sin can affect how we understand our desires and discover our need. While there have been many debates, especially in the twentieth century, about whether humans have natural desires for God, an account of fundamental need as an underlying structure of desires provides another helpful avenue to travel in these debates.[47] Instead of seeing human nature as already directed toward the divine, fundamental need is more neutral as an intrinsic property of human nature. However, while the need is intrinsic to human nature, the need satisfier is extrinsic to human nature. This, I believe, may provide a mediating position in the nature/grace debates.[48]

Sin as Harm

Since the criteria for what makes something a fundamental need include a determination about harm and well-being, such a picture also comports with a canonical description of the human person. While the biblical language used is often that of sin and blessing, these have a basic overlap with harm and well-being. Therefore, before looking at blessing, we will turn to sin.

Throughout the biblical canon, sin plays a prominent role, a role often related to deprivation. While the nature of sin may extend beyond deprivation, that sin's consistent consequence is the withdrawal of the divine presence supports at least a privative aspect. Sin inhibits flourishing, creating a barrier to experiencing God's personal presence. As Cornelius Plantinga notes, "Nothing about sin is its own; all its power, persistence, and plausibility are stolen goods. Sin is not really an entity but a spoiler of entities, not an organism but

---

45. This line of thinking comes out in Sarah Coakley's work: "It is not that physical 'sex' is basic and 'God' ephemeral; rather, it is God who is basic, and 'desire' the precious clue that ever tugs at the heart, reminding the human soul—however dimly—of its created source." This statement is found in her critique of Freud. Coakley, *God, Sexuality, and the Self*, 10.

46. K. Tanner, *Christ the Key*, 133. She references Gregory of Nyssa, *On Virginity* 12.

47. De Lubac, *Mystery of the Supernatural*; Parker, "Reformation or Revolution?," 81.

48. This is probably wishful thinking, but it is a possibility worth raising.

a leech on organisms. Sin does not build shalom; it vandalizes it."[49] Since the theory of need proposed by Thomson recognizes that harm is constituted by its inhibiting the meeting of a fundamental need, then this understanding of harm seems to map well onto the role that sin plays by inhibiting a second-personal relation to the divine presence.[50]

The integration of Tanner's and Thomson's works also helps drive home the weightiness of sin while not undermining the goodness of human nature itself. On this account, sin harms humans—it keeps them from strongly participating in the divine life. However, it does not undermine the need, even as it inhibits the meeting of that need.[51] So, sin is egregious since it keeps us from attaining what we require to flourish as the kinds of creatures we are (which is consonant with the way God wants us to be).[52] Sin's pervasiveness thwarts our recognition of our fundamental need and is environmental as well as internal. In other words, "Missing what we need, we substitute other things for it: created inputs replace a divine one as our central formative principle. By this means we are forced to work in ways we are not designed to. Nothing we do, consequently, is satisfying for us."[53] So, while human nature maintains its integrity, the meeting of its most fundamental need is thwarted. Sin deprives humankind of participating in its most God-glorifying end, which is identical to its greatest extent of flourishing.

One might argue that this dispositional need implies that the Genesis account sets God up to have placed the man and woman in a state of harm. To be made incomplete, lacking the very source of their flourishing, would be seen as cruel. However, in the same way that God is not typically deemed cruel because of creating humans to need water and food to survive, neither is it cruel that God would give humans another constitutional need. What would appear cruel is if God did not also provide the means to meet this need. However, not only did God give a context for these needs to be met, but God also went to great lengths to maintain that context. The intended environment for meeting these needs was a context of abundance, not only of food and water but also of God's life-giving presence. So, while humans were meant to be creatures of a special need in a context of abundance, we

---

49. Plantinga, *Not the Way It's Supposed to Be*, 89.

50. The question of whether harm is state based or event based is not critical to this discussion. However, I do not see why these are mutually exclusive and could not both be viable according to the biblical data. For articulations and defenses of both views, see Hanser, "Metaphysics of Harm"; Hanser, "Still More on the Metaphysics of Harm"; J. Thomson, "More on the Metaphysics of Harm," 436.

51. K. Tanner, *Christ the Key*, 65.

52. K. Tanner, *Christ the Key*, 62–63.

53. K. Tanner, *Christ the Key*, 68.

are still creatures of this special need, but in a context of scarcity.[54] God then entered into that context of scarcity, offering abundant life (John 10:10) while also experiencing human need and human suffering in the process of overcoming human sin.[55]

This framing of human sinfulness also leads to an additional benefit of a needs-based anthropology. On the one hand, sin is severely egregious because it impedes the meeting of a fundamental human need, thereby causing harm. On the other hand, this severity does not impugn the value or *telos* of the human person. While sin impedes the ability to depend on the divine presence and become like the true image, God's intention *that* humanity become like this true image remains constant. Therefore, one's dignity and value are grounded in God's intentions, not in our actualization of any particular capacities or functions.

Furthermore, while many fundamental human needs, such as a need for food or water, are physiologically pronounced (especially through desires)— the fundamental human need for God's second-personal presence may not be phenomenologically pronounced. This notion bears out consistently in the biblical witness as humans fail to recognize their fundamental need to relate to God's personal presence. Yet if sin is a mode of deprivation, deprivation is not always felt. In other words, humans can live in a state of harm and be unaware of this.[56] Such unawareness does not negate the reality of the need.[57] Recalling Thomson's story of the fictitious planet of Kakapos (discussed in chap. 2

54. Again, desire could feature in at this juncture as another divinely given gift to help humans realize their fundamental need for union with Godself. As with thirst indicating the need for hydration, perhaps God has built in other signs of longing that point the human person to search for God. The Christian tradition is rich with thinking along these lines; however, the technical category of need may provide even better metaphysical legs on which these arguments might stand.

55. Of course, this still raises questions about how someone needs to recognize their need and how much, specifically, they need to know content about the object of that need in order for it to be met. This needs-based anthropology does not require a specific soteriological model to work, but it does provoke questions about (1) whether God would willingly harm human beings who may not ever have epistemic access to know that they have this need (due to stage of development, time, culture, ability, etc.) and (2) how much cognitive content one must have of the object of one's need (opening possibilities for relational soteriologies over intellective soteriologies).

56. Such a picture might draw the charge of some kind of cosmic paternalism, and I think this picture is open to that if (1) God is male (not just Jesus), (2) God did not provide a way to know about this harm, (3) God did not value human agency, or (4) God only cared about maintaining power. Since I reject each of these claims, I do not believe this is some form of paternalism. However, this picture does maintain a strong Creator/creature distinction. On this account, the Creator is justified in instructing the human creature regarding what they need, since their nature was intentionally formed (or directed) to have those needs.

57. G. Thomson, *Needs*, 16.

above), we can be ignorant of the harm we are experiencing.[58] Throughout the Hebrew Bible and New Testament, true life, the path of wisdom, is indicated. Simultaneously, the way of death, the path of folly, is also clear. However, people can be ignorant of a fundamental need, and a failure to understand their need does not negate its reality. In the same way, they can remain unaware of their true identity, but this ignorance does not negate its actuality.

A needs-based anthropology can recognize the depth of sinfulness, since this impedes the fundamental human need for a second-personal relationship with God. However, such an account does not then degree humanness or lead to a devaluation of the human person, as if they are somehow less human if they do not recognize this need.

Significance of Community

While this book has focused on humanity's fundamental need for a second-personal relationship with God, which is then relied on and made possible through the incarnate Logos, the implications for this constitutional human need are necessarily communal as well. When humans do not get their fundamental need met through dependence on the divine presence, the corollary good of human community experiences privation. As Thomson explains,

> It is an important feature of the concept "harm" that the things we are deprived of when we are harmed have both primary and secondary value. If something is both a primary and a secondary good, then it is doubly bad to lack it. Harm typically does reinforce itself in this way: the things we lack when we are harmed are things which are harmful to lack. In this sense, harm has an ongoing quality, and is the opposite of flourishing. The good things which we have and appreciate when we flourish themselves lead us on to further goods, and so on.[59]

So, when a person depends on the personal divine presence, this is a primary good and is not pursued for any other end. This relation benefits human community, especially with others who are also dependent on the divine presence. A secondary good comes about when community members are built up in their mutual dependence on the divine presence, which also has a unifying effect on this community, causing even more goods to arise. In this present age, the collective of human persons unified by their dependence on the personal divine presence is the church. The presence of God continues to expand in the world today, not just through individual persons but through the whole

---

58. G. Thomson, *Needs*, 36.
59. G. Thomson, *Needs*, 39–40.

body living out the power of that presence in their lives corporately. This significance is attested by the need for community in the garden and the role of the expanded community in the eschaton.

Furthermore, in between these times Israel and, later, the church are intended to enter into God's presence and expand God's presence into the world around them. The adoption as God's children, especially in the new covenant reality, emphasizes the relation of spiritual siblings in a new mode of intimacy. Malatesta, in his work on 1 John, makes this relation explicit. He argues that the Spirit, Father, and Jesus "ground and determine the interpersonal relationships of the members of the community among themselves (see 1,3). The community will be a family of brothers and sisters who live in mutual love to the degree that they are all children of the same Father, have Jesus as their brother, and are guided by the same Holy Spirit."[60] Thus, the human need for dependence on God's Spirit constitutes the condition that unifies the spiritual community, rendering an expanding family of God, adopted through the Son.[61]

Greater Cross-Testament Continuity

Since the Old Testament saints needed to relate to God's personal presence just as much as humans from any other era of salvation history, God's presence with them was still a gift of God's Spirit. This need opens up greater continuity between the scriptural testaments, as the work of Word and Spirit are, in Tanner's account, graciously active throughout human history, meeting this ongoing human need. In an article wherein she responds to commentators on *Christ the Key*, Tanner states, "If we are created in Christ's image, then we are created to be something like what Christ is even before his coming—to lead a life in service to the beneficent Father's mission for the world as that is shaped according to the pattern of the Word through the power of the Holy Spirit."[62] In salvation history, this took many forms, including the tabernacle, the temple, theophanies, anointed prophets, and much else that God gave to Israel. God's action in and with Israel reveals that God chooses to continue

---

60. Malatesta, *Interiority and Covenant*, 324.

61. The development of this ecclesiology as it relates to the fundamental human need defended here is too rich not to make a comment about how this affects who is able to minister as a member of this royal priesthood. Since the fundamental human need to depend on the divine presence and thereby enact the functions of representing God's rule and expanding this presence into all the world is not contingent on sexed differences, it seems problematic to theologically condition these functions to one's sexed embodiment.

62. Soskice, Koster, McFarland, Lösel, McDougall, and Tanner, "*Christ the Key* Book Forum," 345–46.

to provide humans with God's own personal presence and provide for their need for strong participation, even if it had not yet been fully realized. Tanner alludes to something like this when she says, "This gift of the Spirit explains how scripture can call people 'sons of God' prior to the incarnation."[63] God provided ways, by grace, for humankind to participate in the divine life, even if strong participation was not permanently accessible before the incarnation.

Such a continuity helps push against a replacement theology that sees the church as the new Israel. As T. F. Torrance insightfully states, "In the whole historico-redemptive activity of God in Israel the Kingdom of God and the people of God were essentially correlative conceptions, or rather two different aspects, of the one rule of God grounded in creation and made good in redemption. It was to be fulfilled through the saving acts of God in Israel but on fulfilment it would inevitably transcend the boundaries of Israel and take form as the universal kingship of God over all his creation."[64] This way of viewing Israel compels gentiles to view their inclusion among the people of God as an act of God's radical love. Thus, gentiles are invited into the family of God that already existed and can enter into this new kinship because of the *prōtotokos*, Jesus of Nazareth, expanding Israel through himself.

Maintains Primary Principles

The concept of need also supports Tanner's principles of God's radical transcendence and of the noncompetitiveness between the divine and human. Creatures have needs, God does not.[65] Tanner states this clearly: "There is nothing in between God and creatures, no ontological continuum spanning the difference between them, despite what the idea of one creature better imitating God than another might suggest; and therefore there can be no real approximation to the divine on any creature's part."[66] Thus, God meets human needs while humans remain what they are.[67] Humans will never escape their needs, even as they are being met, and thus the discontinuity between God and creatures is further established. However, in "meeting" human needs, God never becomes less of who God is, even as humans become even more of who they are meant to be while remaining human.

63. K. Tanner, *Christ the Key*, 27.
64. T. Torrance, *Theology in Reconstruction*, 199.
65. Although this does raise an interesting question about whether each member of the Trinity needs the others, as briefly mentioned in chap. 9. However, this needs-based anthropology still maintains the primary principle of noncompetitiveness, since how each person of the Trinity needs each other is radically different from how humans need one another or even need God.
66. K. Tanner, *Christ the Key*, 12.
67. K. Tanner, *Christ the Key*, 12.

Well-Being as Flourishing

Finally, the meeting of this need enables a retelling of the Christian narrative as a story of flourishing. The good news is truly good. Herein lies perhaps the greatest case for the value of fundamental need discourse for theology, as summarized by Pennington. Pennington recognizes that the *Bible* is about human flourishing, and he is not alone in this bold assessment.[68] While this should be nuanced (as Pennington himself does) by saying the Bible is about revealing who God is, at the same time, this revelation remains bound to human flourishing, even as it goes far beyond this theme.

Furthermore, this makes even more sense of the incarnation as the "good news" for the whole world. The one who made humanity also intended for this creation to thrive and created the means for this flourishing—even if this meant dying and rising again to bring this about for human creatures. Pennington goes on to say, "The proclamation of both the Jewish and Christian Scriptures is that the God of Abraham, Isaac, Jacob, and (Father of) Jesus offers the only true, full, and enduring human flourishing available in the world."[69] Notably, the Scriptures are even more centrally about the magnificence and power of God, whose very Being brings about this environment. "Receiving God's grace," Tanner maintains, "becomes a requirement for simply being a human being fully alive and flourishing."[70] Such flourishing is only possible through participation in that which is not in ourselves and comes from without. Pulling from the inescapability criterion for fundamental need, we can say that the only viable course of action for meeting that need is Christ. Fundamental human need and Christ are inseparable. Humans are intended not just for weak imaging of the divine but for strong imaging. Such strong imaging is concentrated in the person of Jesus Christ, whom the New Testament depicts as the faithful human being in whom God's image subsists because he is the God-man. Thus, when humans sin, they excise themselves and other created life from experiencing full flourishing. When applied to Jesus, this also means that even though he did not sin, he still entered a world conditioned by sin as he revealed the path to true flourishing through himself.[71]

---

68. Pennington, *Sermon on the Mount*, 290–94, 309.
69. Pennington, *Sermon on the Mount*, 290–91.
70. K. Tanner, *Christ the Key*, 60.
71. Flourishing consistently features in the works of patristic theologians, wherein by participating in Christ's identity, a person experiences flourishing. Beeley cites the support of several thinkers: Athanasius, *Orationes contra Arianos* 1.38, 41–43; Gregory of Nyssa, *Against Eunomius* 3.3.67–68; Maximus Confessor, *Opuscule* 7.81C. Beeley, "Christ and Human Flourishing," 129, 133.

Anticipating Objections to a Needs-Based Anthropology

It seems to me that the primary objections to a needs-based anthropology would parallel the objections to a desire-based anthropology and which we have already briefly addressed in chapter 9 as they relate to Tanner's work. These have become known as the "nature/grace" debates and have been especially prominent in Roman Catholic thought. The two primary views are extrinsicism and intrinsicism: "In extrinsicism, the supernatural acts outside of nature and is alien to human nature. Intrinsicism, on the other hand, emphasizes that nature and grace are intertwined, such that there is no such thing as a natural end. Human nature is oriented toward the supernatural. Since human beings desire a supernatural end they do not have a 'pure nature.' It is already directed towards the supernatural."[72] The objection lodged against intrinsicists is that by denying any kind of "pure nature," a nature that can exist apart from the supernatural, they seem to obligate God to give grace (on my account, God's personal presence) for humans to reach their intended end. Thus, God's absolute freedom is undermined. Further, because nature cannot be understood apart from grace, human nature has no integrity unto itself.

My response is that if a need for grace was divinely determined to be central to what it means to be human at or even before creation, then the "act of creation just is the ordination of eschatological consummation."[73] In other words, by choosing not only to create but also how to create humankind, God remains free. By creating creatures of this kind, "human," creatures who need a second-personal relation to God to be united with God, God willingly obligated Godself to meet this need. Furthermore, the voluntary obligation of God to provide for this unique human need no more undermines God's graciousness than the fact that creatures need hydration obligated God to create water. In other words, if humankind's need for God's personal presence undermines God's graciousness, then all creaturely needs that must be met by external inputs thereby undermine God's grace. However, since being a creature as opposed to *a se* characterizes creatureliness, having needs is bound to being a creature. So, God's graciousness is gratuitous at every turn—not only in God's *creating* human beings at all but also in his intending for humans to have this need that only God could meet. God, knowing that this need would, in some way, constitute humanness, willingly obligated Godself to provide for this need through the lasting gift of Godself.[74]

---

72. Parker, "Reformation or Revolution?," 81.

73. Cortez, *ReSourcing Theological Anthropology*, 66. See also K. Tanner, *Christ the Key*, 116.

74. Balthasar raises a similar point in *Dare We Hope "That All Men Be Saved"?*: "God owed the created being whatever is in accordance with his wisdom and will and, given that, whatever

Regarding the second objection, while I agree that we cannot talk about full human flourishing apart from grace, we can speak of degreed flourishing and a nature in a state of lack. Thus, this unique need tells us a good deal about how God desires to relate to humans and how having a mutable nature is an intentional aspect of being human. Again, Tanner's work in *Christ the Key* is helpful here, wherein she discusses the plasticity of human nature as distinct from the rest of the creaturely kingdom.[75] Yet as unique as this human nature may be in its openness to the divine, it cannot of its own accord unify itself with divinity.

Furthermore, discussion of capacities and properties that have a natural end is still possible on the intrinsic account, whereby human nature remains intelligible. However, these "must be understood as penultimate realities meant to serve the higher telos of eschatological consummation."[76] The discussion of need is also helpful here, because there are degrees of meeting a need. For example, the need for food is fundamental; however, this need may not be a part of our constitution in the eschaton. Therefore, it would not fit the criterion of being inescapable. However, we can have fruitful conversations about instrumental needs and fundamental needs of a nonspiritual sort, which all contribute to discussions of what it means to be human. While human nature cannot be understood exhaustively apart from grace, it can still be understood accurately apart from grace. Recalling our example above, a meerkat is still a meerkat even if it is not eating bugs. A human is still a human even if she is not relating to God's personal presence.

Another objection might be that the claim about someone not realizing they are not flourishing is not falsifiable because a person may not know if they are being harmed. Further, there are many other ways to flourish, even without this need being met, so a lack of flourishing related to the divine-human relationship may be hard to discern. I think this is a valid point. However, if we return to abduction, this theological proposal can perhaps be

---

his goodness allows to become manifest; in this sense, God's justice is an expression of what befits (*decentia*) himself, through which he guarantees himself what he owes himself. On the other hand, he owes the created being whatever befits that being, for instance, in the case of man, that he has hands or that the animals are subject to him. But this second sort of indebtedness is dependent upon the first. For if God gives a created being what is owed, that does not mean that he himself is a debtor, since, after all, he is not ordered toward his creatures, but they are ordered toward him. That they exist at all, and are what they are, is due not to God's justice but solely to his goodness and generosity (a.1 ad 3), which means that his justice—in respect of both himself and his creatures—is to be seen as a mode of his goodness" (88). I am grateful to Natalie Carnes for supplying this reference.

75. K. Tanner, *Christ the Key*, 39–40.

76. Cortez, *ReSourcing Theological Anthropology*, 67, pulling from his interpretation of de Lubac.

helpfully supplemented by looking at testimonies and studies that attest to people's second-personal relationships with God and whether this positively correlates with their flourishing. Relatedly, because there are many aspects to flourishing—union with God is our ultimate end, but there are many penultimate ends (relationships with community, family, meaningful work, emotional health, etc.)—one might be flourishing in relationship with God but not be flourishing in all ways. We see this come out even in the apostle Paul's words, when he rejoices even in a state of physical need (Phil. 4:11–13). At the same time, the relationship between penultimate and ultimate needs is an area of research that would benefit from engagement.

CONCLUSION

This book has proposed that humans were created for an intended receptivity—a need without lack. The realization of this need involves dynamic growth, so that the dispositional need for a second-personal relation to God requires ongoing fulfillment. Additionally, this need was intended to be discovered in a context of abundance, an abundance of what—or, better, who—would continually meet this need. When sin entered the narrative, however, scarcity and toil took the place of abundance and rest. Thus, this need was not intrinsically an imperfection but a receptivity integral to what it means to be human. While having needs is typically understood negatively, on this view, such need indicates the greatest creaturely dignity God could have granted humankind—that it is created to be dynamically satisfied in and through communion with the triune life of God. Such communion is made possible through the incarnation of the Logos, who puts on *human* form so that all humanity might reach its intended end of union with the divine presence and becoming like the true image through the work of the Spirit.

Afterword

Building Bridges and Moving Forward

Given the integrative and constructive nature of this project, many questions likely remain unanswered. Therefore, I would like to conclude with some possible areas that may benefit from further exploration.

One such area is the relationship between analytic theology and liberation theology, a relationship that could be strengthened if scholars in both schools would consider this aspect of dependence.[1] As an example, in Bauckham's commentary on James, he recognizes, "The poor are the paradigm heirs of the kingdom, paradigmatic both in their lack of social status and economic security and in the wholehearted dependence on God in faith that accompanies it."[2] There is much to learn from the poor and disenfranchised as those who may uniquely bear witness to this fundamental need—both to the church and the world. Those who are flourishing regarding a second-personal relation to God while their penultimate needs are not being met could bear witness to parts of the church whose penultimate needs are met but are not flourishing in their second-personal relation to God.

Second, by thinking of one central aspect of flourishing as union with God's presence, we could reexamine the question of what impedes that flourishing. So, if union with God is not compromised, one wonders if some disabilities are merely differences.[3] Utilizing Elizabeth Barnes's distinction

---

1. The value—indeed, the possible necessity—of this linkage is argued for by Sameer Yadav, "Toward an Analytic Theology of Liberation."

2. Bauckham, *James*, 103.

3. "Any state of affairs that prevents perfect union with or worship of God will be absent. But the possibility that some disabilities might have such an effect certainly doesn't entail that

between "bad-difference" and "mere-difference," especially when thinking eschatologically, one can ask, If a disability does not make a person automatically worse off, will it require healing?[4] Given the rhetoric in many spiritual communities regarding the relation of human sin to disability and the supposed necessity of eschatological healing, an anthropology that provides space for some disabilities that are not inhibiting the meeting of this fundamental need would seem prima facie valuable.

This understanding of disability also relates to ecclesiology and eschatology. When sin and death are no longer a part of the human order, perhaps what has been understood as an inhibitor to human-to-human relationships will no longer be experienced as such. For instance, blindness is often perceived as a "bad-difference" given the present state of affairs. However, this is often experienced as harm because there are no infrastructures to accommodate this difference, nor is there human understanding of the full value of someone who is differently sighted. If both of these were addressed, perhaps disabilities that seem like bad-differences could be experienced as mere-differences.

Third, the corporate nature of the image of God also flows from a needs-based anthropology. We are not just individuals with this need for a relation in the divine presence, but also a community of such persons. Under Thomson's rubric, the primary good of meeting a fundamental need would affect secondary goods. This aspect of the image of God—specifically as it relates to Christology and ecclesiology—could use more exegetical study and theological application and has already been alluded to in light of some of Willie Jennings's exhortations throughout this work.[5] We often meet the need for a second-personal relation to God while in community and in communion with those unlike us.[6]

Fourth, a scientific benefit of a needs-based view is its possible compatibility with evolutionary theory.[7] Whether we understand the creation accounts as historically factual, purely literary, or as theologically imaginative, the early Hebrew audience would have understood them as their central origin

---

all disabilities are like that, and I think we have reasons (both testimonial and theological) to believe that not all disabilities would have this negative effect." Timpe, "Defiant Afterlife," 21.

4. Barnes, *Minority Body*, 54.

5. Cf. McDowell's comments (*Image of God*, 210) on the corporate nature of the image of God, which would benefit from further study. Peter-Ben Smit asserts, "For Paul, ecclesiology is ultimately shaped by Christology." *Paradigms of Being in Christ*, 164.

6. Jennings, *Christian Imagination*, 270.

7. While theistic evolutionary accounts that suggest that humans are in the image of God may not be without problems, the evidence continues to grow that evolutionary theory must be taken seriously in discussions of theological anthropology. For a theological perspective on this development and its impact on theological anthropology, see Moritz, "Evolutionary Biology and Theological Anthropology."

story.[8] Yet these were not origin accounts about the "how" in the ways that modern readers would like them to be.[9] Instead, so much of these origin accounts are identity accounts, concerned with questions of why and who. The accounts of Genesis 1 and 2 communicate God's sui generis power and authority, humanity's uniqueness, creation's goodness, and the significance of the divine presence. Those, not the scientific explanation of the world's beginnings, are the illocutions that permeate the rest of the Christian story. A key question would be, How might this need for relating to God's personal presence have evolved?

Relatedly, such an understanding would enable more beneficial engagement with social and empirical sciences. For instance, the importance of surrounding environments to the human person and the unique plasticity of the human person, both emphasized by Tanner, are both well attested in social and developmental psychology.[10] The external context and the human's inner nature are in perpetual dialogue. Tanner states this explicitly: "What is of theological interest about it is its lack of given definition, malleability through outside influences, unbounded character, and general openness to radical transformation."[11] Humans may have evolved to have just such open-ended natures as they now exhibit. Perhaps, by asserting this fundamental need, we are reschematizing existence itself as an instrumental need: humans exist to strongly participate in the triune life. Thus, all needs relating to existing and even surviving might be prioritized as instrumental for this chief end.

Fifth, for those who think that any view of the image of God and human uniqueness necessarily entails a form of speciesism, the needs-based view seems to provide the most modest form of this uniqueness, which is hopefully less open to abuses.[12] However, from a Christian theological perspective, *that* humans are unique in some way is undeniable based on the *imago Dei* and the incarnation of the Logos in human form. However, the mere fact that the human relation to the divine life is unique does not mean that the

8. This list is not meant to exhaust the ways these chapters might be read but to highlight the diversity of ways one might go about reading them.

9. For a development of the idea that identity is central to these accounts from a biblical scholar's perspective, see J. Walton, *Lost World of Genesis One*.

10. This is not to say that other creatures do not depend on their environments; however, the human brain is incredibly plastic compared to other creatures' brains. The most similar brain would be that of the chimpanzee, but upon comparison, the chimpanzee's brain is still more controlled by genetic factors. Gómez-Robles, Hopkins, Schapiro, and Sherwood, "Relaxed Genetic Control," 14799.

11. K. Tanner, *Christ the Key*, 1.

12. On Moritz's terms, this would be called a "non-essentialist" anthropology, as opposed to other anthropologies, which are largely "essentialist." "Evolutionary Biology and Theological Anthropology," 49.

rest of the created world is not intended to experience the divine presence. Bartholomew, drawing from Irenaeus, maintains that "the creation was made for humankind, but this is an administrative anthropocentrism and decidedly not an ontological one. Creation is arranged for the well-being of humans, but this is not its only purpose—it has its own integrity in relation to God. Human dominion over creation is muted in Irenaeus's theology."[13] Grounding human uniqueness in God's divine intentions and in an understanding that these intentions included the function of wise creation care emphasizes God's authority over the created world, not human control over nonhuman creatures.

Such a de-emphasis on human superiority finds support in the opening Genesis accounts, which reveal both a distinctiveness and commonality between nonhuman creatures and human creatures. I have addressed this distinctiveness throughout this book; the focus here is the commonality of all creatures. Bauckham notes that "in Genesis 2:7 God forms the first human from the earth, just as he does all other living creatures, flora, and fauna. Adam's earthiness is emphasized by the wordplay between his name Adam and the Hebrew word for the ground, 'adamah.'"[14] This continuity of the "earthling" with the rest of the created world should temper any theology of dominion. The biological sciences attest to such commonality, as seen in the fact that humans share 99 percent of their DNA with nonhuman creatures.[15] These exegetical and scientific observations should help mitigate the ideology of superiority that can sometimes accompany Christian theological anthropology.

As this leg of the journey ends, minimally, we have seen the value of need for understanding theological anthropology. Maximally, we have seen that God desires to meet our need for union with God's own presence through Jesus and the Spirit. Regardless, I hope that readers will find other ways to improve upon this proposal as we seek to discern what it means to be human in light of what God has revealed in human history and continues to reveal in these present times.

---

13. Bartholomew, *Where Mortals Dwell*, 197; cf. Irenaeus, *Against Heresies* 2.1.1–2.10.4.
14. Bauckham, *Living with Other Creatures*, 4.
15. Daniel Fairbanks, *Relics of Eden: The Powerful Evidence of Evolution in Human DNA* (Amherst, NY: Prometheus Books, 2010), 96.

Bibliography

Aalen, Sverre. "Δόξα [Doxa]." In *The New International Dictionary of New Testament Theology*, edited by Colin Brown, 2:44–52. Grand Rapids: Zondervan, 1986.

Alexander, T. Desmond. *From Eden to the New Jerusalem: An Introduction to Biblical Theology*. Grand Rapids, MI: Kregel, 2008.

———. *From Paradise to the Promised Land: An Introduction to the Pentateuch*. 3rd ed. Grand Rapids: Baker Academic, 2012.

Allison, Dale C. *James: A Critical and Exegetical Commentary*. International Critical Commentary. London: Bloomsbury T&T Clark, 2013.

Alston, William P. *Divine Nature and Human Language: Essays in Philosophical Theology*. Ithaca, NY: Cornell University Press, 1989.

———. "The Indwelling of the Holy Spirit." In *Philosophy and the Christian Faith*, edited by Thomas V. Morris, 121–50. Notre Dame, IN: University of Notre Dame Press, 1988.

Anderson, Gary A. "The Cosmic Mountain: Eden and Its Early Interpreters in Syriac Christianity." In Morales, *Cult and Cosmos*, 367–88.

Anderson, Ray S., and Todd H. Speidell. *On Being Human: Essays in Theological Anthropology*. Eugene, OR: Wipf & Stock, 2010.

Aquinas, Thomas. *Summa Theologiae*. Translated by Fathers of the English Dominican Province. 2nd ed. 1920. https://www.newadvent.org/summa/.

Arcadi, James. "God Is Where God Acts: Reconceiving Divine Omnipresence." *Topoi* 36 (2017): 631–39.

———. *An Incarnational Model of the Eucharist*. Cambridge: Cambridge University Press, 2018.

Arcadi, James M., and James T. Turner, eds. *T&T Clark Handbook of Analytic Theology*. London: Bloomsbury T&T Clark, 2021.

Athanasius. *On the Incarnation of the Word*. Christian Classics Ethereal Library. Accessed October 18, 2021. https://www.ccel.org/ccel/athanasius/incarnation.

Augustine. *The Literal Meaning of Genesis*, vol. 2, *Books 7–12*. Translated by John Hammond Taylor. Ancient Christian Texts. New York: Paulist Press, 1982.

Badcock, Gary D. *Light of Truth and Fire of Love: A Theology of the Holy Spirit*. Grand Rapids: Eerdmans, 1997.

Balthasar, Hans Urs von. *Dare We Hope "That All Men Be Saved"? With a Short Discourse on Hell*. 2nd ed. Translated by David Kipp and Lothar Karuth. San Francisco: Ignatius, 2014.

Barker, Kit. *Imprecation as Divine Discourse: Speech Act Theory, Dual Authorship, and Theological Interpretation*. Winona Lake, IN: Eisenbrauns, 2018.

Barnes, Elizabeth. *The Minority Body: A Theory of Disability*. Oxford: Oxford University Press, 2016.

Barnett, Paul. *The Second Epistle to the Corinthians*. Grand Rapids: Eerdmans, 1997.

Barr, James. "The Image of God in the Book of Genesis: A Study of Terminology." *Bulletin of the John Rylands Library* 51, no. 1 (1968): 11–26.

Barth, Karl. *Church Dogmatics*, vol. III, *The Doctrine of Creation*, part 1. Translated by J. W. Edwards, O. Bussey, and H. Knight. London: T&T Clark, 1958.

Bartholomew, Craig. *Where Mortals Dwell: A Christian View of Place for Today*. Grand Rapids: Baker Academic, 2011.

Bauckham, Richard. "The Incarnation and the Cosmic Christ." In *Incarnation: On the Scope and Depth of Christology*, edited by Niels Henrik Gregerson, 25–58. Minneapolis: Fortress, 2013.

———. *James*. London: Routledge & Kegan Paul, 1999.

———. *Jesus and the God of Israel: God Crucified and Other Studies on the New Testament's Christology of Divine Identity*. Grand Rapids: Eerdmans, 2008.

———. *Living with Other Creatures: Green Exegesis & Theology*. Waco: Baylor University Press, 2011.

———. *The Theology of the Book of Revelation*. New Testament Theology. Cambridge: Cambridge University Press, 1993.

Beale, Gregory K. *The Temple and the Church's Mission: A Biblical Theology of the Dwelling Place of God*. Downers Grove, IL: InterVarsity, 2004.

Beale, Gregory K., and Mitchell Kim. *God Dwells among Us: Expanding Eden to the Ends of the Earth*. Downers Grove, IL: InterVarsity, 2015.

Beasley-Murray, George R. *John*. 2nd ed. Word Biblical Commentary 36. 1999. Reprint, Grand Rapids: Zondervan, 2015.

BeDuhn, Jason David. "'Because of the Angels': Unveiling Paul's Anthropology in 1 Corinthians 11." *Journal of Biblical Literature* 118, no. 2 (1999): 295–320.

Beeley, Christopher A. "Christ and Human Flourishing in Patristic Theology." *Pro Ecclesia* 25, no. 2 (2016): 126–53.

Beetham, Christopher A. *Echoes of Scripture in the Letter of Paul to the Colossians.* Boston: Brill, 2008.

Bird, Phyllis A. "'Male and Female He Created Them': Gen 1:27b in the Context of the Priestly Account of Creation." *Harvard Theological Review* 74, no. 2 (1981): 129–59.

Block, Daniel I., and U. Cassuto. *A Commentary on the Book of Exodus.* Jerusalem: Magnes, 1976.

Briggs, Richard S. "Humans in the Image of God and Other Things Genesis Does Not Make Clear." *Journal of Theological Interpretation* 4, no. 1 (2010): 111–26.

Briggs, Robert A. *Jewish Temple Imagery in the Book of Revelation.* New York: Lang, 1999.

Brock, Gillian, and David Miller. "Needs in Moral and Political Philosophy." In *Stanford Encyclopedia of Philosophy.* Stanford University, 1997–. Article published April 11, 2019. https://plato.stanford.edu/archives/sum2019/entries/needs/.

Brown, Jeannine K. "Creation's Renewal in the Gospel of John." *Catholic Biblical Quarterly* 72, no. 2 (2010): 275–90.

Brown, Raymond. *The Gospel according to John I–XII.* Anchor Bible 29. London: Continuum, 1971.

Bruce, F. F. *The Epistle to the Hebrews.* Grand Rapids: Eerdmans, 1990.

Burge, Gary M. *John.* NIV Application Commentary. Grand Rapids: Zondervan, 2000.

Burrows, E., SJ. "Some Cosmological Patterns in Babylonian Religion." In Morales, *Cult and Cosmos,* 27–48.

Bustion, Olivia. "Autism and Christianity: An Ethnographic Intervention." *Journal of the American Academy of Religion* 85, no. 3 (September 2017): 653–81.

Carr, Wesley. "Imago Dei." In *The New Dictionary of Pastoral Studies,* edited by Wesley Carr, Donald Capps, Robin Gill, Anton Obholzer, Ruth Page, Deborah van Deusen Hunsinger, and Rowan Williams, 169. New ed. London: SPCK, 2002.

Charry, Ellen T. *God and the Art of Happiness: An Offering of Pastoral Doctrinal Theology.* Grand Rapids: Eerdmans, 2011.

Choi, Sungho, and Michael Fara. "Dispositions." In *Stanford Encyclopedia of Philosophy.* Stanford University, 1997–. Article published July 26, 2006. Substantive revision June 22, 2018. https://plato.stanford.edu/entries/dispositions/.

Clines, D. J. A. "Image of God." In *Dictionary of Paul and His Letters*, edited by Gerald F. Hawthorne, Ralph P. Martin, and Daniel G. Reid, 427. Downers Grove, IL: InterVarsity, 1994.

———. "The Image of God in Man." *Tyndale Bulletin*, no. 19 (1968): 53–103.

Clough, David L. *On Animals*. Vol. 1, *Systematic Theology*. London: Bloomsbury T&T Clark, 2012.

Coakley, Sarah. *God, Sexuality, and the Self: An Essay "On the Trinity."* New York: Cambridge University Press, 2013.

———. *The New Asceticism*. London: Bloomsbury Continuum, 2016.

Cockayne, Joshua. "Contemporaneity and Communion: Kierkegaard on the Personal Presence of Christ." *British Journal for the History of Philosophy* 25, no. 1 (2017): 41–62.

Cockerill, Gareth Lee. *The Epistle to the Hebrews*. New International Commentary on the New Testament. Grand Rapids: Eerdmans, 2012.

Coffey, David. "The Whole Rahner on the Supernatural Existential." *Theological Studies* 65, no. 1 (February 2004): 95–118.

Cole, Graham A. *He Who Gives Life: The Doctrine of the Holy Spirit*. Wheaton: Crossway, 2007.

Coloe, M. L. "Theological Reflections on Creation in the Gospel of John." *Pacifica* 24, no. 1 (2011): 1–12.

Congar, Yves. *The Mystery of the Temple*. Westminster, MD: Newman Press, 1962.

Cortez, Marc. *Christological Anthropology in Historical Perspective: Ancient and Contemporary Approaches to Theological Anthropology*. Grand Rapids: Zondervan, 2016.

———. "Idols, Images, and a Spirit-ed Anthropology: A Pneumatological Account of the *Imago Dei*." In *Third Article Theology: A Pneumatological Dogmatics*, edited by Myk Habets, 267–82. Minneapolis: Fortress, 2016.

———. "The Madness in our Method: Christology as the Necessary Starting Point for Theological Anthropology." In Farris and Taliaferro, *Ashgate Research Companion to Theological Anthropology*, 15–26.

———. *ReSourcing Theological Anthropology*. Grand Rapids: Zondervan, 2018.

———. *Theological Anthropology: A Guide for the Perplexed*. London: T&T Clark, 2010.

Craigie, Peter C., and Marvin E. Tate. *Psalms 1–50*. 2nd ed. Word Biblical Commentary 19. Nashville: Nelson, 2004.

Crisp, Oliver D. "A Christological Model of the *Imago Dei*." In Farris and Taliaferro, *Ashgate Research Companion to Theological Anthropology*, 217–30.

———. "Desiderata for Models of the Hypostatic Union." In *Christology, Ancient and Modern: Explorations in Constructive Dogmatics*, edited by Oliver Crisp, G. Hunsinger, P. J. Leithart, and Fred Sanders, 19–41. Grand Rapids: Zondervan, 2013.

———. "Did Christ Have a Fallen Human Nature?" *International Journal of Systematic Theology* 6, no. 3 (July 2004): 270–88.

———. *Divinity and Humanity: The Incarnation Reconsidered*. 1st ed. Cambridge: Cambridge University Press, 2007.

Crittenden, Paul. "David Coffey: Reshaping Traditional Theology." *Irish Theological Quarterly* 83, no. 4 (2018): 310–28.

Cuneo, Terence. *Ritualized Faith: Essays on the Philosophy of Liturgy*. Oxford Studies in Analytic Theology. Oxford: Oxford University Press, 2016.

Davis, Ellen F. *Scripture, Culture, and Agriculture: An Agrarian Reading of the Bible*. New York: Cambridge University Press, 2008.

DeFranza, Megan K. *Sex Difference in Christian Theology: Male, Female, and Intersex in the Image of God*. Grand Rapids: Eerdmans, 2015.

de Lubac, Henri. *The Mystery of the Supernatural*. Reprint. New York: Crossroad, 1998.

Dewick, Edward Chisholm. *The Indwelling God: A Historical Study of the Christian Conception of Divine Immanence and Incarnation, with Special Reference to Indian Thought*. Oxford: Oxford University Press, 1938.

Dion, Paul-Eugène. "Image et ressemblance en Araméen ancien (Tell Fakhariyah)." *Science et esprit* 34, no. 2 (May 1982): 151–53.

Dumbrell, William J. *Covenant and Creation: An Old Testament Covenant Theology*. 2nd ed. Exeter: Paternoster, 2013.

———. *The Search for Order*. Grand Rapids: Baker, 1994.

Dunn, James D. G. *Christology in the Making: An Inquiry into the Origins of the Doctrine of the Incarnation*. 2nd ed. London: SCM, 2003.

———. *The Epistles to the Colossians and to Philemon: A Commentary on the Greek Text*. New International Greek Testament Commentary. Grand Rapids: Eerdmans, 1996.

———. *The Theology of Paul the Apostle*. Grand Rapids: Eerdmans, 1998.

Duvall, J. Scott, and J. Daniel Hays. *God's Relational Presence: The Cohesive Center of Biblical Theology*. Grand Rapids: Baker Academic, 2019.

Erickson, Millard. *Christian Theology*. Grand Rapids: Baker, 1998.

Estelle, Bryan D. *Echoes of Exodus: Tracing a Biblical Motif*. Downers Grove, IL: InterVarsity, 2018.

Fairbanks, Daniel. *Relics of Eden: The Powerful Evidence of Evolution in Human DNA*. Amherst, NY: Prometheus Books, 2010.

Farris, Joshua R., and Charles Taliaferro, eds. *The Ashgate Research Companion to Theological Anthropology*. New ed. Burlington, VT: Ashgate, 2015.

Faur, José. "The Biblical Idea of Idolatry." *Jewish Quarterly Review* 69 (1978): 1–15.

Fee, Gordon D. *God's Empowering Presence: The Holy Spirit in the Letters of Paul*. Peabody, MA: Hendrickson, 1994.

———. *Paul, the Spirit, and the People of God*. Reprint. Grand Rapids: Baker, 1996.

———. *Pauline Christology: An Exegetical-Theological Study*. Peabody, MA: Hendrickson, 2007.

Ferguson, Sinclair B. *The Holy Spirit*. Downers Grove, IL: InterVarsity, 1996.

Fishbane, Michael. "The Sacred Center: The Symbolic Structure of the Bible." In Morales, *Cult and Cosmos*, 389–408.

Fitzmyer, Joseph A. "Glory Reflected on the Face of Christ (2 Cor. 3:7–4:6) and a Palestinian Jewish Motif." *Theological Studies* 42, no. 4 (December 1981): 630–44.

Gane, Roy. "'Bread of the Presence' and Creator-in-Residence." *Vetus Testamentum* 42, no. 2 (1992): 179–203.

Garr, W. Randall. *In His Own Image and Likeness: Humanity, Divinity, and Monotheism*. Culture and History of the Ancient Near East 15. Boston: Brill, 2003.

Gentry, Peter J., and Stephen J. Wellum. *Kingdom through Covenant: A Biblical-Theological Understanding of the Covenants*. Wheaton: Crossway, 2012.

Gómez-Robles, Aida, William D. Hopkins, Steven J. Schapiro, and Chet C. Sherwood. "Relaxed Genetic Control of Cortical Organization in Human Brains Compared with Chimpanzees." *Proceedings of the National Academy of Sciences* 112, no. 48 (December 2015): 14799–804.

Goranson Jacob, Haley. *Conformed to the Image of His Son: Reconsidering Paul's Theology of Glory in Romans*. Downers Grove, IL: IVP Academic, 2018.

Gordon, James R. "ReThinking Divine Spatiality: Divine Omnipresence in Philosophical and Theological Perspective." *Heythrop Journal* 59 (2018): 534–43.

Graham, Elaine. "Towards a Theology of Desire." *Theology & Sexuality* 1 (September 1994): 13–30.

Green, Joel B. *Body, Soul, and Human Life: The Nature of Humanity in the Bible*. Grand Rapids: Baker Academic, 2008.

———. "What Does It Mean to Be Human? Another Chapter in the Ongoing Interaction of Science and Scripture." In *From Cells to Souls and Beyond: Changing Portraits of Human Nature*, edited by Malcolm Jeeves, 188–93. Grand Rapids: Eerdmans, 2004.

Green, Joel B., Scot McKnight, and I. Howard Marshall, eds. *Dictionary of Jesus and the Gospels*. 2nd ed. Downers Grove, IL: InterVarsity, 1992.

Greggs, Tom. *Dogmatic Ecclesiology*. Volume 1, *The Priestly Catholicity of the Church*. Grand Rapids: Baker Academic, 2019.

Grenz, Stanley J. "Jesus as the Imago Dei: Image-of-God Christology and the Non-Linear Linearity of Theology." *Journal of the Evangelical Theological Society* 47, no. 4 (December 2004): 617–28.

Gross, Walter. "Die Gottebenbildlichkeit des Menschen im Kontext der Priester-schrift." *Theologische Quartalschrift* 161 (1981): 244–64.

Gunton, Colin E. *Christ and Creation: The Didsbury Lectures, 1990*. Reprint. Eugene, OR: Wipf & Stock, 2005.

Guthrie, George H. *2 Corinthians*. Baker Exegetical Commentary on the New Testament. Grand Rapids: Baker Academic, 2015.

Habets, Myk. *The Anointed Son: A Trinitarian Spirit Christology*. Eugene, OR: Pickwick Publications, 2010.

Hafemann, Scott J., and Paul R. House, eds. *Central Themes in Biblical Theology: Mapping Unity in Diversity*. Nottingham: Inter-Varsity, 2007.

Hamilton, James M., Jr. *God's Indwelling Presence: The Holy Spirit in the Old & New Testaments*. Nashville: B&H, 2006.

Hansen, G. Walter. *The Letter to the Philippians*. Grand Rapids: Eerdmans, 2009.

Hanser, Matthew. "The Metaphysics of Harm." *Philosophy and Phenomenological Research* 77, no. 2 (September 2008): 421–50.

———. "Still More on the Metaphysics of Harm." *Philosophy and Phenomenological Research* 82, no. 2 (March 2011): 459–69.

Haran, Menahem. *Temples and Temple-Service in Ancient Israel: Inquiry into the Character of Cult Phenomena and the Historical Setting of the Priestly School*. Oxford: Oxford University Press, 1979.

Harland, P. J. *The Value of Human Life: A Study of the Story of the Flood (Genesis 6–9)*. Leiden: Brill, 1996.

Hawthorne, Gerald. *The Presence and the Power: The Significance of the Holy Spirit in the Life and Ministry of Jesus*. Eugene, OR: Wipf & Stock, 2003.

Hays, J. Daniel. *The Temple and the Tabernacle: A Study of God's Dwelling Places from Genesis to Revelation*. Grand Rapids: Baker Books, 2016.

Hays, Richard B. *Echoes of Scripture in the Gospels*. Waco: Baylor University Press, 2016.

———. *Reading Backwards: Figural Christology and the Fourfold Gospel Witness*. Waco: Baylor University Press, 2014.

Heim, Erin H. "In Him and through Him from the Foundation of the World: Adoption and Christocentric Anthropology." In *Christ and the Created Order*, vol. 2 of

Perspectives from Theology, Philosophy, and Science, edited by Andrew B. Torrance and Thomas H. McCall, 129–50. Grand Rapids: Zondervan, 2018.

———. "Paths beyond Tracing Out: The Hermeneutics of Metaphor and Theological Method." In *The Voice of God in the Text of Scripture: Explorations in Constructive Dogmatics*, edited by Oliver D. Crisp and Fred Sanders, 112–26. Grand Rapids: Zondervan, 2016.

Herzfeld, Noreen. "Image of God." In *New SCM Dictionary of Christian Spirituality*, edited by Philip Sheldrake, 361–63. London: SCM, 2013.

Himmelfarb, Martha. *Ascent to Heaven in Jewish and Christian Apocalypses*. New York: Oxford University Press, 1993.

Holmes, Christopher R. J. *The Holy Spirit*. Edited by Michael Allen and Scott R. Swain. Grand Rapids: Zondervan Academic, 2015.

Horowitz, Maryanne Cline. "The Image of God in Man—Is Woman Included?" *Harvard Theological Review* 72, no. 3–4 (July 1979): 175–206.

Horst, Friedrich. "Face to Face: The Biblical Doctrine of the Image of God." *Union Seminary Magazine* 4, no. 3 (July 1950): 259–70.

Horton, Michael S. *People and Place: A Covenant Ecclesiology*. Louisville: Westminster John Knox, 2008.

Houston, James M. *The Heart's Desire: Satisfying the Hunger of the Soul*. Vancouver: Regent College Publishing, 2001.

Hutchison, J. C. "The Vine in John 15 and Old Testament Imagery in the 'I Am' Statements." *Bibliotheca Sacra* 168, no. 669 (2011): 63–80.

Inman, Ross D. "Omnipresence and the Location of the Immaterial." *Oxford Studies in Philosophy of Religion* 8 (2017): 167–206.

———. "Retrieving Divine Immensity and Omnipresence." In *T&T Clark Handbook of Analytic Theology*, edited by James M. Arcadi and James T. Turner Jr., 127–40. London: Bloomsbury T&T Clark, 2021.

Jennings, Willie James. *The Christian Imagination: Theology and the Origins of Race*. New Haven: Yale University Press, 2010.

Jensen, David H. *God, Desire, and a Theology of Human Sexuality*. Louisville: Westminster John Knox, 2013.

Jenson, Philip. "Genesis 1–3 and the Tabernacle." Lecture given at St. Mary's College, University of St. Andrews, February 22, 2018.

Jervis, L. Ann. "'But I Want You to Know . . .': Paul's Midrashic Intertextual Response to the Corinthian Worshipers (1 Cor 11:2–16)." *Journal of Biblical Literature* 112, no. 2 (1993): 231–46.

Johnson, Luke Timothy. *Hebrews: A Commentary*. Louisville: Westminster John Knox, 2006.

Jónsson, Gunnlaugur A. "The Image of God: Genesis 1:26–28 in a Century of Old Testament Research." Coniectanea Biblica: Old Testament Series 26. Uppsala: Almqvist & Wiksell, 1988.

Joüon, Paul. *Grammaire de l'hébreu biblique*. Rome: Biblical Institute Press, 1923.

Kamitsuka, Margaret D. *The Embrace of Eros: Bodies, Desires, and Sexuality in Christianity*. Minneapolis: Fortress, 2010.

Kearney, Peter J. "Creation and Liturgy: The P Redaction of Ex 25–40." *Zeitschrift für die Alttestamentliche Wissenschaft* 89, no. 3 (1977): 375–87.

Keener, Craig S. *Acts: An Exegetical Commentary*. Vol. 2. Grand Rapids: Baker Academic, 2013.

———. *1–2 Corinthians*. Cambridge: Cambridge University Press, 2010.

Kilner, John F. *Dignity and Destiny: Humanity in the Image of God*. Grand Rapids: Eerdmans, 2014.

———. "Humanity in God's Image: Is the Image Really Damaged?" *Journal of the Evangelical Theological Society* 53, no. 3 (September 2010): 601–17.

Kline, Meredith G. *Images of the Spirit*. Reprint. Eugene, OR: Wipf & Stock, 1999.

Koester, Craig R. *Dwelling of God: The Tabernacle in the Old Testament, Intertestamental Jewish Literature, and the New Testament*. Washington, DC: Catholic Biblical Association of America, 1989.

———. *Revelation: A New Translation with Introduction and Commentary*. Anchor Yale Bible. New Haven: Yale University Press, 2014.

Kreitzer, Larry Joseph. "Christ and Second Adam in Paul." *Communio Viatorum* 32, no. 1–2 (1989): 55–101.

Kroll, Kimberley. "Indwelling without the Indwelling Holy Spirit: A Critique of Ray Yeo's Modified Account." *Journal of Analytic Theology* 7 (2019): 124–41.

Kruse, Colin G. *Paul's Letter to the Romans*. Grand Rapids: Eerdmans, 2012.

Kwon, Yon-Gyong. "Αρραβων [*Arrabōn*] as Pledge in Second Corinthians." *New Testament Studies* 54, no. 4 (October 2008): 525–41.

Lagrange, Marie-Joseph. *Le judaïsme avant Jésus-Christ*. Paris: Gabalda, 1931.

Lambdin, Thomas O. *Introduction to Biblical Hebrew*. New York: Scribner's Sons, 1971.

Lambrecht, Jan. "Transformation in 2 Cor 3,18." *Bibliotheca Sacra* 64 (1983): 243–54.

Lamp, Jeffrey S. "Wisdom in Col 1:15–20: Contribution and Significance." *Journal of the Evangelical Theological Society* 41, no. 1 (1998): 45–53.

Lane, William L. *Hebrews 1–8*. Word Biblical Commentary 47A. Nashville: Nelson, 1991.

Leidenhag, Joanna. "The Challenge of Autism for Relational Approaches to Theological Anthropology." *International Journal of Systematic Theology* 23, no. 1 (2021): 109–34.

———. "Does the Indwelling of the Holy Spirit Require a Neurotypical Brain?" New Visions in Theological Anthropology, University of St Andrews. Accessed October 11, 2021. https://set.wp.st-andrews.ac.uk/does-the-indwelling-of-the-holy-spirit -require-a-neurotypical-brain/.

Leidenhag, Joanna, and R. T. Mullins. "Flourishing in the Spirit: Distinguishing Incarnation and Indwelling for Theological Anthropology." In *The Christian Doctrine of Humanity: Explorations in Constructive Dogmatics*, edited by Oliver D. Crisp and Fred Sanders, 182–99. Grand Rapids: Zondervan, 2018.

Levenson, J. D. "Cosmos and Microcosm." In Morales, *Cult and Cosmos*, 227–48.

———. "The Temple and the World." *Journal of Religion* 64, no. 3 (July 1984): 275–98.

Levison, John R. *Filled with the Spirit*. Grand Rapids: Eerdmans, 2009.

Lincoln, Andrew T. *Ephesians*. Word Biblical Commentary 42. 1990. Reprint, Grand Rapids: Zondervan, 2014.

———. *The Gospel according to Saint John*. Grand Rapids: Baker Academic, 2013.

Loke, Andrew Ter Ern. *A Kryptic Model of the Incarnation*. Burlington, VT: Routledge, 2014.

Lossky, Vladimir. *In the Image and Likeness of God*. Translated by T. E. Bird. Crestwood, NY: St. Vladimir's Seminary Press, 1974.

Macaskill, Grant. *Union with Christ in the New Testament*. Oxford: Oxford University Press, 2013.

Malatesta, Edward. *Interiority and Covenant*. Rome: Biblical Institute Press, 1978.

Marcus, Joel. "Son of Man as Son of Adam, Part II: Exegesis." *Revue Biblique* 110, no. 3 (July 2003): 370–86.

Marshall, I Howard. "Being Human: Made in the Image of God." *Stone-Campbell Journal* 4, no. 1 (2001): 47–67.

Massey, Preston T. "Gender versus Marital Concerns: Does 1 Corinthians 11:2–16 Address the Issues of Male/Female or Husband/Wife?" *Tyndale Bulletin* 64, no. 2 (2013): 239–56.

McCall, Thomas. *Against God and Nature: The Doctrine of Sin*. Wheaton: Crossway, 2019.

———. "Relational Trinity: Creedal Perspective." In *Two Views on the Doctrine of the Trinity*, edited by Jason S. Sexton, 113–37. Grand Rapids: Zondervan, 2014.

McDowell, Catherine L. *The Image of God in the Garden of Eden: The Creation of Humankind in Genesis 2:5–3:24 in Light of the Mīs Pî Pīt Pî and Wpt-r Rituals of*

Mesopotamia and Ancient Egypt. Siphrut: Literature and Theology of the Hebrew Scriptures. Winona Lake, IN: Eisenbrauns, 2015.

McFarland, Ian. "Spirit and Incarnation: Toward a Pneumatic Chalcedonianism: Spirit and Incarnation." *International Journal of Systematic Theology* 16 (2014): 143–58.

———. *The Word Made Flesh.* Louisville: Westminster John Knox, 2019.

McGrath, Alister E. *Christian Theology: An Introduction.* 6th ed. Malden, MA: Wiley-Blackwell, 2016.

McKirland, Christa L. "Did Jesus Need the Spirit? An Appeal for Pneumatic Christology to Inform Christological Anthropology." *Perichoresis* 19, no. 2 (2021): 43–61.

———. "Image of God and Divine Presence: A Critique of Gender Essentialism." In *Discovering Biblical Equality*, 3rd ed., edited by Ronald W. Pierce, Cynthia Long Westfall, and Christa L. McKirland, 282–309. Downers Grove, IL: InterVarsity, 2021.

McKnight, Scot. *The Letter of James.* Grand Rapids: Eerdmans, 2011.

Merrill, E. H. "Image of God." In *Dictionary of the Old Testament: Pentateuch; A Compendium of Contemporary Biblical Scholarship*, edited by T. Desmond Alexander and David W. Baker, 441–45. Downers Grove, IL: InterVarsity, 2003.

Mettinger, T. N. D. "Abbild oder Urbild? 'Imago Dei' in traditionsgeschichtlicher Sicht." *Zeitschrift für die Alttestamentliche Wissenschaft* 86, no. 4 (1974): 403–24.

Meyers, Carol L. *The Tabernacle Menorah: A Synthetic Study of a Symbol from the Biblical Cult.* 2nd ed. Piscataway, NJ: Gorgias, 2003.

Michaels, J. Ramsey. *1 Peter.* Word Biblical Commentary 49. Waco: Word, 1988.

Middleton, J. Richard. *The Liberating Image: The* Imago Dei *in Genesis 1.* Grand Rapids: Brazos, 2005.

———. *A New Heaven and a New Earth: Reclaiming Biblical Eschatology.* Grand Rapids: Baker Academic, 2014.

Moffitt, David M. "It Is Not Finished: Jesus's Perpetual Atoning Work as the Heavenly High Priest in Hebrews." In *So Great a Salvation*, edited by Jon C. Laansma, George H. Guthrie, and Cynthia Long Westfall, 157–75. London: Bloomsbury T&T Clark, 2019.

Moo, Douglas J. *The Letters to the Colossians and to Philemon.* Pillar New Testament Commentary. Grand Rapids: Eerdmans, 2008.

Moore, Sebastian. *Jesus the Liberator of Desire.* New York: Crossroad, 1989.

Morales, L. Michael, ed. *Cult and Cosmos: Tilting toward a Temple-Centered Theology.* Biblical Tools and Studies 18. Leuven: Peeters, 2014.

———. *Who Shall Ascend the Mountain of the Lord? A Biblical Theology of the Book of Leviticus.* Downers Grove, IL: InterVarsity, 2015.

Moreland, J. P., and Scott B. Rae. *Body & Soul: Human Nature & the Crisis in Ethics*. Downers Grove, IL: InterVarsity, 2000.

Moritz, Joshua M. "Evolutionary Biology and Theological Anthropology." In Farris and Taliaferro, *Ashgate Research Companion to Theological Anthropology*, 45–56.

Newman, Carey C. *Paul's Glory-Christology: Tradition and Rhetoric*. Leiden: Brill, 1992.

Nolland, John. *Luke 9:21–18:34*. Word Biblical Commentary 35B. 1993. Reprint, Grand Rapids: Zondervan, 2016.

O'Brien, Peter. *Colossians–Philemon*. Word Biblical Commentary 44. 1978. Reprint, Grand Rapids: Zondervan, 2014.

Oppenheim, A. L. *Ancient Mesopotamia: Portrait of a Dead Civilization*. Chicago: University of Chicago Press, 1964.

Palmer, J. "Bread." In *Dictionary of Jesus and the Gospels*, edited by Joel B. Green, Scot McKnight, and I. Howard Marshall, 83–86. Downers Grove, IL: InterVarsity, 1992.

Parker, Gregory W., Jr. "Reformation or Revolution? Herman Bavinck and Henri de Lubac on Nature and Grace." *Perichoresis* 15, no. 3 (October 2017): 81–95.

Pawl, Faith Glavey. "Exploring Theological Zoology: Might Non-Human Animals be Spiritual (but Not Religious)?" In *The Lost Sheep in Philosophy of Religion: New Perspectives on Disability, Gender, Race, and Animals*, edited by Blake Hereth and Kevin Timpe, 163–82. New York: Routledge & Kegan Paul, 2019.

Peeler, Amy. "Imaging Glory: 1 Corinthians 11, Gender, and Bodies at Worship." In *Beauty, Order, and Mystery: A Christian Vision of Human Sexuality*, edited by Gerald L. Hiestand and Todd Wilson, 151–64. Downers Grove, IL: InterVarsity, 2017.

Pennington, Jonathan T. *The Sermon on the Mount and Human Flourishing: A Theological Commentary*. Grand Rapids: Baker Academic, 2017.

Peppiatt, Lucy. "Life in the Spirit: Christ's and Ours." In *The Christian Doctrine of Humanity: Explorations in Constructive Dogmatics*, edited by Oliver D. Crisp and Fred Sanders, 165–81. Grand Rapids: Zondervan, 2018.

———. "Man as the Image and Glory of God, and Woman as the Glory of Man: Perspicuity or Ambiguity?" *Priscilla Papers* 33, no. 3 (Summer 2019): 12–19.

———. *Rediscovering Scripture's Vision for Women: Fresh Perspectives on Disputed Texts*. Downers Grove, IL: InterVarsity, 2019.

Peterson, Ryan S. *Imago Dei as Human Identity*. Winona Lake, IN: Eisenbrauns, 2016.

Phythian-Adams, W. J. *The People and the Presence*. Oxford: Oxford University Press, 1942.

Pitre, Brant. *Jesus and the Last Supper*. Grand Rapids: Eerdmans, 2015.

Plantinga, Cornelius, Jr. *Not the Way It's Supposed to Be: A Breviary of Sin*. Reprint. Grand Rapids: Eerdmans, 2009.

Porteous, N. W. "Image of God." In *The Interpreter's Dictionary of the Bible*, edited by Keith R. Crim, 2:682–85. Nashville: Abingdon, 1993.

Porter, Steven L., and Brandon Rickabaugh. "The Sanctifying Work of the Holy Spirit: Revisiting Alston's Interpersonal Model." *Journal of Analytic Theology* 6, no. 1 (2018): 112–30.

Ridderbos, Herman N. *Paul: An Outline of His Theology*. Grand Rapids: Eerdmans, 1997.

Roberts, Alexander, ed. *The Ante-Nicene Fathers: The Writings of the Fathers Down to A.D. 325*. Vol. 1, *The Apostolic Fathers with Justin Martyr and Irenaeus: 1*. New York: Cosimo Classics, 2007.

Rowe, C. Kavin. "Biblical Pressure and Trinitarian Hermeneutics." *Pro Ecclesia* 11, no. 3 (August 2002): 295–312.

Rowland, Christopher, and Christopher R. A. Morray-Jones. *The Mystery of God: Early Jewish Mysticism and the New Testament*. Compendia Rerum Iudaicarum Ad Novum Testamentum. Section 3, Jewish Traditions in Early Christian Literature, vol. 12. Boston: Brill, 2009.

Ryken, Leland, James C. Wilhoit, and Tremper Longman III. *Dictionary of Biblical Imagery*. Downers Grove, IL: InterVarsity, 1998.

Schreiter, R. "Peacemaking and Reconciliation." In *Global Dictionary of Theology: A Resource for the Worldwide Church*, edited by William A. Dyrness and Veli-Matti Kärkkäinen, 637–41. Downers Grove, IL: InterVarsity, 2008.

Schuele, Andreas. "Made in the 'Image of God': The Concepts of Divine Images in Gen 1–3." *Zeitschrift für die Alttestamentliche Wissenschaft* 117, no. 1 (2005): 1–20.

———. "The Spirit of YHWH and the Aura of Divine Presence." *Interpretation: A Journal of Bible & Theology* 66, no. 1 (January 2012): 16–28.

Schuppert, Fabian. "Distinguishing Basic Needs and Fundamental Interests." *Critical Review of International Social and Political Philosophy* 16, no. 1 (January 2013): 24–44.

Silva, Moisés. *Philippians*. Grand Rapids: Baker Academic, 2005.

Smail, Thomas A. *Reflected Glory*. London: Hodder & Stoughton, 1975.

Smit, Peter-Ben. *Paradigms of Being in Christ: A Study of the Epistle to the Philippians*. Eugene, OR: A&C Black, 2013.

Smith, James K. A. *Desiring the Kingdom: Worship, Worldview, and Cultural Formation*. Vol. 1 of *Cultural Liturgies*. Grand Rapids: Baker Academic, 2009.

Soskice, Janet Martin, Hilda P. Koster, Ian A. McFarland, Steffen Lösel, Joy Ann McDougall, and Kathryn Tanner. "*Christ the Key* Book Forum." *Theology Today* 68, no. 3 (October 2011): 310–47.

Spence, Alan. "Christ's Humanity and Ours." In *Persons, Divine and Human: King's College Essays in Theological Anthropology*, edited by Christoph Schwöbel and Colin Gunton, 74–97. Edinburgh: T&T Clark, 1992.

Strauss, Mark L. "Jesus and the Spirit in Biblical and Theological Perspective: Messianic Empowering, Saving Wisdom, and the Limits of Biblical Theology." In *The Spirit and Christ in the New Testament and Christian Theology: Essays in Honor of Max Turner*, edited by I. H. Marshall, V. Rabens, and C. Bennema, 266–84. Grand Rapids: Eerdmans, 2012.

Stubbs, David L., and John D. Witvliet. *Table and Temple: The Christian Eucharist and Its Jewish Roots*. Grand Rapids: Eerdmans, 2020.

Stump, Eleonore. "Omnipresence, Indwelling, and the Second-Personal." *European Journal for Philosophy of Religion* 5, no. 4 (2013): 29–53.

———. *Wandering in Darkness: Narrative and the Problem of Suffering*. Oxford: Oxford University Press, 2012.

Tanner, Kathryn. *Christ the Key*. Cambridge: Cambridge University Press, 2010.

———. *God and Creation in Christian Theology: Tyranny and Empowerment?* Oxford: Blackwell, 1988.

———. *Jesus, Humanity and the Trinity: A Brief Systematic Theology*. Minneapolis: Fortress, 2001.

Tanner, Norman P. *The Councils of the Church: A Short History*. New York: Independent Publishers Group, 2001.

Taylor, Elanor. "More on Dispositions?" Talk given at Building Foundations in Science-Engaged Theology Seminar, private forum, June 14, 2021.

Terrien, Samuel L. *The Elusive Presence: Toward a New Biblical Theology*. Religious Perspectives 26. San Francisco: Harper & Row, 1978.

———. "Proclamation and Presence: Old Testament Essays in Honour of Gwynne Henton Davies." *Catholic Biblical Quarterly* 33, no. 4 (October 1971): 567–68.

Thiselton, Anthony C. *The First Epistle to the Corinthians: A Commentary on the Greek Text*. Grand Rapids: Eerdmans, 2000.

Thompson, Marianne. *Colossians and Philemon: A Two Horizons Commentary*. Grand Rapids: Eerdmans, 2005.

Thomson, Garrett. "Fundamental Needs." *Royal Institute of Philosophy Supplement* 80 (2005): 175–86.

———. *Needs*. International Library of Philosophy. New York: Routledge & Kegan Paul, 1987.

Thomson, Garrett, Scherto Gill, and Ivor Goodson. *Happiness, Flourishing and the Good Life: A Transformative Vision for Human Well-Being*. New York: Routledge & Kegan Paul, 2020.

Thomson, Judith Jarvis. "More on the Metaphysics of Harm." *Philosophy and Phenomenological Research* 82, no. 2 (2011): 436–58.

Timpe, Kevin. "Defiant Afterlife—Disability and Uniting Ourselves to God." Lecture presented at the Annual Logos Conference, University of Notre Dame, May 25, 2018.

———. *Free Will in Philosophical Theology*. Bloomsbury Studies in Philosophy of Religion. New York: Bloomsbury, 2014.

Torrance, Alan. *Persons in Communion: Trinitarian Description and Human Participation*. London: T&T Clark, 2010.

Torrance, T. F. *Theology in Reconstruction*. Grand Rapids: Eerdmans, 1965.

Towner, W. Sibley. "Clones of God: Genesis 1:26–28 and the Image of God in the Hebrew Bible." *Interpretation* 59, no. 4 (October 2005): 341–56.

Treier, Daniel. "The Incarnation." In *Christian Dogmatics*, edited by Michael Allen and Scott R. Swain, 216–42. Grand Rapids: Baker Academic, 2016.

Trible, Phyllis. *God and the Rhetoric of Sexuality*. New ed. Philadelphia: Augsburg Fortress, 1978.

Turner, James T., Jr. "The *End* of Things: Resurrection and New Creation." In *T&T Clark Handbook of Analytic Theology*, edited by James M. Arcadi and James T. Turner, 423–36. London: T&T Clark, 2021.

———. "Temple Theology, Holistic Eschatology, and the Imago Dei: An Analytic Prolegomenon." *TheoLogica: An International Journal for Philosophy of Religion and Philosophical Theology* 2, no. 1 (March 2018): 95–114.

Turner, Max. "Jesus and the Spirit in Lucan Perspective." *Tyndale Bulletin* 32 (1981): 3–42.

———. *Power from on High: The Spirit in Israel's Restoration and Witness in Luke-Acts*. Eugene, OR: A&C Black, 1996.

———. "The Significance of Spirit Endowment for Paul." *Vox Evangelica* 9 (1975): 56–70.

———. "'Trinitarian' Pneumatology in the New Testament? Towards an Explanation of the Worship of Jesus." *Asbury Theological Journal* 57 (2002): 167–86.

Um, Stephen. *The Theme of Temple Christology in John's Gospel*. London: Bloomsbury, 2006.

Vanhoozer, Kevin J. "Holy Scripture." In *Christian Dogmatics*, edited by Michael Allen and Scott R. Swain, 30–56. Grand Rapids: Baker Academic, 2016.

Vidu, Adonis. "*Filioque* and the Order of the Divine Missions." In *The Third Person of the Trinity: Explorations in Constructive Dogmatics*, edited by Oliver D. Crisp and Fred Sanders, 21–35. Zondervan Academic, 2020.

———. "Triune Agency, East and West: Uncreated Energies or Created Effects?" *Perichoresis* 18 (2020): 57–75.

von Rad, Gerhard. "εἰκών [eikōn]: D. The Divine Likeness in the OT." In *Theological Dictionary of the New Testament*, vol. 2, edited by Gerhard Kittel, translated by Geoffrey Bromiley, 390–92. Grand Rapids: Eerdmans, 1965.

———. *Genesis: A Commentary*. 2nd ed. London: SCM, 1963.

Vos, Geerhardus. "The Eschatological Aspect of the Pauline Conception of the Spirit." 1912. Reprinted in *Redemptive History and Biblical Interpretation: The Shorter Writings of Geerhardus Vos*, edited by Richard B. Gaffin Jr., 91–125. Phillipsburg, NJ: P&R, 2001.

Walton, Heather. "Theology of Desire." *Theology & Sexuality* 1 (September 1994): 31–41.

Walton, John H. *Genesis*. NIV Application Commentary. Grand Rapids: Zondervan, 2001.

———. *The Lost World of Genesis One*. Downers Grove, IL: InterVarsity, 2009.

Watson, Francis. *Text and Truth: Redefining Biblical Theology*. Grand Rapids: Eerdmans, 1997.

Weinandy, Thomas. *The Father's Spirit of Sonship: Reconceiving the Trinity*. Eugene, OR: Wipf & Stock, 2011.

Weinfeld, Moshe. "Sabbath, Temple and the Enthronement of the Lord: The Problem of the *Sitz im Leben* of Genesis 1:1–2:3." In Morales, *Cult and Cosmos*, 149–60.

Wenham, Gordon J. *Genesis 1–15*. Word Biblical Commentary 1. Waco: Word, 1987.

———. *Numbers: An Introduction and Commentary*. Downers Grove, IL: InterVarsity, 2008.

———. "Sanctuary Symbolism in the Garden of Eden Story." In Morales, *Cult and Cosmos*, 161–66.

Westermann, Claus. *Genesis*. Translated by David Green. London: T&T Clark, 1987.

———. *The Genesis Account of Creation*. Minneapolis: Fortress, 1968.

Wiggins, David. *Needs, Values, Truth: Essays in the Philosophy of Value*. 3rd ed. Oxford: Oxford University Press, 1998.

Williams, Michael D. "First Calling: The Imago Dei and the Order of Creation Part II." *Presbyterion* 39, no. 2 (September 2013): 75–97.

Wilson, Gerald. *Psalms*. Vol. 1. NIV Application Commentary. Grand Rapids: Zondervan, 2002.

Witherington, Ben, III. *The Indelible Image: The Theological and Ethical Thought World of the New Testament*, vol. 1, *The Individual Witnesses*. Downers Grove, IL: InterVarsity, 2009.

Wolterstorff, Nicholas. *Divine Discourse: Philosophical Reflections on the Claim That God Speaks*. Cambridge: Cambridge University Press, 1995.

Wood, William. *Analytic Theology and the Academic Study of Religion*. Oxford: Oxford University Press, 2021.

Wright, N. T. *After You Believe: Why Christian Character Matters*. New York: HarperOne, 2012.

———. *Colossians and Philemon*. Grand Rapids: Eerdmans, 1996.

———. *Jesus and the Victory of God*. Christian Origins and the Question of God 2. Minneapolis: Fortress, 1997.

———. "Romans." In *The New Interpreter's Bible: A Commentary in Twelve Volumes*, 10:393–770. Nashville: Abingdon, 2002.

Yadav, Sameer. "Toward an Analytic Theology of Liberation." In *Voices from the Edge: Centering Marginalized Voices in Analytic Theology*, edited by Michelle Panchuk and Michael Rea, 47–74. New York: Oxford University Press, 2020.

Yarnold, E. "The Trinitarian Implications of Luke and Acts 1." *Heythrop Journal* 7 (1966): 18–32.

Yee, Gale A. *Jewish Feasts and the Gospel of John*. Eugene, OR: Wipf & Stock, 2007.

Author Index

Scripture Index

Subject Index

DATE DUE

GAYLORD   PRINTED IN U.S.A.